THE DEVELOPMENT DIPLOMAT

THE DEVELOPMENT DIPLOMAT

WORKING ACROSS BORDERS, BOARDROOMS, AND BUREAUCRACIES TO END POVERTY

FATEMA Z. SUMAR

NEW DEGREE PRESS

THE DEVELOPMENT DIPLOMAT
Working Across Borders, Boardrooms, and Bureaucracies to End Poverty

ISBN   978-1-63676-495-5   *Paperback*
         978-1-63730-413-6   *Kindle Ebook*
         978-1-63730-414-3   *Ebook*

To Zahra, Safya, and Insiya,
who were Mamma's pride and joy, and
who are my head, heart, and soul, and
to Nageeb, who makes us all whole.

PRAISE FOR
THE DEVELOPMENT DIPLOMAT

———

"*The Development Diplomat* is a triumph! Buy it for every young person in your life who wants a career in either diplomacy or development; who wants to make the world a better place by lifting people out of poverty while navigating the shoals of politics. Fatema Z. Sumar tells gripping tales — from helicopter rides in the Himalayas to thugs at the door in Colombo — that highlight the necessity of truly bringing development and diplomacy together. She's also a mom, a South Asian woman in largely white offices, a Muslim breaking barriers at every turn, and a wonderful storyteller."

> — *Anne-Marie Slaughter,* CEO *of New America and author of "Why Women Still Can't Have It All"*

"Fatema Z. Sumar's insightful journey working in over thirty developing countries provides a roadmap for those individuals who strive to make a difference in pursuit of poverty alleviation through public service. This exceptional volume is long overdue. While there have been numerous one-off books on both foreign policy and international development assistance, Sumar forges a different path, pursuing an analytic framework that integrates development, foreign policy, and national security. She calls the implementers of this approach 'development diplomats.' As she so importantly discusses throughout this exceptional text, when development and foreign policy officials work together in pursuit of a common objective, transformative change can and will happen. When one looks at the challenges the world faces today, from the reemergence of radicalism in Afghanistan to the equitable distribution of the COVID vaccine, Sumar's unique development diplomat approach is not only sensible but also essential. I strongly recommend this book, which I'm sure will contribute to a better world."

— *William Frej, former White House National Security Director for Development Issues and* USAID *Mission Director in Poland, Indonesia, Central Asia, and Afghanistan; Career Minister (retired)*

"Fatema Z. Sumar has been on the front lines of diplomacy and development for years. There is no one better placed to write such an important and timely book about tackling global poverty. From Capitol Hill to the State Department to Asia and beyond, Fatema's journey and personal story is one of courage and perseverance. Told through the eyes of a true practitioner and expert, *The Development Diplomat* is a must-read for anyone interested in how the United States can still have a big and positive impact abroad through its development and aid programs."

— *Richard Verma, former US Ambassador to India*

"In this rich and readable book on American aid and foreign policy, Fatema Z. Sumar takes the reader through events that changed the course of history—and of her life. The first-person account of what it takes to succeed is also an honest and riveting account of a purpose-driven life."

— *Homi Kharas, Senior Fellow at The Brookings Institution*

"Fatema Z. Sumar has a clear vision for a world without poverty. Her creative approach brings diplomats, development experts, and civil society together to tackle problems which exist worldwide. As a diplomat who worked closely with Fatema when she served on Capitol Hill and at the State Department, I have seen firsthand her dedication to achieving sustainable development goals. Her writing takes the reader to countries around the world exploring innovative ways to alleviate injustice and economic inequality. This book is a must-read for anyone who shares her vision for a better world."

— *Ambassador Susan M. Elliott, President and CEO of National Committee on American Foreign Policy and former US Ambassador to Tajikistan (retired)*

"Amongst the vast trove of books on foreign policy, relatively few tackle the topic of foreign assistance, so Fatema Z. Sumar's *The Development Diplomat* is a very welcomed study of the immensely important but also frustratingly difficult challenge of development. She brings a rich background to bear on her book's focus on South and Central Asia from her work in Congress, the Millennium Challenge Corporation, and the State Department where our work intersected. In addition to her case studies, her twenty-one recommendations on ways to most effectively pursue diplomacy and development in tandem are a must-read."

— *Laura Kennedy, former Deputy Assistant Secretary of State and US Ambassador to Turkmenistan and to the Conference on Disarmament (retired)*

"Young professionals seeking a path into careers in international development and policy — especially those historically excluded from these fields — will benefit from how Fatema Z. Sumar illuminates professions of international affairs. She unpacks how foreign policy and international development practitioners can work together to address challenges without glossing over the failures along the way. I know *The Development Diplomat* will inspire future generations to join her in the fight against global poverty."

— *Carmen Iezzi Mezzera, Executive Director of the Association of Professional Schools of International Affairs*

"Fatema Z. Sumar introduces you to the world of the development diplomat, bridging dreams of a better world with the challenges of making positive political, economic, and social changes real. Through personal stories, Sumar brings her humanity and experience to a story we must all make our own: how to build a better and more inclusive world. Her book is a must-read for anyone interested in the fascinating intersection of development practice and diplomacy."

— *Sam Worthington, CEO of InterAction*

"With an unusual combination of conceptual clarity and narrative flair, Fatema Z. Sumar explores one of humanity's great policy challenges: how to sustainably improve quality of life for people around the world. Her moving and often gripping personal story amplifies her vision of a new generation of 'development diplomats' who bring diverse voices to the table and entrepreneurially marshal all the resources, skills, and assets at our disposal – diplomatic, development, and more – to create a sense of hope and optimism for even the most marginalized among us. Sumar powerfully illuminates how crossing traditional silos to achieve a better future for all is not only politically smart and ethically necessary, it can also be professionally exhilarating, leading to a career of impact, meaning, and genuine fulfillment. Development professionals – from civil society, government, and business – will find this book a provocative look at how creative deal-making across silos can catapult us toward a more peaceful, prosperous, and pluralist world for all."

— *Khalil Z. Shariff, CEO of Aga Khan Foundation USA and Canada*

"In this very personal account, Fatema Z. Sumar makes the case for integrating diplomacy and development in order to fight global poverty more effectively. Along the way, she shares her own experiences about juggling work and parenthood, giving readers who are earlier in their careers a first-hand view of what it takes to make a difference in the world while still doing right by the people you love the most. May her compelling story inspire others to also pursue such impactful careers!"

— *Kristin M. Lord, President and CEO of IREX*

"Fatema Z. Sumar has written a personal and passionate guide for merging diplomacy and development to produce better policies for better lives. The insights and clear analysis will appeal to established professionals and the next generation of global leaders."

— *Doug Frantz, former Deputy Secretary-General of the Organization for Economic Cooperation and Development (OECD)*

"Fatema Z. Sumar makes a powerful argument for an integrated and cross-disciplinary approach to solving one of the world's most complex problems. Having worked with her for years watching her apply these practices on a global scale, I know her approach is tested and practical. This is an essential lens for public officials, civil society organizations, businesses, and others pursuing the achievable objective of ending poverty."

— *Mohamad Ali, Board Member of Oxfam America*

"Anyone who doubts the positive impact that immigrants continue to make on American society, or wonders whether our development partnerships abroad make a difference, or thinks that all public servants exist and work in silos need only read this terrific work by Fatema Z. Sumar – a first-generation South Asian immigrant who became one of the outstanding next-generation development diplomats and whose experience in the corridors of Congress, the hallways of the State Department, and the myriad roads and pathways of nations across the globe have made her one of America's most productive Sherpas in international development."

— *Doug Wilson, former Assistant Secretary of Defense for Public Affairs*

"With ample doses of inspiration and perspiration, Fatema Z. Sumar brings a personal focus to change-making in the world of development. By applying a sharp analytical lens to the realities on the ground, she illustrates how real progress can be driven at the intersection of diplomacy and development. She takes us behind the curtain and guides us through the ups and downs of deal-making in some of the most fragile and conflictive places on the planet. *The Development Diplomat* is a key read for anyone aspiring to move the needle in today's complex web of global issues."

— *Carl F. Muñana, former CEO of Inter-American Investment Corporation*

"Fatema Z. Sumar blends compelling personal stories, an international development primer, and a rousing call for action in this remarkable book that takes us from the side of the New Jersey Turnpike to the steppes of Mongolia. A must-read for anyone interested in solving the biggest international challenges."

— *Naheed Nenshi, Mayor of Calgary, Canada*

"Fatema Z. Sumar shares her personal experience as a diplomat and development practitioner to provide guidance for the next generation. Her enthusiasm and dedication shine through. Her book's reflections and advice are well worth the time of those who want to enter public service and make a difference."

— *Christopher Kojm, former Chairman of the National Intelligence Council and Professor of Practice at the Elliott School of International Affairs, George Washington University*

"Diplomacy plays a critical role in shaping international development priorities and funding, as we have seen during the COVID-19 pandemic. In *The Development Diplomat*, Fatema Z. Sumar provides an insider's look into how diplomacy can work — and fall short — in addressing major global challenges like climate change and poverty. I strongly recommend this book to those interested in how diplomacy can shape and launch initiatives that lift up and empower underprivileged populations, and tackle the world's biggest problems."

— *Bart Edes, Professor of Practice at McGill University and former North American Representative for the Asian Development Bank*

"Fatema Z. Sumar courageously uses her personal life experience to showcase how technically correct solutions, while necessary, are not sufficient to make change happen. Often, political and administrative feasibility are also needed to get things done in development. She calls upon public policy schools to better equip students to ensure long-term sustainable change by teaching them how to build broad-based coalitions, break down silos, work flexibly, and develop emotional intelligence. A must read for those considering a career in international development."

— *Salimah Samji, Director of Building State Capability at the Center for International Development, Harvard University*

NOTE TO READER

———

As this book was going to print, the Taliban quickly and unexpectedly captured control of Afghanistan in August 2021. Given the timing of events, the book does not address the situation in Afghanistan following the Taliban takeover, although it includes many historical references involving Afghanistan, Pakistan, and Central Asia that are more relevant than ever in understanding America's role in the region. Time will tell the impact the Taliban will have on the broader development agenda.

CONTENTS

TIMELINE OF KEY MILESTONES

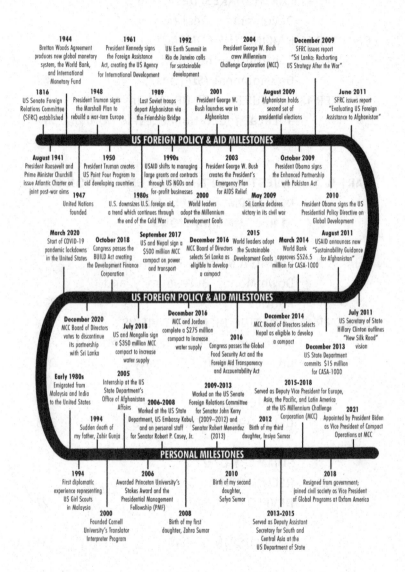

1944
Bretton Woods Agreement produces new global monetary system, the World Bank, and International Monetary Fund

1961
President Kennedy signs the Foreign Assistance Act, creating the US Agency for International Development

1992
UN Earth Summit in Rio de Janeiro calls for sustainable development

2004
President George W. Bush crew Millennium Challenge Corporation (MCC)

December 2009
SFRC issues report "Sri Lanka: Recharting US Strategy After the War"

1816
US Senate Foreign Relations Committee (SFRC) established

1948
President Truman signs the Marshall Plan to rebuild a war-torn Europe

1989
Last Soviet troops depart Afghanistan via the Friendship Bridge

2001
President George W. Bush launches war in Afghanistan

August 2009
Afghanistan holds second set of presidential elections

June 2011
SFRC issues report "Evaluating US Foreign Assistance to Afghanistan"

US FOREIGN POLICY & AID MILESTONES

August 1941
President Roosevelt and Prime Minister Churchill issue Atlantic Charter on joint post-war aims

1950
President Truman creates US Point Four Program to aid developing countries

1990s
USAID shifts to managing large grants and contracts through US NGOs and for-profit businesses

2003
President George W. Bush creates the President's Emergency Plan for AIDS Relief

October 2009
President Obama signs the Enhanced Partnership with Pakistan Act

1947
United Nations founded

1980s
U.S. downsizes U.S. foreign aid, a trend which continues through the end of the Cold War

2000
World leaders adopt the Millennium Development Goals

May 2009
Sri Lanka declares victory in its civil war

2010
President Obama signs the US Presidential Policy Directive on Global Development

March 2020
Start of COVID-19 pandemic lockdowns in the United States

October 2018
Congress passes the BUILD Act creating the Development Finance Corporation

September 2017
US and Nepal sign a $500 million MCC compact on power and transport

December 2016
MCC Board of Directors selects Sri Lanka as eligible to develop a compact

2015
World leaders adopt the Sustainable Development Goals

March 2014
World Bank approves $526.5 million for CASA-1000

August 2011
USAID announces new "Sustainability Guidance for Afghanistan"

US FOREIGN POLICY & AID MILESTONES

December 2020
MCC Board of Directors votes to discontinue its partnership with Sri Lanka

July 2018
US and Mongolia sign a $350 million MCC compact to increase water supply

December 2016
MCC and Jordan complete a $275 million compact to increase water supply

December 2014
MCC Board of Directors selects Nepal as eligible to develop a compact

July 2011
US Secretary of State Hillary Clinton outlines "New Silk Road" vision

2016
Congress passes the Global Food Security Act and the Foreign Aid Transparency and Accountability Act

December 2013
US State Department commits $15 million for CASA-1000

Early 1980s
Emigrated from Malaysia and India to the United States

2005
Internship at the US State Department's Office of Afghanistan Affairs

2009-2013
Worked on the US Senate Foreign Relations Committee for Senator John Kerry (2009–2012) and Senator Robert Menendez (2013)

2015-2018
Served as Deputy Vice President for Europe, Asia, the Pacific, and Latin America at the US Millennium Challenge Corporation (MCC)

1994
Sudden death of my father, Zahir Gunja

2006-2008
Worked at the US State Department, US Embassy Kabul, and on personal staff for Senator Robert P. Casey, Jr.

2012
Birth of my third daughter, Insiya Sumar

2021
Appointed by President Biden as Vice President of Compact Operations at MCC

PERSONAL MILESTONES

1994
First diplomatic experience representing US Girl Scouts in Malaysia

2006
Awarded Princeton University's Stokes Award and the Presidential Management Fellowship (PMF)

2010
Birth of my second daughter, Safya Sumar

2018
Resigned from government; joined civil society as Vice President of Global Programs at Oxfam America

2000
Founded Cornell University's Translator Interpreter Program

2008
Birth of my first daughter, Zahra Sumar

2013-2015
Served as Deputy Assistant Secretary for South and Central Asia at the US Department of State

TRAVEL LOG

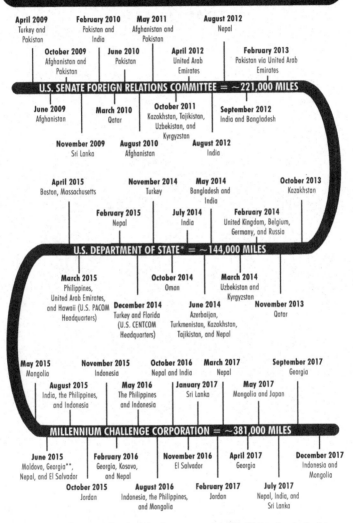

US GOVERNMENT TRAVEL LOG ~750,000 MILES

April 2009
Turkey and Pakistan

October 2009
Afghanistan and Pakistan

February 2010
Pakistan and India

June 2010
Pakistan

May 2011
Afghanistan and Pakistan

April 2012
United Arab Emirates

August 2012
Nepal

February 2013
Pakistan via United Arab Emirates

U.S. SENATE FOREIGN RELATIONS COMMITTEE = ~221,000 MILES

June 2009
Afghanistan

November 2009
Sri Lanka

March 2010
Qatar

August 2010
Afghanistan

October 2011
Kazakhstan, Tajikistan, Uzbekistan, and Kyrgyzstan

August 2012
India

September 2012
India and Bangladesh

April 2015
Boston, Massachusetts

February 2015
Nepal

November 2014
Turkey

July 2014
India

May 2014
Bangladesh and India

February 2014
United Kingdom, Belgium, Germany, and Russia

October 2013
Kazakhstan

U.S. DEPARTMENT OF STATE* = ~144,000 MILES

March 2015
Philippines, United Arab Emirates, and Hawaii (U.S. PACOM Headquarters)

December 2014
Turkey and Florida (U.S. CENTCOM Headquarters)

October 2014
Oman

June 2014
Azerbaijan, Turkmenistan, Kazakhstan, Tajikistan, and Nepal

March 2014
Uzbekistan and Kyrgyzstan

November 2013
Qatar

May 2015
Mongolia

August 2015
India, the Philippines, and Indonesia

November 2015
Indonesia

May 2016
The Philippines and Indonesia

October 2016
Nepal and India

January 2017
Sri Lanka

March 2017
Nepal

May 2017
Mongolia and Japan

September 2017
Georgia

MILLENNIUM CHALLENGE CORPORATION = ~381,000 MILES

June 2015
Moldova, Georgia**, Nepal, and El Salvador

October 2015
Jordan

February 2016
Georgia, Kosovo, and Nepal

August 2016
Indonesia, the Philippines, and Mongolia

November 2016
El Salvador

February 2017
Jordan

April 2017
Georgia

July 2017
Nepal, India, and Sri Lanka

December 2017
Indonesia and Mongolia

*Excludes travel taken from 2006-2008 for work at the State Department to countries including Afghanistan, Kyrgyzstan, Kazakhstan, and Belgium. **Georgia refers to the Eastern European country in the Caucasus region and not the U.S. state.

TRAVEL MAP

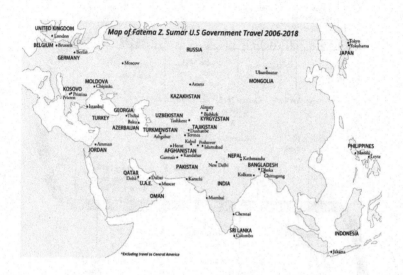

Map of Fatema Z. Sumar U.S Government Travel 2006-2018

*Excluding travel to Central America

ACRONYMS

ADB	Asian Development Bank
A/S	Assistant Secretary
BCL	Briefing Checklist
CASA	Central Asia South Asia
CASAREM	Central Asia South Asia Regional Energy Market
CEO	Chief Executive Officer
CODEL	Congressional Delegation
COIN	Counterinsurgency
COVID-19	Coronavirus Disease 2019
DAS	Deputy Assistant Secretary
DCA	Development Credit Authority
DFC	US Development Finance Corporation
DRL	US State Department Bureau of Democracy, Human Rights, and Labor
ECC	Electoral Complaints Commission
EUR/ACE	US State Department Office of the Coordinator of US Assistance to Europe and Eurasia
FSOs	Foreign Service Officers
GATT	General Agreement on Tariffs and Trade
GDP	Gross Domestic Product
GNI	Gross National Income

GNP	Gross National Product
GOA	Government of Afghanistan
HFAC	US House Foreign Affairs Committee
HSGAC	US Senate Homeland Security and Governmental Affairs Committee
HST	Harry S. Truman
IBRD	International Bank for Reconstruction and Development
ICRC	International Committee of the Red Cross
IDA	International Development Association
IDB	Islamic Development Bank
IDPs	Internally Displaced Persons
IMF	International Monetary Fund
INGOs	International Nongovernmental Organizations
INL	US State Department Bureau of International Narcotics and Law Enforcement Affairs
ISAF	International Security Assistance Force
KLB	Kerry-Lugar-Berman legislation on Pakistan
LTTE	Liberation Tamil Tigers of Eelam
MAIL	Afghanistan Ministry of Agriculture Irrigation and Livestock
MCA	Millennium Challenge Account
MCC	US Millennium Challenge Corporation
MDGs	Millennium Development Goals
MW	Megawatt
NATO	North Atlantic Treaty Organization
NGOs	Nongovernmental Organizations
NJ	New Jersey
NSC	National Security Council
OAPA	Office of Afghanistan and Pakistan
ODA	Official Development Assistance
OEF	Operation Enduring Freedom
OHCHR	UN Office of the High Commissioner for Human Rights

OMB	Office of Management and Budget
OPIC	Overseas Private Investment Corporation
P	US State Department Under Secretary for Political Affairs
PEPFAR	President's Emergency Plan for AIDS Relief
PM	US State Department Bureau of Political-Military Affairs
PMF	Presidential Management Fellowship
POTUS	President of the United States
PPP	Public-Private Partnership
PPP	Purchasing Power Parity
SCA	South Central Asia
SCA/A	US State Department Afghanistan desk
SCA/FO	US State Department SCA Front Office
SDGs	Sustainable Development Goals
SES	Senior Executive Service
SFRC	US Senate Foreign Relations Committee
SLFP	Sri Lanka Freedom Party
SRAP	US Special Representative for Afghanistan and Pakistan
STAFFDEL	Staff Delegation
TIP	Translator Interpreter Program
TUTAP	Turkmenistan, Uzbekistan, Tajikistan, Afghanistan, and Pakistan
UN	United Nations
UNGA	UN General Assembly
UNHCR	UN High Commissioner for Refugees
UNP	United National Party
US	United States
USAID	US Agency for International Development
USG	US Government
USUN	US Mission to the United Nations

AUTHOR'S NOTE

From a young age, I felt strongly connected to the stories and lives of people all around the world. Maybe it was because my extended family was spread across so many countries. Perhaps I grew up watching and internalizing my parents' struggle in leaving behind their families and countries of origin to escape generational poverty and try their luck in America. I did not know how, but even as a child, I wanted to create impact at scale and, true to the cliché, make the world a better place. As a first-generation Muslim immigrant of South Asian descent, I never expected to one day represent the United States of America as a diplomat and development official. I never planned on being a development diplomat.

Many people in careers like mine may share a similar moment of inspiration early on in their adult lives when they pick a job or an internship to make a difference in people's lives. They may start in their country's Foreign Service or work for a nongovernmental organization (NGO). They could participate at local levels in villages or cities or at regional or global levels working for nonprofit organizations, foundations, governments, multilateral institutions, or even the private sector. That initial foray may set them down a more permanent career path into the fields of foreign policy and international development, working in jobs that are deeply meaningful and become part of their life's mission.

In these positions, some people fluidly work across foreign policy and international development, recognizing the importance of both fields to promote shared security, stability, and prosperity. Others, as they deepen their expertise and knowledge and rise through the ranks, work deep within their own silos and are unable or unsure how to reach across the artificial divide. They may receive little formal training or exposure to each other's worlds, particularly if they are focused largely on their organization's internal bureaucracy. Promotions and job placements may rely on performance within their respective fields, with few formal incentives or opportunities to work across silos to learn more about the other part of the equation.

When foreign policy and development officials constructively come together in a common cause, transformative change can happen. Success can result in major new anti-poverty initiatives, new investments in physical and social infrastructure, and policy and institutional reforms addressing the root causes of poverty. When they talk past each other and fail to decipher the language and culture of their counterparts, the moment to fight poverty at scale can be lost in a heartbeat.

The space between foreign policy and international development can be filled by development diplomats, practitioners in both fields who successfully work together to achieve big things, as I witnessed in my career. Thanks to the Presidential

Management Fellowship (PMF), the flagship US government leadership development program for civil servants, I moved between agencies and branches of the US government. I also received formal training on many parts of the complex US bureaucracy early in my career.

I first trained as a diplomat and political aide in the national security and foreign policy worlds, with multiple stints at the US State Department and working for three senators in the US Congress, John Kerry, Robert Menendez, and Bob Casey Jr. During these experiences, I kept running headfirst into the field of international development, witnessing what both botched efforts and transformative investments looked like. I wanted to make a meaningful difference, particularly at national and regional levels, to reduce poverty at scale. Over time, I moved over to the Millennium Challenge Corporation (MCC), a US government development agency, and Oxfam America, an international nongovernmental organization (INGO), to build sustainable programming from the bottom up. Throughout this journey, I realized the silos dividing the foreign policy and development communities could be bridged with creative thinkers who speak fluently across both worlds.

This book draws on my insights from traveling to more than sixty countries, about half of them visited while officially representing the US government as a development diplomat from 2006 to 2018. It does not include any material from work I have done for the US government since then. The book takes the reader behind the scenes of what these types of careers look like and why they are some of the best jobs in the world, even though they can take a personal toll, especially for women managing family responsibilities. The stories shared here are deeply personal and my own recollection of events backed up by the historical record. Any mistakes in the book are mine alone.

As I traveled three-quarters of a million miles around the world on behalf of the United States, I found the work to be exhilarating, exhausting, rewarding, and unrelenting. Sometimes there were moments of danger and personal sacrifice. It meant drinking hundreds of cups of tea to advance diplomatic negotiations. Progress could take years; failure could take minutes. Above all, the struggle of juggling motherhood with a career on the road never ended, as I experienced with each of my three children.

Inspired by my parents and in-laws, this book is for anyone interested in creating a world free from the injustice of poverty. The stories and lessons shared here enable us to invest in the next generation of development diplomats, who are trained and equipped to achieve transformative results.

For our future diplomats, development experts, humanitarians, and peacemakers, this book is especially for you. May these words inspire you to pursue your own path committed to public service. May these stories encourage you to find new ways to break old barriers. In doing so, may you find and unleash your inner power to change the world for good.

INTRODUCTION

HIGH ABOVE THE MONGOLIAN STEPPE
I could not tear my gaze from the tiny airplane window. As I absorbed the sights of Inner Mongolia down below, time hung suspended as centuries seamlessly crisscrossed the green steppe, arid desert, and the Great Wall of China. Just hours before, I had walked that very wall during a layover but was now on the move again, lost in thoughts meandering through space and time.

There rode Genghis Khan and his tribesmen, I thought, looking for twelfth-century horsemen on the plains below. The Mongol Empire, which Genghis Khan and his successors carved out by uniting many of the nomadic, warring tribes of Northeast Asia, became the largest contiguous empire in history. Though often remembered by Westerners for his cruelty and destruction, Chinggis Khan, as referred to by Mongolians, is a national hero and source of immense pride in his present-day country. Synonymous with the grandeur of the ancient Silk Road connecting trade, commerce, art, and culture across Asia, Europe, and Africa, Genghis Khan laid the foundation for the modern world, including concepts of the rule of law, diplomatic immunity, religious coexistence, secular politics, and the free exchange of ideas. He is one of the most influential men in history and forever cemented Mongolia's place, changing the course of the world.[1]

A thousand years later, the work to build a thriving country continued, leading to my return to the capital, Ulaanbaatar, in December 2017. My head spun with the events of the past few days as I wrapped up seventy-two whirlwind hours spanning the ninety-five-degree heat of Indonesia with the negative twenty-degree freeze of Mongolia on official United States government business. The challenge of packing a carry-on suitcase for these extreme climates foreshadowed the complex negotiations in each country to advance our poverty-fighting agenda.

As I drummed my fingers on the seat armrest, I wondered, *Did we make people's lives better? Are we reducing poverty? Is all this travel taking me away from my kids worth it?*

On my thirty-eighth birthday, on behalf of the US government development agency called the Millennium Challenge Corporation (MCC), I met with the Mongolian prime minister, foreign minister, and other officials to finalize a way forward on a $350 million grant investment to increase bulk water supply in Ulaanbaatar.[2] After years of analysis and dis-

---

1   Jack Weatherford, *Genghis Khan and the Making of the Modern World* (New York: Crown Publishing Group, 2004), 3-10.
2   "MCC Regional Deputy Vice President Visits Mongolia, Meets with Senior Government Officials on MCC Compact Development Progress," US Millennium Challenge Corporation, press release, December 6, 2017.

cussion, both of our countries were eager to make this partnership work to improve the lives of the Mongolian people.

Mongolia held a special place in my heart, perhaps because it was so unique. Roughly two and a half times the size of Texas, but with only one-eighth of the population, it is the most sparsely populated nation in the world, with about three million people.[3] Because of the seventy million livestock, I always ran into more animals than humans when visiting the countryside. Though about a quarter of its people historically lived nomadic lifestyles, massive internal migration from rural areas to the city capital nearly tripled Ulaanbaatar's size. In less than three decades, Ulaanbaatar represented almost half of the country's population and three-quarters of its economic activity.[4]

The mining industry played a critical role in growing Mongolia's economy as it transitioned from socialism in 1990. I had never seen anything as massive as the Tavan Tolgoi coal mine and Oyu Tolgoi copper mine while in Ömnögovi Province in the South Gobi region of Mongolia. For a brief time, as the country experienced double-digit growth from 2011 to 2013, mainly due to a mining boom, Mongolia was the world's fastest-growing economy. A collapse in the price of coal and copper, the country's largest exports, however, led to a sharp economic downturn starting in 2014. This economic crisis exacerbated growing inequalities, accelerated internal

3   Karen Sessions, "Congressional Notification Transmittal Sheet," US Millennium Challenge Corporation, June 11, 2018.

4   Hiraga, Uochi, and Doyle, "Counting the Uncounted—How the Mongolian Nomadic Survey is Leaving No One Behind," *World Bank Blogs*, April 18, 2020.

migration and urbanization, and reversed nearly a decade of poverty reduction with roughly one in three people living below the poverty line.[5]

In speaking with female herders, migrants, and business leaders during my visits, I learned poverty disproportionately affected women in Mongolia. They shared their struggles to take care of their families under such tough economic conditions. Even though women were more likely to be better educated than men due to the Communist Party's legacy in the twentieth century, essentially proclaiming equality between men and women, traditional norms and values prevented women from achieving full equality and resulted in massive inequities in pay.[6]

The 2014 economic downturn was felt most acutely in Ulaanbaatar. Following decades of rapid urbanization, most of the city's residents lived in sprawling, low-density, peri-urban settlements called the "ger areas." The ger areas lacked basic services such as electricity, heat, and water supply. As I toured the gers, homes referred to as yurts in Central Asian countries, families living on the outskirts of Ulaanbaatar shared their challenges in moving from the countryside to the city. The imminent shortage of water was a particularly pressing problem, resulting from increased pollution and contamination of the Tuul River, which supplied the city's water needs. At current rates, the demand for water would outstrip supply by 2021, hindering job opportunities and

5   "The World Bank in Mongolia Overview," The World Bank, updated April 6, 2021.

6   Eliza Cochran, "6 Facts about Women's Rights in Mongolia," The Borgen Project (blog), December 17, 2020.

overall quality of life. Accordingly, Mongolia asked MCC to consider a significant investment in the water sector in the capital.[7]

The United States wanted to help Mongolians fight poverty and seize new market-oriented economic opportunities as part of its overall foreign policy priorities. Sustainable development in Mongolia was in both countries' collective interests, as Mongolia characterized the United States as its most important "third neighbor" in balancing the influence of China and Russia. Lifting people out of poverty was more than altruism or the right thing to do. Sustained economic growth would help countries like Mongolia transition to middle-income status, creating stability and more opportunities for a broader-based partnership with the United States and other democracies.

As a diplomat and development official, I knew we were on the cusp of a historic breakthrough if we could finally seal the deal. We spent the past three years undertaking analysis and discussing potential investments that could tackle the binding constraints to economic growth, particularly in the water sector. Progress in international development, though, is not always linear. As we considered various interventions, we worked through many ways to achieve sustainable growth, such as options regarding financing terms, policy and institutional reforms, tariff implications, and environmental and social standards. We considered each option against the backdrop of shifting political agendas when governments

---

7   Sessions, "Congressional Notification Transmittal Sheet," 2018.

changed hands and geopolitical headwinds that informed our policy choices.

On my December 2017 trip, our teams were convinced we found a way to provide a sustainable supply of water to fend off an impending water crisis and sustain private-sector-led economic growth. My job was to deliver the news of the United States' plan. *Will the Mongolians agree with our proposals? Will they accept our terms? Will we accept theirs?*

With significant US grant money at stake, the investment was a top priority between our two countries. Success required negotiations between both countries but also within each country's bureaucracy. For instance, I spent as much time negotiating with the Mongolians as I did with the US Ambassador and American counterparts across the US government, particularly the State Department, the White House, and Congress. The complex discussions involved economic analysis and technical knowledge of the Mongolian water sector. It also required political savviness and emotional intelligence to appreciate the broader political climate in the region and the pressures both governments faced on an investment this large. To succeed, we needed international development and foreign policy to work together. Failure could set back our anti-poverty efforts for the next generation. I refused to fail.

TWO TO TANGO

When most people think about tackling poverty, development experts like humanitarians, doctors, teachers, farmers, engineers, and economists fighting the good fight may come to mind. Indeed, their work is fundamental to building infrastructure, investing in education and health care systems, and increasing access to services and opportunities. This is particularly true to improve the lives of women and girls who make up more than two-thirds of the world's illiterate people.[8] To scale up sustainable development solutions, however, these experts cannot succeed on their own. They must partner with civil society, the private sector, and governments.

Civil society includes nongovernmental organizations and people who understand and reflect the needs of the populations they serve. The private sector is important to stimulate conditions for economic growth to generate revenue for the state. And governments are responsible for the welfare of their people. Governments can play a critical role in advancing inclusive and sustainable economies by implementing policy and institutional reforms, bringing together public and private sector resources, enforcing the rule of law and human rights, and prioritizing economic and social development in their national strategies. Institutionalizing these solutions, however, can take years or even decades, often taking twists and turns before breakthroughs are achieved.

Traditionally when it comes to partnering with governments, development officials work with technical line ministries in areas such as finance, education, public works, or health. Sustainable development, though, depends on securing political buy-in, which often requires partnering more broadly outside these lanes. For instance, development officials may also need

---

8   "Rural Women and the Millennium Development Goals," Inter-Agency Task Force on Rural Women, United Nations, 2012, accessed May 10, 2021.

to build relationships with political leaders, foreign affairs ministries, and opposing political parties, who could come to power in numerous election cycles and determine the outcome of a major development initiative. Working more intentionally in a deeply political space requires a unique set of skills development experts may not have. Politics, geopolitics, history, and the strategic context of the bilateral relationship are important dimensions to consider in managing these types of relationships to build critical political support for poverty-fighting efforts.

This is where diplomats come in. The foreign policy community represented by a country's foreign affairs ministry, or State Department in the case of the United States, can help navigate political waters for international development. People may think about foreign policy and the work of diplomacy through the lens of treaties, security pacts, or international meetings. Diplomats, however, can and do play critical roles in supporting the international development agenda. Diplomats are experts in politics and policy and should be able to leverage this knowledge in sophisticated ways to address critical gaps for the development community if both sides partner in smart ways. On the other hand, diplomats who lack expertise in economic affairs, political economy, international development, and social justice can unintentionally undermine development progress and set back efforts years in the making, especially if foreign aid is used for political purposes in lieu of fighting poverty. Prioritizing security issues in foreign policy at the expense of the basic needs of the most vulnerable can also create tensions in how foreign assistance dollars are spent.

Ultimately, securing long-term political support from governments and local populations is critical for sustainable development, as I observed in many countries like Mongolia and Pakistan. Success requires understanding the needs and incentives of all relevant stakeholders, as I experienced in Afghanistan and Jordan. During the time it takes to design and implement projects, governments may come and go, with different political parties championing varying development agendas, as I saw repeatedly in Nepal and Sri Lanka.

As someone with a foot in both diplomacy and development, I spent my career working across these silos in dozens of countries around the world. While leading regional development projects connecting Central and South Asia, I observed that getting all parties to agree on a single development strategy and timeline grounded in data and evidence, which could survive politically without politicizing the aid, could be challenging. While development experts were largely apolitical in designing and implementing poverty reduction programs, foreign policy officials pursued development strategies that furthered their national political agenda, as in the case of Afghanistan. Development professionals could comfortably take years developing or implementing pro-poor projects as long as the funding existed. At the same time, foreign policy officials pressed for more immediate deliverables and public announcements aligned to a finite political cycle, as I witnessed in Sri Lanka.

Diplomats and development officials can share the same goal to support a pro-poor agenda, but for different reasons. Development experts, for instance, may focus on increasing economic growth, promoting democracy and good governance, addressing systemic inequalities, or expanding social services to vulnerable populations to create a better functioning and fair society. Foreign policy officials, on the other hand, value cementing a strategic alliance between countries or promoting security and stability to advance their political agenda. Both parties may agree on shared development priorities but may have different points of views on what projects to fund, how much to spend, conditions and timing of the aid, and other considerations. These differences can be sufficient to prevent development projects from moving forward despite shared interests to fight poverty.

When diplomats and development officials successfully come together, they have a chance to pursue transformative change. It does not always work, and sometimes politics trump development. Still, the opportunity to fight poverty becomes that much harder if diplomats and development experts cannot work together on a shared vision. It can also result in lost opportunities for advancing national security and foreign policy goals.

Having worked in both fields across multiple US administrations, I understood each community's distinct languages and cultures, allowing me to see how we were often speaking past each other. I saw my role, in part, to translate across teams and build bridges to find creative ways forward. A fruitful partnership between international development experts and foreign policy diplomats required a collective road map of shared language, priorities, timelines, terms of financing, and policy reforms to advance anti-poverty efforts. Success relied on what I am referring to as "development diplomacy," defined here as leveraging diplomacy to achieve development objectives to end poverty.

On the night of my birthday in Ulaanbaatar, I received flowers and a card at my hotel from Mongolian Prime Minister Ukhnaagiin Khurelsukh. I was touched by the kind gesture and hoped it signified we were on the right path. My meetings on this winter visit were not easy, as I delivered potentially tough news on what the United States could and could not fund given our conditions and processes. I did not know how our Mongolian partners would react and did not want to cause any rifts in the bilateral relationship.

Successful diplomacy required threading the needle between each countries' development processes and political priorities involving extensive consultations in both the United States and Mongolia with our economists, infrastructure specialists, foreign affairs colleagues, technical line ministries, finance experts, and politicians. Representing the US government at such senior levels was a weighty responsibility, and I felt the piercing eyes of Washington, DC from six thousand miles away. *I hope I don't screw this up. So much rests on this visit.*

Months later, I exhaled when the United States and Mongolia signed a historic $350-million investment to increase the supply of water to Ulaanbaatar by more than 80 percent. The Mongolian government also committed up to $111.8 million of additional resources, one of the largest country contributions ever made by an MCC partner country at that time.[9] The

---

9   "MCC Mongolia Water Compacts Starts 5-Year Timeline with Entry into Force," US Millennium Challenge Corporation, press release, April 5, 2021.

funds would be used over a five-year timeline to construct new groundwater wells, a state-of-the-art water purification plant, and a new plant for treating and recycling wastewater, and the development and implementation of policy, legal, regulatory, and institutional reforms for long-term sustainability of Ulaanbaatar's water supply.

Together, these investments would create new jobs and increase the supply of water to Ulaanbaatar by more than 80 percent, ensuring a firm footing for the country to sustain its future economic growth.[10] After years of negotiations within the US government and various agencies of the Mongolian government, with dozens of development officials and foreign policy experts in each country tirelessly working together, both countries shared a joint vision on how best to fight water poverty in Ulaanbaatar.

I was one part of a larger collective effort, but proud to play a role in advancing sustainable and inclusive development to reduce poverty in Mongolia. As I looked through my airplane window high above the Mongolian steppe on my return home in December 2017, the last trip of my US government career at that point in my life, I realized I had unintentionally morphed into a "development diplomat." Perhaps this was my inner power, this ability to build bridges between worlds to have an impact at scale and, in my small way, change the world for good. There are many types of diplomacy including: nuclear diplomacy, science diplomacy, public diplomacy, gunboat diplomacy, and vaccine diplomacy. I decided to

---

10   Ibid.

capture some of my experiences in working on "development diplomacy," the sole focus of this book.

Drawing mainly on my experiences in Asia, which are applicable globally, the book is organized into four parts to help understand different perspectives. Part I provides a foundational overview of how development and diplomacy work within the US government and are learning chapters for those new to either field. Parts II and III focus on my time in the US legislative and executive branches, respectively, where I saw diplomacy and development come together or fall apart, including behind-the-scenes views of what happens in these jobs. Part IV shares lessons learned and twenty-one recommendations for policymakers to consider in investing in a new generation of development diplomats. Throughout the book, I share personal insights on how challenging it can be to manage this line of work as a woman, mother, and member of a minority.

Imagine if we created a whole cadre of development diplomats trained with the necessary skills from the onset of their careers to work across the international development and foreign policy divides. When done right, development diplomacy can result in programming built to withstand political turbulence, leading to sustainable and inclusive growth. This transformative investment can lead to greater political and economic stability, security for the most vulnerable, and increased opportunities for bilateral and regional partnerships. A minimal investment in our most important poverty-fighting asset—our people—can yield exponential development, security, and political benefits.

As we work to combat COVID-19, climate change, growing inequality, and security challenges, development diplomats are invaluable partners in meeting the world's Sustainable Development Goals (SDGs), a global commitment to end poverty by 2030, so all people enjoy peace and prosperity. If we can partner in more creative ways, as many of us hoped to do when we started our careers, together, we can change the world and end poverty once and for all.

PART I

UNPACKING DEVELOPMENT AND DIPLOMACY

When you get these jobs that you have been so brilliantly trained for, just remember that your real job is that if you are free, you need to free somebody else. If you have some power, then your job is to empower somebody else. This is not just a grab-bag candy game. This is the time for every artist in every genre to do what he or she does loudly and consistently. It doesn't matter to me what your position is. You've got to keep asserting the complexity and the originality of life, and the multiplicity of it, and the facets of it. This is about being a complex human being in the world, not about finding a villain. This is no time for anything else than the best that you've got.

—*Toni Morrison*[11]

---

11   Toni Morrison, "The Truest Eye," interview by Pam Houston, *O, The Oprah Magazine*, November 2003.

CHAPTER 1

DRIVING THE ROAD TO FIGHT POVERTY
WHY THE UNITED STATES LEADS GLOBAL DEVELOPMENT EFFORTS

- **Fight for others to have the same rights you enjoy.**
- **There are no borders or walls to protect us from poverty and inequality.**
- **Seeing things from all sides can bring people together.**

A DISCOVERY ON THE NEW JERSEY TURNPIKE

I found my spine and life's calling on the New Jersey Turnpike as a child in the early 1990s. We were heading south away from Exit 9 and the crowded strip malls and diners that dot Central Jersey. My father, Zahir Gunja, confidently drove his beloved Toyota Previa. This bluish-gray van, more akin to a humpback whale, represented more than a car to him. It proudly fit all four of his daughters, his doctor wife, his patriarchal father, his special needs brother, and probably half of our visiting relatives from India if we ignored seatbelts (we did; it was the early 1990s after all). The van symbolized hard-fought, middle-class status breaking from the generational poverty he experienced for most of his life. The Previa was his manifestation of the American Dream.

Without warning, my father steered the car into the shoulder of the New Jersey Turnpike, coming to an abrupt halt as cars whizzed by.

"Pappa, what are you doing? We can't stop here. It's dangerous," I cried out.

"Nothing's wrong; calm down," he replied. "It's *zohor namaz* time. We are going to stop here for our afternoon prayers."

"We can't do that," I replied, aghast. "Everyone is going to stare at us and think we are weird."

"No one will even notice; they are driving so fast," my father responded. "Even if they do, who cares?"

Within minutes, my parents unfolded their *masalas,* or prayer rugs, on the uneven, sloped grass bordering the shoulder's asphalt. After checking and rechecking his trusty prayer compass to make sure we faced southeast toward Mecca, Saudi Arabia, Pappa called out the *azan,* the Muslim call to prayer. I followed him in ritual, prostrating rigidly in submission to *Allah.* As I prayed outwardly, I seethed inwardly. I hoped none of my friends could see me. My father, however, had no patience for my chagrin, saying something that stuck with me ever since.

"Fatema, don't forget who you are. We came to this country to have freedoms and opportunities we did not have at home in India and Malaysia. Your job is to exercise these freedoms and make sure everyone has the same opportunities wherever they are in the world. Never be ashamed of who you are. Fight for others to have the same rights."

As a child, I did not understand the weight of his words and could not get past being different. A devout Muslim immigrant family, we stuck out in school, on the soccer field, and now even on our highways. To the outside world, we had funny-sounding names even in the Americanized versions we adopted for our teachers and friends.

Our days and nights were filled with prayer, even when we should have been doing our homework or could have been playing. "*Allah* first; everything else second," became the unofficial motto in our house. I could not appreciate the anchor religion provided my parents as they struggled to immigrate to a new country far from home, assimilate in a land of foreign tongues and cultures, and escape a history of generational poverty. Nor could I grasp the power of living in different worlds and having exposure to so many languages, cultures, and countries from an early age.

What I could see in front of me was what it meant to be poor. Whether in central Jersey or halfway around the world in Asia, I recognized the differences between people who had fancy houses and cars and those who struggled just to make ends meet. I recalled family trips to Mumbai, India, where many lived in densely crowded conditions with few amenities while orphans begged in the streets. On family visits to

Johor Bahru, Malaysia, I sometimes stayed in the rundown, crowded flats where my mother and her siblings grew up, places the government would demolish years later because of the decrepit conditions.

On the home front, I remember my parents whispering late at night when they thought everyone was sleeping, concerned about how to pay the bills to avoid taking an interest-based loan, which was culturally forbidden in our religion. With money always tight, we saved every penny and splurged on little. I watched in envy as my friends played with their new Cabbage Patch Kids and enjoyed individual ice cream cones while my sisters and I made do with hand-me-downs and shared treats. While we always had a roof over our heads, healthy meals, and access to quality education and healthcare thanks to my parents' incredible work ethic, it was never a guarantee that their economic futures could be so radically different than their pasts.

I did not appreciate then how my parents' success or failure depended not only on their individual actions, but on systems of governance, taxation, and policy priorities that could purposefully keep them poor or help them succeed. I did not comprehend poverty was man-made, a deliberate choice by governments to invest in some people while ignoring the basic needs of others. Although my parents worked tirelessly to make a better life for themselves and their children, they would have never entered the middle class without US policies on immigration, education, and homeownership enabling their success and eventually, my own. Perhaps it was fitting I chose to work on public policy for the US government as an adult. As the world's superpower, the United States decided the fates of many nations and people, including my parents. I wanted to influence this power for good.

FROM THE ASHES OF WORLD WAR II

Before the United States entered World War II, it started planning for peace. US President Franklin Delano Roosevelt knew he could not make the same mistakes President Woodrow Wilson and his predecessors had made. Failure to properly plan following World War I resulted in years of restrictive trade and tariff policies, US isolationism, and the collapse of national banks and economies. Within a decade, the world witnessed the Great Depression and the rise of Adolf Hitler and Nazi Germany.

In August 1941, several months before the Pearl Harbor attacks officially drew the United States into war, President Roosevelt and British Prime Minister Winston Churchill secretly met and issued a barely three-hundred-word-long joint statement. Later dubbed the Atlantic Charter, this document mapped out American and British goals for the world after the end of World War II.[12] The Atlantic Charter laid the groundwork for the post-war world, codifying a set of principles focused on "sovereign equality, self-determination and democracy, collective security and international law, and equal commercial access and treatment."[13] Among the eight principles of the charter, the fourth and fifth clauses, respectively, emphasized lowering trade barriers and fos-

---

12   Stewart M. Patrick, "Remembering the Atlantic," *Council on Foreign Relations* (blog), August 16, 2011.

13   Ibid.

tering global economic cooperation and advancement of social welfare.[14]

The Atlantic Charter inspired several major international agreements and took place amid events that shaped the post-World War II era, particularly the dismantling of the British Empire. These changes set the stage for a post-colonial world order conceived by colonial powers in the global North that represented the richest and most industrialized countries at the time. This new architecture included the creation of the United Nations (UN), the General Agreement on Tariffs and Trade (GATT), and the Bretton Woods system, which created the International Monetary Fund (IMF) and the International Bank for Reconstruction and Development (IBRD), now known as the World Bank Group. In July 1944, at a beautiful resort nestled in the White Mountains in New Hampshire, the Bretton Woods conference resulted in a new global financial system. The negotiations produced a framework for economic cooperation and development for a more stable and prosperous global economy.[15]

The United States played a key role in setting up and running the Bretton Woods system. It created the IMF to monitor exchange rates and lend reserve currencies to nations with balance-of-payments deficits. It charged the IBRD to provide financial assistance for reconstruction after World War

---

14 Ibid.
15 Laura Knoy, "Transcript: 75 Years Ago: N.H.'s Bretton Woods Conference Reshaped World Economic Policy," *The Exchange,* New Hampshire Public Radio, July 8, 2019.

II and the economic development of less developed countries.[16] These institutions had an outsized impact in shaping the post-World War II global order, stabilizing international currencies, rebuilding a war-torn Europe, and shaping global norms to fight poverty. Although the Bretton Woods system dissolved in 1970, the World Bank and IMF still function today as critical institutions to collectively promote long-term economic development, poverty reduction, and monetary cooperation and provide policy advice to preserve global macroeconomic and financial stability.[17,18]

While the United States championed new multilateral institutions in the aftermath of World War II, it also pursued major bilateral initiatives such as the Marshall Plan. From 1947 to 1949, US Secretary of State George Marshall invested more than fifteen billion dollars in financial and technical assistance in war-torn Europe. These resources allowed Europe to rebuild its infrastructure, strengthen its economy, halt the spread of communism, and stabilize the region from threats of future world wars.[19] The Marshall Plan became a key catalyst for the formation of the North Atlantic Treaty Organization (NATO), a military alliance between North American and European countries established in 1949, to promote regional stability.[20]

---

16 Sandra Kollen Ghizoni, "Creation of the Bretton Woods System," Federal Reserve History, November 22, 2013.

17 James Chen, "Bretton Woods System and Agreement," Investopedia, updated April 28, 2021.

18 "The IMF and the World Bank," International Monetary Fund, accessed April 10, 2021.

19 "USAID History," US Agency for International Development, updated May 7, 2019.

20 "Marshall Plan," HISTORY, updated June 5, 2020.

Efforts like the Bretton Woods system and Marshall Plan significantly influenced the modern-day concept of international development, prioritizing free markets and capitalism, social protection to help the poor and vulnerable cope with crises and shocks, and foreign assistance programs for countries at risk of instability. It also firmly intertwined development efforts with foreign policy goals. For instance, President Harry S. Truman formally proposed an international development assistance program called the 1950 Point Four Program. The Point Four Program focused on creating markets for the United States by reducing poverty and increasing production in developing countries, diminishing the threat of communism by helping countries prosper under capitalism.[21]

The Point Four Program also laid the foundation for the creation of the US Agency for International Development (USAID).[22] During the 1950s, as Africa and Asia experienced the breakup of colonial empires, fears of a communist takeover in the developing world dominated US foreign policy interests. Then-Senator John F. Kennedy seized upon a novel making waves at the time titled, *The Ugly American*. It critiqued the heavy-handed approach of the United States in Southeast Asia and called for grassroots efforts to improve poor people's lives to successfully counter communism.[23] As development expert Daniel F. Runde writes:

21 "USAID History," USAID, updated May 7, 2019.
22 Ibid.
23 Daniel F. Runde, "US Foreign Assistance in the Age of Strategic Competition," Center for Strategic and International Studies, May 14, 2020.

[Senator Kennedy] famously sent a copy [of the book] to each of his Senate colleagues as "required reading." Once he became president, Kennedy used *The Ugly American*'s ideas as the blueprint for the Peace Corps and for the Foreign Assistance Act of 1961, which founded USAID. USAID became the coordination vehicle for much of US foreign aid and expanded the focus of foreign assistance beyond just economic development to areas like agriculture, health, and education. The central themes of the Marshall Plan were retained with the creation of USAID.[24]

Each decade in the post-WWII era brought a different focus for US development efforts. In the 1950s and 1960s, USAID focused on massive capital and technical assistance to rebuild Europe and other poverty hotspots to fight the spread of communism. In the 1970s, USAID invested in a basic human needs approach centered on hunger, population planning, health, education, and human resource development. In the 1980s, the United States used foreign assistance to stabilize currencies and financial systems and promote free-market principles. With the fall of the Berlin Wall and the breakup of the Soviet Union, the top priority in the 1990s centered on establishing functioning democracies with open, market-oriented economic systems and responsive social safety nets.[25]

---

24 Ibid.
25 "USAID History," USAID, updated May 7, 2019.

In the 2000s, at the height of US wars in Afghanistan and Iraq, USAID shifted to a war footing, investing billions in these two countries on massive nation-building efforts to fight counterterrorism and focusing on other high-priority conflict areas. In the early 2010s, the Obama administration moved away from large, contractor-based models of development to support localization efforts where power and resources could be given to those on the ground. This shift turned into the Trump administration's "Journey to Self-Reliance," emphasizing an expansion of partnership and decision-making closer to those directly affected.[26]

Today, USAID is the US government's primary development agency working in more than one hundred developing countries to end extreme poverty and promote resilient, democratic societies.[27] The agency is headed by an administrator, who is appointed by the US president and confirmed by the US Senate.[28] Each USAID country office or mission is led by a Mission Director, who is responsible for implementing and overseeing all country-level development funds and programs. The Mission Director is part of the Country Team at the US Embassy under the direction of the US Ambassador.[29]

In addition to USAID, over twenty US government agencies manage foreign assistance programs and range in mission and scale, covering everything from investing in large-scale

---

26 Ibid.
27 Ibid.
28 "Office of the Administrator," US Agency for International Development, updated January 20, 2017.
29 "ADS Chapter 102 Agency Organization," US Agency for International Development, revised June 27, 2017.

infrastructure to community-driven development to job creation.[30] Some of these agencies are relatively young, such as the Millennium Challenge Corporation (MCC), which President George W. Bush created in 2004 as a new way to partner with low-income countries that meet particular good governance criteria.[31] In 2018, Congress formed the newest agency, the Development Finance Corporation (DFC), by merging the Overseas Private Investment Corporation (OPIC) and the USAID's Development Credit Authority (DCA), to provide low-cost and low-risk financing for businesses to open or expand operations in low-income countries to increase employment and economic growth.[32]

These aid agencies serve dual missions: to reduce poverty and to support US foreign policy objectives. It is why USAID receives overall policy guidance and budget approvals from the US Department of State and why even independent aid agencies that do not report to the White House, like the DFC or MCC, have the US Secretary of State as Chair of their Board of Directors. Just as in the post-WWII era when the United States was fighting communism, today's US development priorities still require political support from the foreign policy community for any major initiative to succeed. Critics of the current system would like to see development and humanitarian aid play a more independent role, separate from foreign policy considerations, and not follow the path Canada, Australia, Norway, and the United Kingdom have taken

30 "Agencies: Overview," ForeignAssistance.gov, updated January 22, 2021.
31 "The Millennium Challenge Account," White House of President George W. Bush, accessed April 20, 2021.
32 "US International Development Finance Corporation Begins Operations," US International Development Finance Corporation, January 2, 2020.

in recent years of folding their development ministries and agencies into their foreign affairs ministries. [33,34]

Viewing development priorities through the lens of foreign policy can bolster support for overall development budgets, particularly in countries viewed as high priority in terms of national security. Conversely, the power imbalance can have adverse consequences on development outcomes, inadvertently politicizing foreign aid for purposes that support security or foreign policy priorities but do not address the highest priority needs for the world's most vulnerable and marginalized.

The interdependent relationship between the foreign policy and development worlds is critical; they are codependent on each other for collective success in promoting political and economic security. Development professionals can find themselves at the mercy of their diplomatic counterparts in foreign affairs agencies, who may have the power to hold up resources for development initiatives, particularly in Washington and other capitals. On the other hand, foreign policy officials may consider development budgets relatively rigid and inflexible to address real-time needs and challenges on the ground. Development diplomats who can navigate between these worlds must understand and appreciate foreign policy considerations in successfully implementing development strategies without sacrificing the development agenda to foreign policy priorities.

33 Abby Young-Powell, "What Happens when an Aid Department is Folded?" *Devex*, December 18, 2019.

34 William Worley, "Breaking: DFID Merged with FCO," *Devex*, June 16, 2020.

To break this down in simple terms, consider a Venn diagram with a circle each for foreign policy and development officials. Each circle shares the same goals to advance policy initiatives such as reducing poverty, but their points of view may differ. The foreign policy community may support or oppose a proposed development project on political grounds. The development community may support or oppose the same project on economic and social grounds.

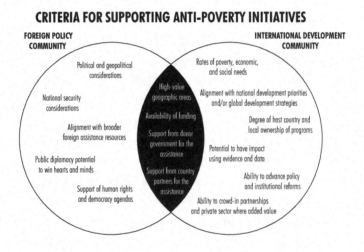

CRITERIA FOR SUPPORTING ANTI-POVERTY INITIATIVES

FOREIGN POLICY COMMUNITY

INTERNATIONAL DEVELOPMENT COMMUNITY

Political and geopolitical considerations

National security considerations

Alignment with broader foreign assistance resources

Public diplomacy potential to win hearts and minds

Support of human rights and democracy agendas

High-value geographic areas

Availability of funding

Support from donor government for the assistance

Support from country partners for the assistance

Rates of poverty, economic, and social needs

Alignment with national development priorities and/or global development strategies

Degree of host country and local ownership of programs

Potential to have impact using evidence and data

Ability to advance policy and institutional reforms

Ability to crowd-in partnerships and private sector where added value

On complex projects like building infrastructure or investing in large-scale capacity building initiatives, the proposed projects may only go successfully forward when these circles intersect. Expanding the size of the intersecting circle takes a lot of strategic planning and coordination on budgets, timelines, policy conditions, and congressional support. It requires development diplomacy. As the world races to recover and rebuild from COVID-19, we must dramatically scale up efforts to expand the size of the intersecting circle.

THE ROAD FROM RIO

In recent years, the international community called for dramatic new collective action to fight poverty. There was a basic recognition that no one country or actor could end global poverty by itself. With everyone focused on the same goals and timelines, the world could accelerate progress in lifting millions and even billions from the brink of survival.

Following a decade of major UN conferences and summits, like the 1992 Earth Summit in Rio de Janeiro calling for sustainable development, world leaders came together in September 2000 at the UN in New York City to adopt the United Nations Millennium Declaration.[35,36] The Declaration, codified in a series of eight Millennium Development Goals (MDGs), committed the world to a new global partnership, aiming to reduce extreme poverty by 2015.[37] With the MDGs as a north star, the 2000–2015 period produced the most successful anti-poverty movement in world history, with more than one billion people lifted out of extreme poverty (although much of the massive poverty reduction took place in India and China, two countries not particularly tied to the MDG agenda).[38,39] According to the Millennium Development Goals Report 2015, gains included combating hunger,

---

35 "United Nations Conference on Environment and Development, Rio de Janeiro, Brazil, 3-14 June 1992," United Nations, accessed June 5, 2021.

36 "Millennium Summit (6-8 September 2000)," United Nations, accessed June 5, 2021.

37 "News on Millennium Development Goals," United Nations, accessed June 5, 2021.

38 "Goal 1: Eradicate Extreme Poverty & Hunger," United Nations, accessed June 5, 2021.

39 "India, China Played Central Role in Global Poverty Reduction: United Nations," *Press Trust of India*, updated July 7, 2015.

expanding access to health care and education, creating new jobs and economic opportunities, improving sanitation, and increasing access to clean drinking water.[40]

There was much to celebrate, but the job was far from finished. Over 10 percent of the world's population, more than 766 million people, still faced poverty.[41] Women and girls, even those who benefited from gains in education and health services, continued to face structural gender power dynamics. "Progress on these other measures has been slow," according to London School of Economics and Political Science professor Naila Kabeer. "UN Women has estimated that, at the present pace of change, it will take fifty years before [women] achieve parity in parliament and eighty years to achieve equality in the economy."[42]

In September 2015, the world came together once again at the UN. During a historic meeting, leaders resolved by 2030 to

...end poverty and hunger everywhere; to combat inequalities within and among countries; to build peaceful, just and inclusive societies; to protect human rights and promote gender equality and the empowerment of women and girls; and to ensure the lasting protection of the planet and its natural resources.[43]

40 "Millennium Development Goals Report 2015," United Nations, 2015.

41 "1: End Poverty in all its Forms Everywhere," The World Bank, accessed June 5, 2021.

42 Naila Kabeer, "Gender Equality, the MDGs and the SDGs: Achievements, Lessons and Concerns," *International Growth Centre* (blog), October 1, 2015.

43 General Assembly Resolution 70/1, *Transforming Our World: The 2030 Agenda for Sustainable Development*, A/RES/70/1 (25 December 2015).

These aspirations were translated into seventeen Sustainable Development Goals (SDGs) that would sustain the gains already made to reduce extreme poverty while scaling up efforts to end poverty, particularly for women and girls who were often left behind. Despite the global commitment, identifying the funding and resources to achieve the SDGs was challenging, with a financing gap of around two and a half to three trillion dollars a year.[44] Although the global financial system, rewritten after World War II through efforts like the Bretton Woods system, successfully generated wealth at unprecedented levels with gross world product and global gross private sector financial assets estimated at over eighty trillion dollars and $200 trillion, respectively, it did not automatically repurpose this wealth toward equitable and inclusive economic growth.[45] Critics of the Bretton Woods system argued in many cases, it did the opposite by replicating colonial models of power that kept resource allocations and decision-making on how money should be spent in developing countries in the global North. [46,47]

Today, developing countries still lose trillions of dollars due to illicit financial flows, tax evasion and avoidance, money

---

44 "United Nations Secretary General's Road map for Financing the 2030 Agenda for Sustainable Development 2019-2021," United Nations, 2019.

45 *World Investment Report 2014: Investing in the SDGs: An Action Plan*, UN Conference on Trade and Development (United Nations, 2014).

46 "Inequality Crisis Worsens as World Bank and IMF Persist With Failed Policies," Bretton Woods Project, April 4, 2019.

47 Bastian Becker, "Colonial Legacies in International Aid: Policy Priorities and Actor Constellations," in *From Colonialism to International Aid. Global Dynamics of Social Policy*, ed. Carina Schmitt (Palgrave Macmillan, Cham. 2020), 161-162.

laundering, and corruption. According to anti-poverty organization Oxfam, corporate tax dodging costs poor countries at least one hundred billion dollars every year. Africa alone loses fourteen billion dollars in tax revenues due to the super-rich using tax havens.[48] To put this in perspective, this amount would be enough money to provide an education for 124 million children, prevent the deaths of almost eight million mothers, babies, and children a year, pay for health care to save the lives of four million children, and employ enough teachers to get every African child into school.[49] Developing countries face tough choices and trade-offs in growing their economies. They need to make hard decisions to service their debts, choosing between revenues, spending, and taxes on the rich and poor. In its Foreign Aid 101 report, Oxfam reports:

> According to the IMF, the number of low-income countries that cannot pay their debts or are at high risk of being unable to do so, has doubled since 2013, reaching two out of every five in total. Since 2000, more low-income countries have been taking loans from China or domestic creditors at much higher interest rates than loans from multilaterals like the World Bank. Investments in education and health care result in higher tax revenues and gross domestic product (GDP) over decades, not years. Financing anti-poverty programs with loans only end up deepening poverty as governments raise taxes on staples like food to generate the revenues

---

48 "Inequality and Poverty: The Hidden Costs of Tax Dodging," Oxfam International, accessed May 10, 2021.

49 Ibid.

to pay back debts. Despite this predictable negative impact, many donors are providing "aid" as loans instead of grants. African economies are spending up to five times more on debt payments than they are on health care.[50]

Just as in the aftermath of World War II, US leadership will be critical for global success in delivering both quantity and quality of aid. As the world's wealthiest nation, the United States provides more foreign aid—money, technical assistance, and commodities—than any other country in absolute terms, about $34.6 billion in official development assistance as of 2019.[51] Its share of aid, though, is a smaller proportion of its gross national income (GNI) than any other wealthy nation, a mere 0.16 percent in 2019.

This means the United States proportionally gives less than other countries with fewer resources and roughly the same proportion as Portugal and Slovenia.[52] Rich countries, especially the United States, consistently fail to honor their commitment made at the UN in 1970, to spend a minimum net amount of 0.7 percent of their gross national product (GNP) for foreign aid. As a result, developing countries forego an estimated $5.7 trillion in aid that could have been used to eradicate hunger and extreme poverty.[53]

---

50 Ritu Sharma, "Foreign Aid 101 A Quick and Easy Guide to Understanding US Foreign Aid, Fifth Edition," Oxfam America, 2021.

51 Ibid.

52 Ibid.

53 Emma Seary, "50 Years of Broken Promises," Oxfam International, October 2020.

A push exists within civil society to increase US foreign aid, but US domestic politics makes that difficult to achieve. When polled, most Americans think their government spends a massive amount on foreign aid, something like 25 percent of the federal budget. Foreign aid, however, is less than 1 percent of the entire US federal budget.[54] Poverty-focused development aid is half of that at 0.5 percent.[55] Embarrassingly, as Oxfam points out, the average American spends more on Halloween costumes ($268), jewelry ($174), and sporting goods ($158) each year than the US government spends on fighting poverty around the world ($65).[56]

While cutting foreign aid has almost zero effect in reducing the US national debt, it has disastrous consequences in safeguarding the welfare of millions of people worldwide, putting our shared security at risk. Most Americans may not realize or care that each US dollar spent abroad generates significant returns on investment in promoting stability, generating demand for US goods, building stable trading partners, promoting human rights and social justice, leveling the playing field for women and girls, protecting against global health pandemics, and demonstrating the goodwill of the American people. Increasing the overall amount and quality of humanitarian, development, and security aid is critical for US leadership on the world stage, especially as poverty continues to get worse.

---

54 George Ingram, "What Every American Should Know about US Foreign Aid," Brookings Institution, October 15, 2019.
55 Sharma, "Foreign Aid 101," Oxfam, 2021.
56 Ibid.

Today, our collective last-mile efforts to end hunger, achieve full gender equality, improve health services, and get every child in school face existential challenges. We must pay particular attention to a rapidly warming planet, the largest human migrations in history due to conflict and natural hazards, global pandemics like COVID-19, and diminished US global leadership in the aftermath of the Trump administration. The good news is the world knows how to eradicate extreme poverty. With as little as two trillion dollars in purchasing power parity, the equivalent of just 0.14 percent of global GDP, we can end extreme poverty if we choose to do so.[57]

PANDEMICS AND POVERTY

Here is a hard truth: We are going backward in our collective efforts to end poverty. For a while, we were on the right track, especially when you consider about 80 percent of the world's population lived in extreme poverty in the 1960s.[58] During most of my life, the world made incredible progress in fighting extreme poverty with sharply reduced rates of mortality and hunger, bringing that number closer to 10 percent.[59]

In 2020, however, during the COVID-19 pandemic, we undid twenty-five years of progress in just twenty-five weeks.[60] By one metric, the pandemic left the world with

---

57   Ginette Azcona, "From Insights to Action Gender Equality in the Wake of COVID-19," UN Women, 2020.

58   Peter Beaumont, "Decades of Progress on Extreme Poverty Now in Reverse Due to COVID," *The Guardian*, February 3, 2021.

59   Ibid.

60   "Poverty: Overview," The World Bank, updated October 7, 2020.

the worst job crisis in over ninety years, with hundreds of millions of people underemployed or out of work.[61] The World Bank estimates up to 120 million more people are living in extreme poverty below the poverty line of $1.90 a day, with the total expected to rise to about 150 million by the end of 2021.[62] By some estimates, the economic fallout from COVID-19 could push half a billion more people into poverty.[63] This increase represents a rise of 6 to 8 percent from pre-COVID-19 levels.[64] South Asia accounts for around 60 percent of the new poor, followed by sub-Saharan Africa, East Asia, and the Pacific.[65]

Low-income countries will not be the only ones to suffer the consequences. According to the World Bank, middle-income countries may be home to 82 percent of the new poor.[66] Compared to the chronic poor, new poor populations are more likely to engage in informal services and manufacturing instead of agriculture and live in congested urban environments with their work affected by lockdowns and mobility restrictions.[67] Crises are never gender-neutral in how they affect people, and COVID-19 is no exception, as explained by UN Women:

61 "Mega-rich Recoup COVID-losses in Record-time yet Billions will Live in Poverty for at least a Decade," Oxfam International, press release, January 25, 2021.

62 "Poverty," The World Bank, October 7, 2020.

63 "Half a Billion People could be Pushed into Poverty by Coronavirus, Warns Oxfam," Oxfam International, press release, April 9, 2020.

64 Ibid.

65 Christoph Lakner et al., "Updated Estimates of the Impact of COVID-19 on Global Poverty: Looking Back at 2020 and the Outlook for 2021," *World Bank Blogs*, January 11, 2021.

66 "Poverty," The World Bank, October 7, 2020.

67 Ibid.

While men reportedly have a higher fatality rate, women and girls are especially hurt by the resulting economic and social fallout. Impacts on women and girls have worsened across the board. Women are losing their livelihoods faster because they are more exposed to hard-hit economic sectors. According to a new analysis commissioned by UN Women and [the UN Development Program], by 2021, around 435 million women and girls will be living on less than $1.90 a day—including forty-seven million pushed into poverty because of COVID-19.[68]

Consider that we are living in a world where a handful of people, mostly men, have more wealth than the 4.6 billion people who represent 60 percent of the planet's population.[69] Put another way, the twenty-two richest men in the world have more wealth than all the women in Africa. Meanwhile, the poor get poorer and more marginalized.[70] Underfunded public services result in societies where only the rich can afford a decent education, quality health care, or a life of dignity.

The statistics are sombering, and the stakes are high, especially when factoring in the effects of climate change on the developing world. The World Bank estimates climate change could push an additional 132 million people below the poverty line by 2030.[71] According to the US Global Leadership Coalition:

---

68 Azcona, "From Insights to Action," UN Women, 2020.
69 "5 Shocking Facts about Extreme Global Inequality and How to Even It Up," Oxfam International, accessed May 10, 2021.
70 Ibid.
71 "Climate Change: Overview," The World Bank, updated March 23, 2021.

The impacts of the COVID-19 pandemic are likely to exacerbate the impact of climate-driven challenges and disrupt efforts to address them. Climate-driven disasters threaten to overwhelm local health systems at a time when they are already under extreme stress, and the costs of damage and recovery from a natural disaster, when compounded with the pandemic, are estimated to be as much as 20 percent higher than normal.[72]

With 2020 tying as the hottest year ever recorded, the global economic recovery from COVID-19 will have to factor in multiple dimensions that disproportionately affect the poor. The problem is compounded by the consequences of extreme weather, devastation from droughts and floods, and conflicts over diminishing natural resources such as water.[73]

Successful leadership in meeting these new global challenges requires new ways of working across governments, the private sector, and civil society. We need new types of partnerships to leverage capital, human resources, and sheer political will across these sectors. We must imagine new configurations of how bureaucracies can work more efficiently together to solve interdependent problems. This challenge is our collective opportunity to change the world for good.

On the New Jersey Turnpike, my father charged me with a big mandate during my childhood: to fight for others to

---

72 "Climate Change and the Developing World: A Disproportionate Impact," US Global Leadership Coalition, March 2021.

73 Ibid.

have opportunities. I wanted to be part of something bigger than me, part of a global effort to tackle the world's toughest challenges. I initially saw diplomacy as the road to making that happen. I decided to start right away.

CHAPTER 2

NAVIGATING THE CORRIDORS OF DIPLOMACY

HOW THE US STATE DEPARTMENT WORKS TO FIGHT POVERTY

- Leadership is not about rank or title since anyone can lead at any point.
- Learn the language first before you speak.
- Work across silos, not just deep within them.

MALAYSIAN WATER DIPLOMACY

I first represented the United States as a development diplomat when I was fourteen years old, thanks to a bulletin board I stumbled across two years earlier in 1992. Peeking out from the flurry of bright-colored paper posters tacked up in the Girl Scouts office, a plain white paper caught my eye with the word "Malaysia" bolded in all caps.

What's this all about? On instinct, I tore down the ad. Like my mother, Sakina Gunja, and her siblings, I was born in Malaysia in the city of Johor Bahru on the southern tip of the mainland, just across from Singapore. After studying at Darbhanga Medical College, my mother returned to Bihar, India—with me in tow—to finish her medical internship. According to her accounts, her time in Bihar included some of the roughest years of her life, experiencing widespread power outages, student protests, and poverty. At the same time, she was raising a child on her own while my father worked as an industrial engineer in Stockton, California. If not for my great-aunt, Umme Massey, who moved from Bombay to Bihar to help raise me during this time, my mother claims she would not have made it. Eventually, my mother and I rejoined my father in the United States when I was a toddler, first living in California and then New Jersey, where I spent the rest of my childhood. I hardly ever came across anything related to Southeast Asia in Central Jersey. Bubbling with excitement, I rushed home to tell my parents about the ad.

It turns out, the Delaware Raritan Girl Scouts Council of Central New Jersey was looking for Girl Scouts to represent the United States on a diplomatic exchange in Malaysia with their national Girl Guides Association. With the theme of "Our Water, Our World," the mission centered on the next generation of female leaders in both countries discussing the benefits of water and the dangers of water pollution. Even though I did not have a particular interest or knowledge about environmental issues at this point, I felt compelled to be on this trip. My parents must have been swept up in my enthusiasm because they quickly said yes without fully realizing the commitment required, like needing to cover the costs of the trip. As we raised funds over the next two years, my mom and I also became cultural ambassadors, teaching the American delegation about the Malaysian language, culture, food, and religions. In many ways, my diplomatic role began even before I left the United States.

Many dollars and days later, on August 12, 1994, Malaysia Air flight #95 touched down in Subang International Airport about thirty kilometers west of the capital, Kuala Lumpur. I was excited to be part of this delegation of ten Girl Scouts representing the United States on our first official mission overseas. Proudly dressed in my Girl Scout uniform filled with hard-earned badges and pins, I could not wait to start.

For three weeks, we traveled through the Malaysian states of Selangor, Malacca, Johor, Pahang, and Perak, meeting with government officials and students. We dined with the Malaysian Minister of Education, Dr. Sulaiman bin Daud, and visited schools to discuss the importance of educating and investing in girls. In a briefing with the Ministry of Youth and Sports, we spoke about the role youths play in caring for the environment. We stopped by the University of Malaya to hear a talk by Professor Mohd Al Hassan on "A Primer on Water: A Malaysia Case."

My first sojourn of diplomacy was intoxicating. How surreal to be young but taken seriously in high-level meetings on critical issues such as the environment and water! I loved the dialogue and discussions on development issues. We were forging ties with people on the other side of the world and talking about concrete steps our countries could take. Local Malaysian newspapers picked up on our trip and wrote stories about how their native daughter returned home as an ambassador between the United States and Malaysia. My Malaysian relatives proudly joked with me about my "celebrity status."

For the first time in my life, I saw the value of having a foot in multiple worlds. I realized the more I could relate to others and where they were coming from, the easier it would be to make my case. Even as a teenager, I recognized right away leadership was not about rank or title. Anyone could lead at any point in their life, from any position. On this life-changing trip, I seized the moment to speak to those in power on behalf of those who could not.

The first time I visited the American Embassy in Kuala Lumpur, I was in awe. The embassy exuded power and purpose in its red clay roofing tile with wide verandas and large eave overhangs. The career diplomats we spoke with were bright and motivated to make a difference. They welcomed our views on improving water quality. In my teenage mind, these diplomats could shape environmental outcomes in meaningful ways by exercising the full power of the United States in Malaysia.

"I want that job one day," I said to my fellow Girl Scouts, believing I could change the world for the better as a diplomat. I could not wait to tell my parents everything I experienced.

Unfortunately, I arrived home to find my world turned upside down. At only forty-six years old, my father had become very sick, running high fevers for weeks at a time. The doctors ran nonstop tests trying desperately to solve his medical mystery but could not determine the cause of the illness. Within a few short months, my father died of internal bleeding from a badly botched biopsy. He never heard much of my initial diplomatic foray or lived to see his eldest daughter officially represent the United States of America.

Overnight, I aged a decade as I helped my mother raise three younger siblings on a single income. I slowly started to understand what Pappa meant on the New Jersey Turnpike about being grateful for what we had despite many hardships. His words and legacy lived on. Along with my mother's fighting spirit, my parents' journey strengthened my resolve to be proud of my heritage and fight for others to have opportunity and dignity wherever they lived in the world.

In high school, I started small by co-leading a Girl Scout Brownie troop and volunteering in my town. I studied hard and practiced for my future role on the world stage by participating actively in Model United Nations and Model Congress. In college, thanks to mentors like Joyce Muchan at Cornell University's Public Service Center, I led organizations like the university's largest volunteer program, Into the Streets, and founded the Translator Interpreter Program (TIP) to expand critical language services to those in need. Today, TIP still provides essential language services to over three hundred community agencies in greater Tompkins County, New York.[74] I majored in government and foreign policy, traveled abroad in the Middle East, and studied multiple languages like Arabic and Indonesian (unfortunately, none of them quite stuck).

---

74 "Translator-Interpreter Program," Cornell University Public Service Center, accessed May 10, 2021.

After college, I spoke out against racial profiling in my work with the American Civil Liberties Union, focusing on African American communities decimated by decades of harsh drug laws and Muslim-Americans targeted following the terrorist attacks of September 11, 2001. Eventually, I enrolled in graduate school to pursue foreign policy and fulfill my childhood dream of being a diplomat. I hoped my father would be proud.

THE ACRONYMS OF FOGGY BOTTOM

Diplomacy is essentially the management of a country's relations with other countries for its own strategic and political interests. It is the main instrument of a country's foreign policy. Diplomats represent their country abroad, crafting and implementing foreign policy and leveraging their country's power on critical international issues. Career diplomats usually work through a state's ministry or department of foreign affairs and are supported around the world through embassies and consulates. In the United States, the Department of State is the lead foreign affairs agency responsible for promoting peace and stability in areas of strategic interest. The State Department supports Americans and US businesses abroad, protects US interests overseas, and implements foreign policy priorities around the world. The Department is headed by the Secretary of State, the president's principal foreign policy advisor and chief diplomat.[75]

The Secretary is staffed by political leaders appointed by the White House and career staff from the Foreign Service

---

75 "Diplomacy: The US Department of State at Work," US Department of State, accessed February 9, 2021.

and Civil Service. Foreign service officers (FSOs) are chosen through a highly competitive selection process and rotate assignments every few years among the 270 embassies, consulates, and diplomatic missions around the world, commonly referred to as "posts." Some of these posts are in difficult or even dangerous environments like war zones. Civil servants support the FSOs largely through assignments in Washington, DC, and other domestic locations, bringing deep expertise and historical perspective on a range of issues. Civil servants do not rotate locations or assignments, providing critical continuity to run the Department's core operations. Together, the Foreign Service and Civil Service comprise the backbone of the US diplomatic corps.[76]

Getting a job at the State Department is competitive and prestigious. There are only a few points of entry, such as internships, Foreign Service positions, Civil Service jobs, and fellowships. Despite my fascination with diplomacy from a young age, I initially did not know how to pursue this line of work. It took time to understand the numerous pathways and trade-offs. When my graduate school career advisor, Ann Corwin, encouraged me to apply for the State Department summer internship program between my first and second years of graduate school, I jumped on the chance to live and work in Washington for the first time. I did not know what to expect, but I assumed it would be grand and important. After all, as an intern in the Afghanistan office or "desk," I was getting a security clearance!

I remember the first time I walked into "Main State," the Department's headquarters in the Harry S. Truman (HST)

---

76 Ibid.

building. The limestone façade looked massive and imposing from the outside, tucked away west of the White House in the Foggy Bottom neighborhood and covering an area of four-square blocks. As I entered the official entrance from C and 22nd Streets NW, the approximately 180 flags on the north wall of the lobby grabbed my attention.[77] As I soaked in the colors and shapes from around the world, a flag for each nation with which the United States maintained diplomatic relations, I could feel the magnitude of America being a "superpower."

In my first week on the job, I expected to be immersed in US foreign policy. Instead, my boss, Neil Kromash, threw two folders on my desk.

"Read and memorize these documents," he advised me. "They contain the keys to your success in this building."

I eagerly opened the folders, prepared to see State Department secrets and classified information. Instead, the folders contained a detailed map of the HST building and pages of acronyms. I felt cheated. When I went to respectfully complain to Neil, he looked at me kindly and counseled patience.

"Learn the language first before you speak," he explained.

I quickly came to see the wisdom of Neil's words. HST was a physically massive building, and everyone seemed to speak in code. Architects designed HST to showcase the Department's

---

77   "Extended, Remodeled New State Building," US Department of State, Office of the Historian, accessed June 5, 2021.

power and hierarchy through its vertical plan. The offices and bureaus were arranged in a pyramid style, starting at the top with the Secretary of State's seventh-floor offices and broadening toward the base in decreasing rank order on each subsequent lower floor.

I spent my first few days getting hopelessly lost in the endless corridors of power, literally and figuratively. Using a coded map of floors and hallways running north-south and east-west amid forty-four elevators to find a room took some detective work. I worked on the fourth floor of the 2 Hall, jumping elevators, and crossing odd-numbered corridors to find my bosses' offices two floors up on the even-number side of the building. I learned to plan at least ten minutes of travel time between meetings: five minutes to decipher the coded map and five minutes to run the halls in heels to avoid being late.

Beyond attending meetings, life at the State Department centered around paper, the true religion of the Department. Any policy position, speech, meeting agenda, or talking point needed to be cleared around the building and the world, which meant getting sign-off from any bureau or embassy with a stake on the issue. To write or clear paper, I needed to first decipher the language of the State Department, best expressed through hundreds of acronyms.

"Encourage POTUS to raise USUN vote with GOA during UNGA session on IDP issues," a memo could state, for instance, encouraging the State Department principal to ask the President of the United States (POTUS) to discuss the US vote at the United Nations (USUN) on internally displaced persons

(IDPs) with the head of the Afghan government (GOA) during the upcoming UN General Assembly session (UNGA).

Just learning how to introduce myself took me a week. "I'm an intern in HST working in SCA/A reporting to a DAS in SCA/FO," I may have said to characterize my internship at Main State on the Afghanistan desk.

"I'm currently writing a BCL for the SCA A/S for her meeting with P to be cleared by post and DRL, INL, and EUR/ACE," I may have shared with a colleague to explain the briefing checklist I compiled for the South and Central Asia bureau Assistant Secretary's meeting with the Under Secretary for Political Affairs, which needed clearances from Embassy Kabul and the bureaus responsible for human rights, narcotics and law enforcement, and Central Asia foreign assistance.

I learned even more about the bureaucracy when I accepted the Presidential Management Fellowship (PMF), the flagship US government leadership development program for civil servants, following graduate school. Newly minted as the regional Central Asia Desk Officer at the State Department, a region I initially knew nothing about besides the countries all ending in -stan, I converted fully to my new religion. Success in this world meant getting one's point of view on policy translated into official talking points that survived the clearance process. This required negotiation over words and policy choices with numerous desks and posts to convince higher-ups to accept the proposed language in their meetings and speeches. It also meant navigating how power worked in the hierarchy and understanding how regional and functional bureaus interacted.

For instance, an Assistant Secretary (A/S) and her Deputy Assistant Secretaries (DAS) working on the sixth floor headed a bureau's front office, the nerve center of our foreign policy operations. The most senior official ran each bureau, responsible for a specific region of the world such as South and Central Asia (SCA), where I worked, or a particular function such as Political-Military Affairs (PM). They made the major decisions on foreign policy and development decisions in their respective portfolios and oversaw the work of all embassies in their regions. It could take staff years to work their way up the ranks to work in a bureau's front office as a senior official such as a DAS.

Sometimes there were tensions between regional and functional bureaus over issues such as human rights. DRL, the bureau of Democracy, Human Rights, and Labor, could, for example, take a different stance than a regional bureau like SCA on how a Central Asian country was upholding religious freedom. The bureaus could disagree on the penalties the United States should impose for violating human rights norms. DRL might recommend taking a very hardline approach that SCA opposed on the grounds it would negatively impact the bilateral relationship. In such cases where bureaus could not agree on the way forward, the issue in conflict would be kicked upstairs to bosses on the seventh floor who represented Under Secretaries, Deputy Secretaries, and, of course, the ultimate arbitrator, the Secretary of State.

Working at the State Department required strong writing and analytical skills, curiosity about the world, and deep reverence for rules and order. Junior and mid-career staff implemented policies within their bureaus, coordinating closely with posts and writing or clearing paper all day long to make sure everyone was on the same page. My day-to-day job as a junior staffer required close coordination with the relevant functional bureaus and posts in Central Asia, Moscow, Kabul, Baku, and the broader region. We coordinated through official visits, phone calls, emails, briefing memos, and most of all, through written cables that circulated widely within any government agency relevant to the issue at hand.

Working in a 70,000-person bureaucracy meant strict rules, discipline, and enforcement of hierarchy. Rank mattered in this top-down, decision-making culture and showed up in noticeable ways, such as where one could sit at a table. I remember meetings where everyone shuffled seats whenever a person with a higher rank entered the room to ensure seniority determined who sat by the head of the table. The formality of the building echoed throughout its conference rooms and hallways. Everyone knew their rank and that of others for deciding who could speak at a meeting, sit at a table, or represent the United States. Officers received promotions for demonstrating their policy chops, of course, but also for following these strict rules of engagement.

Due to the massive bureaucracy, successfully negotiating policy, budgets, people, and even office space in the crowded building took enormous skill. Avoiding zero-sum negotiations between bureaus and agencies to pursue win-win solutions required artful practice. The worst outcome could involve a bureau closing ranks and protecting its turf from perceived encroachment from another bureau, preventing new policy ideas from advancing. Success required building trust, a strong network of relationships, and knowledge of how to navigate the bureaucracy both in Washington and abroad.

Regional bureaus and embassies often ended up as the ultimate kingmakers, given their powerful voice on any policy choice affecting their respective region. Victory depended on securing buy-ins from relevant ambassadors and regional front offices. Finding solutions to regional problems was particularly challenging because the Department's budgets, people, and resources were largely organized in bilateral missions around the world. Many speeches by senior Department officials called for grand regional or continental cooperation, but few budgets existed to support regional projects in a significant way. This bilateral division made it more laborious to translate global visions into regional actions.

Deciphering how the State Department worked on the inside became one of my most critical skill sets in navigating the maze of the US government. These foundational skills eventually became the anchor upon which I relied extensively to negotiate successful development outcomes for the US government.

ACROSS BOTH ENDS OF PENNSYLVANIA AVENUE

The thing that most surprised me during my early years at the State Department was the role the Department played on international development. In graduate school, I assumed the work of diplomacy translated narrowly to foreign policy and national security. I did not appreciate the significant role of foreign policy officials on international development, humanitarian assistance, and global health issues. I never studied the development side of the US government, so I missed the critical work of the Department in managing foreign assistance budgets.

The US government's overall budget is divided into twenty categories called budget functions or accounts.[78] The State Department, alongside USAID, the Millennium Challenge Corporation (MCC), the Development Finance Corporation (DFC), and other development agencies, receives funding from the Function 150 account, which covers international affairs. This account includes money for foreign assistance, operation of US consulates and embassies, military assistance for US allies, economic assistance for new democracies, promotion of US exports, dues, and payments to international organizations such as the UN, and international peacekeeping efforts. Historically, 90 percent of this budget is allocated to the State Department and USAID.[79] From 2019 to 2020, 26 percent of the 150 Account supported diplomacy through US embassies and activities that protect American businesses and citizens abroad, such as US passport and consular services.[80]

As the lead US agency coordinating foreign aid, the State Department aligns development and humanitarian priorities with the broader foreign policy agenda. This coordination includes areas such as economic growth, humanitarian crises, contributions to international and multilateral organizations

---

78 Liza Casabona, "What is the Function of the 150 Account?" *The Borgen Project* (blog), April 17, 2015.

79 "Office of Foreign Assistance: About Us," US Department of State, accessed February 9, 2021.

80 Sharma, "Foreign Aid 101," Oxfam, 2021.

like the United Nations and World Bank, facilitating aid to refugees and vulnerable populations, and overseeing global health priorities like fighting HIV/AIDS. This alignment happens through bureaus such as:

- The Office of Foreign Assistance, more colloquially known as the "F" bureau, which provides overall strategic direction for the Department and USAID foreign assistance resources.[81]
- "EB," or the Department's Bureau of Economic and Business Affairs, leads on development finance, investment, and macroeconomic issues, in cooperation with other US government agencies.[82]
- The Bureau of International Organization Affairs, or "IO," with its six diplomatic missions (Geneva, Montreal, Nairobi, New York, Rome, and Vienna), develops and implements U.S. policy at the United Nations and in a wide range of other multilateral organizations.[83]
- Bureaus such as "PRM" for Population, Refugees, and Migration is the humanitarian arm of the State Department, promoting US interests by providing protection, easing suffering, and resolving the plight of persecuted and forcibly displaced people around the world.[84]

---

81   Adva Salinger, "Q&A: What Exactly does the State Department's 'F' Bureau do?" *Devex*, August 14, 2019.

82   "Bureau of Economic and Business Affairs: Our Mission," US Department of State, accessed July 28, 2021.

83   "Bureau of International Organization Affairs: Our Mission," US Department of State, accessed July 28, 2021.

84   "Bureau of Population, Refugees, and Migration: Our Mission," US Department of State, accessed July 28, 2021.

The State Department and development agencies work closely with the White House on foreign assistance. Through its Office of Management and Budget (OMB), the White House considers the overall foreign aid budget and allocation of scarce resources.[85] This analysis could require shifting money from other priorities, across agencies, or requesting additional funds or authorization from Congress. Through its National Security Council (NSC), the White House looks at broader foreign policy and foreign aid strategies of the US government, ensuring each development agency's approach is in line with the overarching US policy priorities.[86]

The State Department examines development priorities through the lens of foreign policy and national security priorities. In other words, outside of humanitarian assistance responding to urgent disasters, the importance of longer-term development funds is weighed against the backdrop of political and foreign policy priorities of a given administration. For instance, the State Department will want to make sure development dollars do not undermine American foreign policy goals by rewarding state sponsors of terrorism. Foreign aid is considered within the context of its ability to actively advance US foreign policy priorities such as promoting peace and stability, upholding democratic norms, empowering women and girls, and protecting human rights.

The US Ambassador, who exercises Chief of Mission authority overseeing all activities of a US diplomatic mission or office abroad, plays a critical role in supporting US foreign

---

85 "Office of Management and Budget," The White House, accessed June 5, 2021.

86 "National Security Council," The White House, accessed June 5, 2021.

aid programs.[87] Soliciting the Ambassador's support for key development initiatives, therefore, is essential. When things work well, the Ambassador can be a powerful ally and staunch supporter of international development initiatives, working closely and constructively with US development agencies to advance a shared mission and raise critical development priorities with the partner country's head of state and key government officials. When development agencies clash with the Ambassador's perspective, the Ambassador's view often carries the day. In theory, independent aid agencies such as MCC face more leeway than an agency like USAID, which is overseen by the State Department, although the basic tensions between foreign policy and development can still exist.

The Secretary of State has final authority for USAID and independent agencies such as DFC and MCC. This oversight is supposed to ensure disparate foreign aid initiatives and policies are stitched up into a coherent strategy so that the US government speaks with one coordinated voice. It requires complex interagency coordination and negotiation, which sometimes goes very smoothly to support anti-poverty initiatives and sometimes falls apart due to competing foreign policy priorities. These spaces between the foreign policy and international development agencies are often not the focus of attention or training for officials in either field, although navigating them strategically can be the difference between success or failure on development priorities.

---

87   Matthew C. Weed and Nina M. Serafino, "US Diplomatic Missions: Background and Issues on Chief of Mission (COM) Authority," Congressional Research Service, March 10, 2014.

The spaces become even more pronounced when working with Congress. Congress exercises oversight responsibilities of the executive branch, including US foreign policy and international development. The Hill executes this mandate in many ways, particularly through its congressional committees such as the Senate Foreign Relations Committee (SFRC) and the House Foreign Affairs Committee (HFAC). These committees have authority to review the budgets and priorities of agencies like the State Department, USAID, DFC, and MCC; approve nominations for senior leadership such as ambassadors and the heads of agencies; authorize legislation and reports on specific policy and development issues within their jurisdiction; and authorize the president to go to war.[88]

Congress and the executive branch can feel like worlds apart, with distinct mandates, cultures, and personalities separating the two. Working successfully with the Hill to implement foreign policy and development priorities is critical for any presidential administration. It can take years to secure the necessary funding for a major development initiative from the initial budget submission through the implementation of the program, so executive agencies need to invest in the long game when building a relationship with Congress.

Despite this critical relationship, too few people move seamlessly between the two branches of government, placing a premium on savvy interlocutors (and lobbyists) who understand how to work across these spaces. The reality is

---

88 Sarah Nitz Nolan, "The Congressional Committee Map: Key Congressional Committees Engaged in US Foreign Assistance," InterAction, accessed February 9, 2021.

most diplomats and development experts are not trained or expected to understand the Hill. Congress is seen as a political machine and insufficiently appreciated or understood at times by development officials and foreign policy experts within the executive branch for the critical role it plays in shaping and overseeing American foreign policy and aid priorities.

In reality, no one agency or branch of government is an island in the ocean of foreign aid; all must work together. Major US development initiatives, such as Power Africa increasing the number of Africans with access to power, the President's Emergency Plan for AIDS Relief (PEPFAR) addressing the global HIV/AIDS epidemic, or Feed the Future tackling the root causes of hunger and malnutrition, only work when the entire US development architecture comes together in a common cause. [89,90,91] Development diplomats that can navigate both the executive and legislative branches can lead the way on transformative American investments to end poverty.

THE SILOS THAT SEPARATE

In many ways, the artificial boundaries separating foreign policy and development start long before the job begins. In colleges and graduate schools, course offerings in these fields are often on distinct academic paths. I needed to choose early in my studies between being a diplomat or a development

---

89 "Power Africa," US Agency for International Development, accessed June 5, 2021.

90 "The United States President's Emergency Plan for AIDS Relief," US Department of State, accessed June 5, 2021.

91 "Feed the Future," Feed the Future, accessed June 5, 2021.

expert, between foreign policy and international development, even though the fields are firmly interconnected and interdependent. There were no requirements to take classes or pursue internships crossing from one lane into the other. The academic silos separating foreign policy and international development were deep and ingrained, mirroring government agencies. I focused on international relations, national security, and peace studies, as well as core requirements in economics and statistics. I managed to graduate with two fancy degrees in government and public policy without ever taking a single development course—my single biggest academic regret.

After graduate school, I received two distinct honors: the Princeton's Stokes Award recognizing academic achievement and public service leadership and the Presidential Management Fellowship (PMF).[92] The Stokes Award foreshadowed my lifelong commitment to following a path of public service and being driven by a mission to serve. The PMF successfully laid the groundwork for my career in government. My biggest decision in accepting the PMF involved selecting which government agency to join. The State Department and foreign policy? USAID and international development? The Treasury Department and international economics? The Defense Department and national security? Greatly influenced by my initial diplomatic sojourn to Malaysia, I prioritized the State Department, choosing my silo and going down the foreign policy rabbit hole.

92   Mel Policicchio, "Stokes Award Winners Look Ahead to Washington," Princeton University School of Public and International Affairs, July 7, 2016.

Fortunately, the PMF provided unique opportunities, allowing me to experience two paid rotations anywhere in government during the two-year fellowship. On the advice of mentors like Christopher Kojm, the Deputy Director of the 9/11 Commission, I took full advantage of the fellowship by accepting assignments overseas at US Embassy Kabul and going to Capitol Hill to work for Senator Robert P. Casey, Jr. as his foreign policy fellow. These experiences gave me a brand-new perspective in appreciating the world beyond Foggy Bottom and the executive branch, particularly in seeing up close the role of Congress in shaping foreign policy and development priorities. When a call came one day in December 2008—soon after I completed the PMF and transitioned into the Civil Service at the State Department—asking if I wanted to work on the Hill, I said yes right away. Who knew one call would change the course of my career?

PART II

OVERSEEING FOREIGN AID FROM CAPITOL HILL

*We rationalized destroying villages in order to save them...
We watched pride allow the most unimportant battles to be
blown into extravaganzas, because we couldn't lose and
we couldn't retreat, and because it didn't matter how
many American bodies were lost to prove that point...
How do you ask a man to be the last man to die for a
mistake?... We are here in Washington to say that the
problem of this war is not just a question of war and
diplomacy. It is part and parcel of everything that we are
trying as human beings to communicate to
people in this country.*

*— John Kerry, testifying before the Senate Foreign
Relations Committee on April 22, 1971*[93]

---

93 "John Kerry: 'How do you Ask a Man to be the Last Man to Die for a
    Mistake?' Vietnam Veterans against the War Testimony—1971," Speakola,
    accessed June 6, 2021.

CHAPTER 3

GARDENING A WARTIME STRATEGY
WORK OF CONGRESSIONAL COMMITTEES ON US FOREIGN POLICY

- Take calculated risks to advance your career.
- Ask tough questions during war to achieve peace.
- When you have the chance, give voice to those who do not have power.

JOB HUNTING ON THE HILL

The first time I met David McKean in December 2008, we stood under a canopy of elm and oak trees in Lower Senate Park on the US Capitol grounds near Union Station in Washington. Moments earlier, we were in his office when the fire alarm rang mercilessly throughout the Senate Russell building, abruptly cutting into our conversation. Just as I mustered the courage to ask him, as Senator John Kerry's Chief of Staff, if he foresaw any job openings, the Capitol Police asked everyone to vacate the US Senate buildings immediately. We joined hundreds of others unceremoniously evacuated into the Senate gardens on that unseasonably warm winter day. I tried unsuccessfully to make small talk during our hallway escapade. The resulting silence in the park stretched uncomfortably as I racked my brain on how to reset the conversation under these odd circumstances.

"You have three minutes before I am leaving for my next meeting," he informed me, giving away little emotion.

I panicked as the sweat started building up despite the cool winter day. *What am I doing here?* I understood little of Hill politics or how these powerfully connected networks operated. When Senator Barack Obama won the November 2008 US presidential election, the White House was not the only institution to change hands. Democrats also swept the Senate and House of Representatives, turning over both the executive and legislative branches of government at the same time.[94] Elections change everything in Washington, even the control of congressional committees and staffing assignments. Getting a job in the Obama-Biden administration or with powerful members of Congress became the hottest game in town.

"Yes, sir, I want to respect your time. I would love to serve on the Senate Foreign Relations Committee (SFRC)," I blurted out before losing my nerve.

I did not know David, and he did not know me. I could tell he struggled to remember why we were meeting in the first place. As a first-generation immigrant, I had no political connections.

---

94 Adam Nagourney, "Obama Wins Election," *The New York Times*, November 4, 2008.

Beyond knocking on a few doors in Pennsylvania during the general election season, I did not have any ties to John Kerry's 2004 presidential campaign. My parents were not donors or Democratic operatives, although they were proud voters who always cast their ballot in each US presidential election. I was just another twenty-something no-name who wanted to change the world. I did not even look the part of a typical Hill staffer as a Muslim American, South Asian woman.

The meeting came together through a former Senate colleague, Richard Kessler. At the time, Rick worked on the Senate Homeland Security and Governmental Affairs Committee (HSGAC). Rick and I often attended similar think tank lunch events during the congressional recesses when I worked as a fellow for Senator Robert P. Casey, Jr. as part of my Presidential Management Fellowship (PMF). It was fun bantering with Rick on the metro rides to and from the events and sharing analysis on the latest foreign policy challenges consuming Washington, usually centered on the US wars in Iraq and Afghanistan.

I did not know then Rick was a consummate Hill staffer well-known to many in both the Senate and House of Representatives. He would go on to become the House Foreign Affairs Committee (HFAC) Staff Director working for Representative Howard Berman. Representative Berman assumed the HFAC Chairmanship in March 2008, filling the vacancy left by former chairman Tom Lantos, who passed away in February 2008.[95]

---

95 Sarah Jane Staats, "New House Foreign Affairs Committee Chairman Howard Berman Vows to Reassert Authorizers Role in Overhaul of US Foreign Assistance," Center for Global Development, March 12, 2008.

As I wrapped up my time in Senator Casey's office to return to the State Department, I passed on my resume to Rick just in case he knew of folks on the Hill looking to hire foreign policy staff. Unbeknownst to me, he forwarded my resume to David when it seemed Senator Kerry would become the incoming SFRC Chairman. Out of the blue, in early December 2008, David emailed me asking to get together.

"You know, working on the Hill can be very tough on a new mom," David observed in the Senate gardens when I mentioned I had a baby. He went on to describe how staffers' lives revolved around their bosses' jam-packed schedules.

"Well, I can't change being a mom, but I promise I'll work hard. You won't regret hiring me," I replied, hoping I convinced him I could handle congressional responsibilities even while coping with the demands of motherhood.

I must have said something right, or maybe David felt generous. A week later, I was face to face with Senator Kerry in the inner sanctum of his second-floor private office in the Senate Russell Building, surrounded by his photos with world leaders, Massachusetts memorabilia, and overflowing bookshelves. Up close, his six-foot, four-inch frame towered over mine by more than a foot, with his full head of thick gray hair parted to the right and his raised, bushy eyebrows adding gravity to his somber and serious patrician face. As his large hand enveloped mine in a firm handshake, my anxiety threatened to derail the entire meeting before it even began. *This guy could have been the President of the United States, and he's meeting with me.*

Senator Kerry motioned for me to join him by his desk as my sweaty palms reached for the closest chair. The furniture and furnishings exuded power and wealth, reminding me of one of the great New England estates from the turn of the century, a far cry from the cramped cubicles I left just an hour ago at my State Department job. Although David joined us for the meeting, he sat far back in the corner of the spacious room out of my sight, leaving me one on one with John Kerry. *Breathe and don't blow this. It's no big deal; you got this...breathe!*

"So, I hear you were in Afghanistan. How are we doing over there?" he asked without preamble before I could even properly introduce myself or settle down into the chair.

"Yes, sir. If I can be honest, we are losing the war and could end up destroying the country and its people in the process if we are not careful," I responded directly as I sat down, crossing and uncrossing my legs as I tried to get comfortable.

For the next forty minutes, he grilled me on what I saw in 2007 during my short time in Kabul working at the US Embassy as an Economics Officer. He spoke as much with his hands as with his mouth, using gestures to great effect to signal the magnitude of an issue when his arms went wide or conveying a deep appreciation for a point of view when his pointer fingers came together. At the end of our conversation, I had no clue if I passed the test since I did not actually understand what was happening. *Was that an interview?* We never discussed an actual job.

I received some clarity days later. David contacted me on Senator Kerry's behalf, asking if I wanted to join the incoming SFRC majority committee staff in January 2009. At the time, I did not realize I was Senator Kerry's very first new SFRC hire and the first mom to join the incoming committee staff.

"You need to start right away in the new year. I don't know yet what your portfolio will be, but we'll figure it out as we settle in," David said. "And, by the way, congratulations."

"Thank you so much, David. I am honored," I replied, committing to a new job on the spot without fully appreciating or thinking through the trade-offs.

Leaving behind a career civil servant position in the executive branch meant giving up job security and predictable promotions for a political job on the Hill with no job guarantees or protections. A political aide on the Hill could be fired anytime for any reason with no transparency on pay or promotion. While a position on a committee staff was more secure than a job in a personal office for a member of Congress, which had high rates of turnover, the average tenure even for committee staff was still only two to five years.[96] Moving from a bureaucratic desk job to a political assignment was risky since my husband just finished law school. We already struggled to pay our mortgage and cover expenses with a new baby.

Nonetheless, I jumped in with both feet because I was hungry to work with an icon like Senator Kerry, someone committed

---

96 "Working on Capitol Hill," Yale Law School Career Development Office, August 2013.

to using his political perch on the committee to solve complex foreign policy challenges. Perhaps I was restless after completing my PMF and craved a more fast-paced lifestyle where I could have a greater impact through legislation, hearings, and reports. The pace of promotion and upward mobility as a civil servant felt slow at the time, given my impatient nature. Taking this job on the spot was the biggest gamble of my entire career. Those three minutes in the Senate gardens changed my life.

AMERICA'S LONGEST WAR

Afghanistan and Pakistan consumed Senator Kerry during his tenure as the Senate Foreign Relations Committee Chairman. His history with the Committee on issues of war and peace long preceded his election to the Senate in 1984. On April 22, 1971, he testified before the Committee on behalf of the group Vietnam Veterans Against the War, famously asking, "How do you ask a man to be the last man to die for a mistake?"[97] Thirty-eight years later, Senator Kerry kept that very question at the forefront of his mind as the United States battled the Taliban in Afghanistan.

The Taliban, a Sunni Islamist nationalist movement founded in the early 1990s, ruled most of Afghanistan from 1996 to October 2001. "Taliban" means "student" in Arabic and Pashto, which is fitting given its ranks were composed of peasant farmers and young men and boys raised in refugee camps and trained in ultraconservative, Saudi-financed, Islamist

---

97 John Kerry, "Transcript: Kerry Testifies Before Senate Panel, 1971," National Public Radio, radio broadcast, April 25, 2006.

religious schools called *madrassas* in neighboring Pakistan. The Taliban and its network of like-minded fundamentalist extremist groups spanned Afghanistan, Pakistan, Kashmir, India, and Central Asia, declaring war against infidels.[98]

Vali Nasr, the Senior Advisor to the US Special Representative for Afghanistan and Pakistan (SRAP) described:

> There is an undercurrent of terror and fanaticism that go hand in hand in the Afghanistan-Pakistan arc, and extends all the way to Uzbekistan. And you can see reflections of it in Bosnia, in Kosovo, in Indonesia, in the Philippines. For instance, in one madrassa in Pakistan, I interviewed seventy Malaysian and Thai students who are being educated side by side with students who went on to the Afghan war and the like. These people return to their countries, and then we see the results in a short while... At best, they become hot-headed preachers in mosques that encourage fighting Christians in Nigeria or Indonesia. And worst case, they actually recruit or participate in terror acts.[99]

By September 1996, the Taliban captured control of Afghanistan's capital Kabul from *mujahedin,* or guerilla factions, who once fought against the Soviets but by the 1990s battled each other.[100] They killed the country's president and declared the founding of the Islamic Emirate of Afghanistan.

---

98 "Terrorist Groups: Afghan Taliban," Counter Terrorism Guide, accessed May 15, 2021.

99 "Interview Vali Nasr," *PBS Frontline,* October 25, 2001.

100 Amos Chapple, "Afghanistan Under the Taliban," *Radio Free Europe/ Radio Liberty,* February 11, 2019.

Overnight, the Taliban imposed radical Islamist customs, interpretations, and jurisprudence of Islamic *Sharia* law on the population, such as extreme and merciless control of women, religious minorities, and political opponents.[101]

Stripping women and girls of basic human rights, "the Taliban regime instituted a system of gender apartheid, effectively thrusting the women of Afghanistan into a state of virtual house arrest. Under Taliban rule, women were stripped of all human rights—their work, visibility, opportunity for education, voice, health care, and mobility," according to the Feminist Majority Foundation.[102] Those found violating Taliban decrees were brutally and publicly beaten, flogged, and killed. Only Pakistan, Saudi Arabia, and the United Arab Emirates recognized the new state.[103]

Leading up to the 2001 attacks on the United States, the Taliban provided a safe haven for al-Qaeda, the terrorist group founded in 1989 by wealthy Saudi Osama bin Laden to mobilize Muslims to fight *jihad* or holy war against the Soviet Union and, later, the United States.[104] Bin Laden exploited popular Muslim grievances against the United States, targeting US support for Israel, US actions in Somalia, and US troops stationed in Saudi Arabia, home of Islam's holiest sites. Al-Qaeda used Afghanistan as a haven from which to freely recruit, train, and

---

101 "Terrorist Groups," Counter Terrorism Guide, May 15, 2021.

102 "The Taliban and Afghan Women," Feminist Majority Foundation, accessed May 15, 2021.

103 Ibid.

104 National Commission on Terrorist Attacks Upon the United States, *The 9/11 Commission Report: Final Report of the National Commission on Terrorist Attacks Upon the United States*, by Thomas H. Kean and Lee H. Hamilton, Y 3.2:T 27/2/FINAL, July 22, 2004, 66.

deploy terrorists globally. They carried out terrorist attacks on the United States, such as the August 1998 bombings on US embassies in Kenya and Tanzania, which killed 224 people, including twelve Americans, and wounded thousands, and the October 2000 bombing of the American destroyer, the USS *Cole,* which killed seventeen American sailors.[105]

On September 11, 2001, al-Qaeda coordinated the hijacking of four commercial airliners from the northeastern United States, crashing into New York City's World Trade Center, destroying parts of the Pentagon in Arlington, Virginia and creating hallowed ground in Shanksville, Pennsylvania.[106] Altogether, the 9/11 terrorist attack killed 2,977 people, surpassing the death toll at Pearl Harbor in December 1941, and sparking a determination across America that we would "never forget."[107]

Senator Kerry supported President George W. Bush's declaration of war against al-Qaeda following the 9/11 attacks and the launch of Operation Enduring Freedom (OEF) in Afghanistan. By the time President Barack Obama assumed office in 2009, however, the war raged on with no end in sight. A Pentagon official told the Senate, "We haven't been fighting there for eight years; we've been fighting for one year eight times in a row," referring to the lack of a cohesive military and political strategy to win the war.[108]

---

105 Ibid.

106 Ibid.

107 Joseph R. Biden Jr., "Remarks by President Biden on the Way Forward in Afghanistan," Treaty Room at The White House, transcript, April 14, 2021.

108 US Congress, Senate, Committee on Foreign Relations, *Afghanistan's Impact on Pakistan,* 111th Cong., 1st sess., 2009, S. Hrg. 111-295, 1.

Despite tens of thousands of US and NATO troops and over $200 billion spent on the war by 2009, the Afghan Taliban still controlled vast amounts of territory and al-Qaeda endured.[109] General Stanley McChrystal, commander of US troops in Afghanistan, immediately asked President Obama for additional troops to decisively defeat the Taliban. But questions remained. Were more troops the right response, especially when the United States killed a top al-Qaeda leader in Somalia in 2009 without a major troop presence?[110] How did the war in Afghanistan affect security in Pakistan and the broader region? Could peace only be achieved through further war?

Senator Kerry believed otherwise. "What's needed is a comprehensive strategy, one that emphasizes the need for the right level of civilian effort as much as for the right military deployment to provide security for that other effort to take hold," he said.[111] There could be no solution to the war without addressing the needs of people, as he saw firsthand as a soldier in Vietnam. "Any strategy that lacks a strong civilian component is doomed."[112]

Afghanistan was one of the poorest places on earth in 2009. According to the UN Office of the High Commissioner for Human Rights (OHCHR), some nine million Afghans,

109 US Congress, Senate, Committee on Foreign Relations, *Exploring Three Strategies for Afghanistan*, 111th Cong., 1st sess., 2009, S. Hrg. 111-321, 4.

110 Jeffrey Gettleman and Eric Schmitt, "US Kills Top Qaeda Militant in Southern Somalia," *The New York Times*, September 14, 2009.

111 US Congress, Senate, Committee, *Exploring Three Strategies for Afghanistan*, 3.

112 US Congress, Senate, Committee on Foreign Relations, *Countering the Threat of Failure in Afghanistan*, 111th Cong., 1st sess., 2009, S. Hrg. 111-291, 2.

representing a third of the population, lived in absolute poverty. Another third lived only slightly above the poverty line, despite some thirty-five billion dollars injected into Afghanistan from 2002 to 2009. The country suffered from the second-highest maternal mortality rate and the third-highest rate of child mortality in the world. Only a quarter of Afghans above the age of fifteen could read and write, with that number even lower for women and nomadic populations.[113]

Decades of fighting by the British, Soviets, and now Americans decimated the country. Afghanistan lacked any strong or centralized government, functioning institutions, or basic infrastructure. Guns and bombs would only go so far. Sustainable economic development and good governance needed to be an integral part of the solution.

HEARING FROM THE EXPERTS

The Senate Foreign Relations Committee (SFRC) was established in 1816 as one of the original ten standing Senate committees. It shaped US foreign policy throughout the years, holding presidents and secretaries of state to account. From debating the purchase of Alaska in 1867, to rejecting the Treaty of Versailles in 1919–1920, to supporting the establishment of the United Nations in 1947 and the passage of the Truman Doctrine in 1947 and the Marshall Plan in 1948, SFRC and the House Foreign Affairs Committee (HFAC), its

---

113 "Human Rights Abuses Exacerbating Poverty in Afghanistan, UN Report Finds," *UN News*, March 30, 2010.

sister committee in the House of Representatives, shared a front-row seat to history.[114]

After the Cold War, a bipartisan spirit prevailed in the foreign relations committees with the adage, "Politics stopping at the water's edge." Unlike partisan committees focused on domestic US policy, the members and staff of the foreign policy committees historically worked across the aisle, leaving partisanship behind as much as possible in representing the United States to the world. Responsible for treaties, legislation, diplomatic nominations, and budget oversight, committee staff exercised their authority by putting together briefings, trips, legislation, reports, investigations, and hearings to conduct oversight of US foreign policy and foreign assistance.

Senator Kerry took his job as chairman seriously, empowering his staff to use all the committee's tools to get to the truth. He frequently brought the committee staff together, inspiring us with his vision for a principled and strategic US foreign policy and speaking frankly with us about both the opportunities and obstacles ahead. He expected us to work hard and honestly for him in representing the people of the United States, never forgetting we were the custodians of US taxpayer dollars and on the front lines of upholding democratic norms and speaking truth to power.

I remember sitting in his personal office or the committee room, listening to him in awe during these private settings without the spotlight of the cameras. Serious, strategic, and

---

114 "Committee History and Rules," Committee on Foreign Relations, US Senate, accessed March 16, 2021.

somber, he shared with staff the heavy burden of safeguarding the country and made us all feel a personal responsibility for protecting the United States. His personal Rolodex likely rivaled that of the White House, and world leaders were just one phone call away. We knew we were working for one of America's greatest foreign policy thinkers and diplomats of all time.

As a newly hired SFRC committee staffer covering South and Central Asia and global Muslim engagement issues in the aftermath of 9/11, I conducted oversight of the Obama administration's policies and budgets in my portfolio. Immediately, my time became engulfed with the war in Afghanistan and neighboring Pakistan. Overnight, I went from working in the large bureaucracy of the State Department alongside thousands of other foreign policy experts to being one of the few advisors on the committee responsible for the direction and strategy of this region. I felt enormous weight on my shoulders to do my job well by being informed of the latest situation on the ground and offering strategic and timely analysis and advice that could save lives. The stakes were high, with no room for error.

Senator Kerry doggedly pursued a way out of the war in Afghanistan. He chaired dozens of hearings, seeking out experts to examine every option and nuance. Hearings were usually open to the public and transcribed as part of the official congressional record. They were a powerful tool in fostering public debate and holding parties accountable. We spent hours behind the scenes with him preparing for these hearings, sorting out who should testify, questions to ask, and issues to raise. Ensuring a wide range of diversity of views from our generals, diplomats, analysts, and development professionals was a top priority.

Bringing in new voices could be challenging, however. We typically tried to put together a roster of hearing witnesses by consensus with our Republican committee colleagues instead of resorting to separate majority and minority witnesses for each party. Usually, it was easier to agree on the names of mainstream witnesses, typically white men well-known in positions of power, connected to Washington networks such as those in influential think tanks, elite academic institutions, or leading civil society organizations. It proved to be much harder to introduce newer names, especially women and people of color who tended to be less known within the Washington Beltway. Despite their relative anonymity, these witnesses often brought firsthand knowledge from communities in conflict and those closest to the ground.

I cheered when we succeeded in diversifying the witness bench, such as when renowned Afghan American author and US envoy for the UN High Commissioner for Refugees (UNHCR) Dr. Khaled Hosseini testified on his perspective on the Afghan refugee crisis.[115] I cringed when we failed to fully appreciate alternative points of view. Even if we successfully invited a new witness, members were not always interested in listening to those unknown.

For instance, during one committee hearing with Ms. Zainub Salbi, the Iraqi American CEO of Women for Women

---

115 US Congress, Senate, Committee, *Countering the Threat of Failure in Afghanistan*, 2.

International, some senators actively disengaged as she spoke passionately about conditions on the ground in Kandahar, a Taliban stronghold. I watched as Ms. Salbi struggled to interject herself in the dialogue largely dominated by men as she spoke alongside the widely respected Ryan Crocker, the former US Ambassador to Pakistan and Iraq, and well-known Australian counterinsurgency expert David Kilcullen.[116]

When Ms. Salbi read from her written testimony, a few senators leaned back in their chairs, pulled out their Blackberries, or spoke to their staff instead of paying attention to her uniquely powerful experience. While some of the senators debated the finer points of military strategy with well-known experts Ambassador Crocker and Dr. Kilcullen for minutes on end, they did not ask Ms. Salbi for her views. As a result, the perspective of civilians in Taliban strongholds, particularly women, was completely missing for most of the hearing.

"Tell her it's okay to interrupt if she wants to make a point," I furiously texted her aide, who was sitting in the audience of the hearing room. "This is her moment; she should seize it!" I frantically typed, worried the entire hearing could go by without due course to her point of view. "Slip her a note."

When Senators Ben Cardin, Bob Casey, and Russ Feingold used their time later during the hearing to specifically call on Ms. Salbi to speak, I exhaled in relief, grateful they would at last tap into her unique insights.[117] Women and minorities

---

116 US Congress, Senate, Committee on Foreign Relations, *Perspectives on Reconciliation Options in Afghanistan*, 111th Cong., 2nd sess., 2010, S. Hrg. 111-761.

117 Ibid.

struggled to be taken seriously as national security or foreign policy experts in congressional hallways of power, but their voices were critical in helping see the bigger picture. Hearings such as these shaped the committee's thinking on wartime strategies and peacetime solutions. They informed how much military support, diplomacy, and foreign assistance the United States should consider in countries around the world. Witness testimony influenced the defense, diplomatic, and development choices of US power abroad. Congressional hearings molded US policy choices, so ensuring diversity of views and perspectives was paramount.

Despite the considerable stress, I loved organizing and attending hearings as a Senate staffer. Turning the door handle to the Senate Dirksen building room 419, the antechamber for the SFRC public committee hearing room 421, always gave me a thrill. The sign on the door said "Private," but I went in anyway, entering the exclusive space where members and congressional staff gathered before a hearing. In that small office cluttered with desks and paper, I joined the committee's senators, witnesses, and other staff, double-checking everyone had what they needed. In those intimate moments where senators and staff spoke freely without the barriers of formality that took over when they ascended the dais of the hearing room, I rubbed elbows with the Washington power set for a split second.

When a hearing began, I joined the other staff entering the hearing room from this antechamber, silently jockeying for a seat on the bench behind Senator Kerry while the committee members settled into their plush armchairs, ready to examine every facet of an intricate policy problem. As I found my seat on the crowded bench and prepared to take notes, I made sure to greet and thank Bertie Bowman, the committee's hearing coordinator and a legend on the Hill.[118] Within the Senate, some people work quietly and behind the scenes with great dignity for the people they serve. Bertie was this person for SFRC, an institution unto himself whose work over the decades ensured the committee functioned through all its political reconfigurations. He brought historical knowledge but also kindness and humor. I saw my job as a staffer to honor and respect his work every time I saw him.

During one SFRC hearing on Afghanistan and Pakistan in 2009, David McKean leaned over from his seat on the bench quite unexpectedly to speak with me.

"You know JK is going to the region soon, right?" he whispered, using the nickname we used to refer to John Kerry. "Want to go with him?"

I looked around, making sure David was really speaking to me and not one of my other colleagues. Senator Kerry did not travel with an entourage, preferring just one or two aides in addition to his Navy military liaison. As the junior staffer covering South and Central Asia at the time, I did not assume I would automatically join him. I quickly nodded, still surprised whenever David spoke to me directly. As one of Senator Kerry's closest and oldest confidants, he was a quiet, serious guy who said little but whose words carried substantial weight.

---

118 Bertie Bowman, *Step by Step: A Memoir of Living the American Dream* (New York: One World, 2009).

Moments later, David scribbled a note, folded it, and placed it on the dais in front of Senator Kerry. The senator quickly glanced at it and abruptly swung his chair around mid-circle. With his glasses perched low on his nose, he tilted his head down to look directly at me while his hands fiddled with the paper. After a moment of silent inspection, he asked, "You want to come with me?"

"Would love to," I managed to squeak out, committing to a trip on the spot without a clue how I would manage childcare on the road. I prayed my mother-in-law could fly in from Calgary, Canada, or my mother could take time off from her full-time job as a psychiatrist in New Jersey to watch my daughter so my husband would not have to fend for himself while holding down a demanding job of his own.

Senator Kerry paused and considered briefly as his chair started swiveling toward the dais. "Okay." He nodded to David, turning his attention again to the hearing without giving me another glance.

It happened so quickly I wondered if I imagined the whole scene as David smiled knowingly. Once again, David intervened in his kind, understated way to shape my future. This time, he got me on the plane to Afghanistan and Pakistan, where I started seeing the power of development diplomacy firsthand.

CHAPTER 4

LANDING ON A CODEL
CONGRESSIONAL TRAVEL
IN WAR ZONES

- Always be prepared to adapt.
- Powerful testimony comes from those on the ground.
- Peace and security cannot exist without economic and social development.

A HOOCH IN THE HINDU KUSH

I finally succumbed to the exhaustion and drifted into a deep sleep. All too quickly, the airman gently but repeatedly shook my shoulder as I struggled to remember where I was.

"Ma'am, we're about to land. You need to tighten your seat belt and close your window shade. We need a dark landing."

"What? Oh, okay. Just give me a moment," I replied as I searched blindly for my thick glasses. I rubbed my eyes and slapped my cheeks, desperate to wake up and focus on the mission at hand.

After nonstop travel from Dulles to Dubai, where we swapped a commercial plane for a US military jet, our plane now circled the narrow valley between the Hindu Kush mountains, preparing to land in Kabul, Afghanistan in October 2009. Landing safely at 6,000 feet in one of the highest altitude capitals in the world during the daytime was challenging enough. Doing so in the middle of the night in complete darkness to avoid incoming fire from the Taliban in the middle of a war raised the stakes. *God, I can't believe I'm here again. I am not cut out for this.*

Blackness and silence engulfed the plane. No one dared to say a word as the hum of the engines filled the space. I held my breath while images of my one-year-old daughter Zahra ran through my head. Her nanny would just now be settling her down for her afternoon nap. Zahra was probably begging for one of her favorite Raffi nursery rhymes or looking for other excuses to avoid sleeping. *Sweet dreams, baby girl. Wish I was with you.* Finally, the landing gear touched the asphalt, and I exhaled.

Within minutes, we exited the cramped plane and thanked the airmen for their service. An advance team from the US military greeted us on the dark tarmac, saluting Senator Kerry and welcoming us to the country. The Pentagon took every possible safety precaution to make sure no harm came to Chairman Kerry and his congressional delegation (CODEL). Led by a member of Congress, CODEL travel typically occurred during congressional recess periods to examine certain facets of US policy. This CODEL took place during the Senate's Columbus Day weekend and included SFRC Chief Counsel Frank Lowenstein, US Navy military liaison Gregory Kausner, and SFRC South and Central Asia staffers Jonah Blank and me.

Together with the support of the Defense Department, State Department, and US Embassies Kabul and Islamabad, we worked for weeks behind the scenes to put together a jam-packed trip to support Senator Kerry's ambitious goals for his long-planned visit to Afghanistan and Pakistan. There were no breaks in the schedule or opportunities to recover from jetlag or enjoy downtime. Senator Kerry liked to cover as much ground as fast as possible. Accordingly, we scheduled every minute, planning multiple opportunities for him to speak directly to troops, diplomats, tribal members, and political leaders to make sense of the way forward.

The information we gathered on this trip would be instrumental in helping flesh out a historic speech he would deliver before the Council on Foreign Relations when he returned to Washington. The speech aspired to lay out America's options in the region, emphasizing our military strategy, political road map, and development objectives.[119] Our collective job was to make sure we could execute his vision on this trip. Thankfully, I previously traveled to both countries, so I knew the lay of the land and could help design the itinerary with firsthand information.

Unlike in most capitals, we did not enter the airport building or go through immigration and customs when we landed. With NATO's International Security Assistance Force (ISAF)

---

119 John Kerry, "Chairman Kerry Delivers Speech on Afghanistan," Council on Foreign Relations' Washington, DC office, US Senate Committee on Foreign Relations, transcript, October 26, 2009.

controlling the military airspace, we stayed on the tarmac instead and bypassed the small building housing the old Kabul International Airport. I did not receive a stamp on my official US passport documenting I entered Afghanistan on Thursday, October 15, 2009. Ironically, despite my numerous visits, I never collected a single stamp from Afghanistan in any of my six diplomatic and official passports, usually bypassing Afghan immigration control via US military checkpoints.

I grabbed my heavy carry-on suitcase from the back of the small plane, all I could bring when traveling with the senator so he could move quickly and never have to check-in luggage on a commercial plane. I joined my colleagues and piled into the caravan of armored Ford Excursion SUVs stationed alongside our plane to take us the remaining few miles to the US Embassy, which, like the airport, was in the Wazir Akbar Khan neighborhood of northern Kabul. Many foreign embassies, and most of Afghanistan's national government institutions like the Presidential Palace, could be found in this posh area. Exhausted from nonstop travel, I noticed little during the nighttime drive of the streets laid out on a grid with Western, two-story houses dating from the 1960s and 1970s.

Somewhere near midnight, I gratefully stumbled into my hooch. These ten-by-twelve-foot container housing units—more commonly referred to as hooches—housed 80 percent of the US civilian and military personnel living in the heavily fortified US Embassy compound. Most hooches were located on the east side of the compound, close to USAID offices.[120]

---

120 Bill Bent, "Life on a Secure Compound in a War Zone is Somewhat Surreal," American Foreign Service Association, September 14, 2014.

When I lived in one in 2007 when I worked at US Embassy Kabul, I crossed the thirty-yard underground tunnel connecting the east side to the west side every day to get to the embassy and to the nicer apartments where senior personnel and families lived. I still remember attending band practice in the evenings in these apartments when I was the lead singer for our makeshift embassy band, "Roads and Power." Since I traveled with a VIP on this October 2009 trip, however, I stayed on the west side closer to the US ambassador's apartment where Senator Kerry stayed.

Despite minimalist conditions rivaling Henry David Thoreau's one-room cabin at Walden Pond, the hooch contained everything one needed—a twin bed with clean sheets, a working toilet and shower, and even a small desk and chair.[121] The tunnel doubled as a bomb shelter when the embassy faced incoming Taliban fire. It served as my first line of defense in case of an incoming enemy attack from rockets or mortar fire. If the "duck and cover" alarm went off, I would curl up and hide under the metal twin bed and wait to be evacuated by the US Marines, as I did in 2007. I usually felt confined in the hooch, but that night my bitterness was forgotten as I gratefully embraced my accommodations, ready to crash. Within moments, I was fast asleep, all thoughts of being back in a war zone forgotten.

A STAFFER'S VIEW OF THE WORLD
I could only afford a few hours of sleep before our day officially started at the US Ambassador's residence over breakfast

---

121 Ibid.

with civilian and military briefings on the war. I needed to look refreshed and polished even when feeling beat up inside. I donned one of my black business suits and pushed my feet into heels as I quickly slapped on mascara and lots of concealer, the irony of dressing as a bureaucrat in the middle of a war not lost on me. After finding some caffeine, I first checked in with the Senator to make sure he had what he needed, and then with the embassy's control officer who managed our schedule.

In addition to scheduling and liaising with the US Embassy's foreign service officers, my job on these trips ranged from mundane tasks such as making sure Senator Kerry had his glasses to taking notes, updating talking points, writing speeches, and providing analysis or feedback on what we were hearing. Sometimes if a meeting was restricted to certain classification levels, like briefings from the intelligence community or to principals only, I would get kicked out of the meeting altogether, waiting patiently outside conference rooms for any crumbs of information I could glean after the fact.

I usually joined the meetings, sitting quietly and trying to be as invisible as possible while frantically capturing insights on paper and in my head. I closely watched Senator Kerry in action, observing his mastery of politics, economics, security, and history. He spoke eloquently, a subject-matter expert on almost any topic before him. He also listened actively, demonstrating emotional intelligence in the way he connected with his interlocutors, making people feel like the most important person in the room. Sometimes I slipped him little notes informing him of critical pieces of information about the subject at hand, pointing out culturally appropriate phrases he could use. I wanted to make sure he knew the latest state of play and was not getting played by a savvy interlocutor. I always got a thrill when he asked a question I just passed along.

Even though I could tell his mind raced a mile a minute looking for solutions to complex problems, outwardly, Senator Kerry appeared patient and in listening mode, providing space for others to offer their views. His large, lanky frame, global fame, and greater-than-life persona dominated the space as he relaxed in his seat, seemingly always at ease whether in a fancy conference room or a makeshift army bunker, whether in his business suit or bomber jacket. He cared deeply about principled US leadership and America's place in the world. It showed. Everyone wanted to meet with him on these foreign visits, even jaded politicians and those who prided themselves on pushing back against what they perceived as American aggression and dominance. Ironically, they were often the first to ask for a photo or selfie after the meeting.

Most of the meetings during our visit took place at the US Embassy to save us the time and trouble of moving around the city, transferring the burden of navigating multiple security checkpoints and securing embassy clearances to enter the US compound to our guests instead. When we did leave the compound, we buckled up in a caravan of armored SUVs accompanied by bodyguards as we raced through the city as fast as possible to avoid potential targeting and security threats. It was a tough way to get to know the country. Through the haze of the tinted windows, I tried hard to catch images of Kabul, searching through the crowded street bazaars filled with men wearing blue jeans or traditional tunics and turbans. Seeing men casually sitting around in pickup trucks and at café tables with Kalashnikov AK-47 rifles threw me for a loop.

I loved seeing women out and about on the streets in Kabul, having regained some semblance of freedom of movement with the fall of the Taliban and its extreme rules confining women to their homes. Many still draped themselves in the famed Kabuli light blue burqa. These full-length *chadarees* covered the entire body, head, and face except for a small region around the eyes. When they were in power, the Taliban required all women to wear the burqa in public. While this condition was no longer the case, many women still wore them due to fears for their safety since the Taliban exercised widespread control and conservative norms remained deeply ingrained. Accordingly, I also covered my arms and legs and wrapped a scarf around my head in all meetings outside of the US Embassy compound as a sign of respect in this male-dominated culture. In many ways, this duality of clothing felt familiar to me as I shifted seamlessly from modern, Westernized dress to traditional Muslim garb, echoing many aspects of my childhood and religious upbringing.

After only twenty-four hours in Kabul, we returned to the airport the following morning to travel to Garmsir, a village in southern Afghanistan. First, we first hitched a ride to the southern province of Kandahar, joining troops and other coalition partners heading down that way onboard a US Air Force C-130 plane.

"Ready for more planes?" Greg Kausner teased me. As an F-14 and F-18 navy pilot, he enjoyed the constant drumbeat of flying.

"Bring it," I replied as I groaned inwardly, knowing what awaited as I entered the cargo hold from the ramp in the rear.

Flying in a C-130 is akin to being in the belly of a beast. The plane is used like a workhorse. Designed to transport cargo and troops and enable medivac, its large, fully pressurized cargo hold can be quickly reconfigured to hold troops, stretchers, tanks, and whatever military equipment needed for battle. As a result, I was convinced Lockheed Martin built it with zero comforts in mind as one of the most utilitarian vehicles on the military market.[122] I failed to appreciate these characteristics on previous trips, suffering instead through the dark and cold.

This time, I felt better prepared and traded my business suits and heels for khakis and hiking shoes for greater comfort. I stuffed an extra pair of neon earplugs into my purse to protect my ears from the noise and dressed in layers just as I learned as a Girl Scout. I was ready for the searing heat of the desert or the frigid air in the skies. I did not bother looking for a good seat since I now knew all the jump seats attached by straps to the sides of the plane were equally uncomfortable. I settled in as much as possible as the deafening noise of the four engines and the darkness of the plane soon lulled me into a catnap. I slept rather soundly as we headed south into Taliban territory.

---

122 Catherine Park, "What to Know about the C130 Hercules Military Aircraft," *11 Alive*, May 2, 2018.

THE HEART OF THE PASHTUNS

An hour and a half later, we arrived at Kandahar Airfield, a NATO base supporting the ISAF mission. Kandahar was Afghanistan's second-largest city and one of the oldest known human settlements. Founded by Alexander the Great around 330 BC, some say the name "Kandahar" evolved from *"Iskandar,"* which is pronounced *"Scandar"* in the local dialect version of the name Alexander.[123] Today, Kandahar is part of the heartland for the Pashtuns, Afghanistan's largest ethnic group, representing their traditional seat of power for more than 300 years.[124] In the late 1990s, the Pashtuns became well-known globally for being the primary group making up the Taliban regime in Afghanistan. Much of the war against the Taliban took place in the south and east of the country, in places home to large Pashtun populations, such as Kandahar and Helmand provinces and bordering Pashtun areas in Pakistan.[125]

We only stayed long enough in Kandahar to thank the troops we flew with for their service. Quickly, we swapped the C-130 for US military helicopters to fly us low over the southern Registan Desert straddling Helmand and Kandahar. As we cut across the dunes and dust-colored compounds where families lived and eked out their daily survival, the desert met the shadow of the Helmand River. The river snaked its way through the terrain on its way to Iran and Pakistan, permitting life to grow along its banks.

123 John E. Hill, *Through the Jade Gate to Rome: A Study of the Silk Routes during the Later Han Dynasty, 1st to 2nd Centuries CE* (Charleston: Book-Surge, 2009), 517-518.

124 "Afghanistan," The World Factbook, Central Intelligence Agency, updated June 9, 2021.

125 Lindsay Maizland and Zachary Laub, "The Taliban in Afghanistan," Council on Foreign Relations, updated March 15, 2021.

"You see down there?" Senator Kerry asked through our headsets, pointing to the trees and farms dotting the landscape alongside mud huts glinting off his sunglasses. "Helmand used to be the breadbasket of Afghanistan, a place where agriculture [like wheat and cotton] thrived on irrigation canals built by American engineers in the 1950s and 1960s."[126]

This period in Afghanistan witnessed a golden age of a more liberal and Western lifestyle while balancing the customs of the country's more conservative factions. During this brief, relatively peaceful era, new buildings were constructed, Western fashion could be seen on both men and women in the cafes and clubs of Kabul, and the country was poised to be on a path of modernization. Both the Soviet Union and the United States courted Afghanistan as part of the Cold War, with the country accepting Soviet machinery and weapons alongside US foreign aid and development assistance.

Following President Dwight Eisenhower's December 1959 trip to Karachi, Pakistan, throngs of Afghans lined the streets in Kabul to welcome the American motorcade. During this trip, President Eisenhower discussed the growing Soviet influence in the region and over time, increased US aid to Afghanistan. Hopes for further modernization stalled in the 1970s when bloody coups, invasions, and civil wars began (and continue to this day).[127]

During the 2000s, drug traffickers and insurgents transformed Helmand into the world's largest producer of opium

---

126 "Chairman Kerry Delivers Speech on Afghanistan," US Senate Foreign Relations Committee, October 26, 2009.

127 Alan Taylor, "Afghanistan in the 1950s and 60s," *The Atlantic*, July 2, 2013.

for heroin. Although the Taliban eradicated opium production in Afghanistan before the war in 2001, by 2009, Afghanistan's opium industry supplied more than 90 percent of the world's heroin and generated an estimated three billion dollars a year in profits.[128] As part of the military expansion in Afghanistan, the Obama administration assigned US troops a lead role in trying to stop the narcotics flow. On the civilian side, the United States phased out eradication of poppy in favor of promoting alternative crops and agriculture development, focusing on increasing agricultural productivity, regenerating the agribusiness sector, rehabilitating watersheds, and irrigation systems, and building capacity in the Afghan Ministry of Agriculture Irrigation and Livestock (MAIL).[129]

Senator Kerry asked us to investigate the administration's counternarcotics strategy earlier in the year. As a result, I visited this very terrain just months prior, in June 2009, on a staff delegation (STAFFDEL) to Helmand province with my SFRC colleague, Doug Frantz. STAFFDELs were trips led by a professional staff member examining certain aspects of US policy of interest to Congress. On our mission, we wanted to understand the illicit drug profits bankrolling the Taliban and fueling the corruption that undermined the Afghan government. To do so, we journeyed into remote Afghan outposts, asking tough questions about the drug trade and corruption. We likely created some enemies along the way from those who wanted Americans to stay out of their business. Our findings from the trip emphasized:

128 US Congress, Senate, Committee on Foreign Relations, *Afghanistan's Narco War: Breaking the Link between Drug Traffickers and Insurgents*, 111th Cong., 1st sess., 2009, Committee Print, 1.

129 Ibid.

The scope of development needed to create jobs, promote alternatives to growing poppy, and train Afghan security forces is enormous. Unlike Iraq, Afghanistan is not a reconstruction project but...a construction project, starting almost from scratch in a country that will probably remain poverty-stricken no matter how much the US and the international community accomplish in the coming years. The administration has raised the stakes by transforming the Afghan war from a limited intervention into a more ambitious and potentially risky counterinsurgency. This transformation raises its own set of questions. How much can any amount of effort by the United States and its allies transform the politics and society of Afghanistan? Why is the United States becoming more deeply involved in Afghanistan nearly eight years after the invasion? Does the American public understand and support the sacrifices that will be required to finish the job? Even defining success remains elusive: Is it to build a nation or just to keep the jihadists from using a nation as a sanctuary?[130]

The June 2009 trip was mentally and physically grinding, made worse by the soaring temperatures and brutal desert heat of the summer months. Flying on helicopters during such conditions was a searing experience, with the avalanche of hot air from the chopper blades hitting our bodies with full force on the tarmac. The heat made every step toward the military birds painful and blinding.

---

130 Ibid.

"Doug, it's like a giant hairdryer is running up and down my body," I complained endlessly. I did not think I would physically survive the blasts of 120-degree heat enveloping us as we hopped helicopters in Taliban territory as if hailing taxis in New York City. Weighed down in my thirty-pound Kevlar army vest, I came close to fainting and vomited a few times.

"You'll be okay; I promise," Doug said sympathetically. "This is what we need to do sometimes to find the truth."

"Well, this must be what hell is like," I replied, recommitting on the spot to my prayers if it meant escaping this inferno.

Thankfully, this October 2009 helicopter ride on the CODEL with Senator Kerry enjoyed the benefit of a cooler fall, giving us all a reprieve from the miserably hot summer. I ignored the pit in my stomach as I sat next to soldiers who were ready on a moment's notice to fire their machine guns and focused instead on the landscape I missed appreciating last time. The serenity of the views from the air masked the turmoil on the ground.

OF TRIBES AND TROOPS

Our helicopters soon landed on the eastern bank of the Helmand River in the Garmsir District. In Pashto, the language spoken by Pashtuns, "Garmsir," means "hot place," which appropriately captured both the climate and insurgent activity. Heavy fighting between US Marines, coalition forces, and Taliban insurgents took place in 2008 along the forty-five miles of river lined with cotton and poppy fields. Marines tried to transform this former Taliban territory by pouring "hundreds of troops and hundreds of millions of dollars into reclaiming this impoverished corner of an already poor province. Crammed bazaars, reoccupied homes, and busy roads are a testament to their efforts," journalist Emma Graham-Harrison writes.[131]

We briefly caught glimpses of the village activity Graham-Harrison described through the narrow slits of our Humvees as we squeezed our way onto the narrow dirt lanes of the bazaars on the way to the provincial Governor's office. Upon arriving, we entered the open-air courtyard. I was stunned to see 275 village elders greet us, men seated cross-legged in their turbans and *salwar khameez* tunics. Helmand Provincial Governor Mangal welcomed Senator Kerry and Lieutenant General Larry Nicholson, the US Commanding General of the Second Marine Expeditionary Brigade of Task Force Leatherneck, with kisses on both cheeks, the traditional Pashtun sign of respect and greeting.

In honor of our visit, the village convened a tribal *jirga*, an Afghan gathering of elders who discuss and decide issues such as dispute resolution. For Pashtun tribes, *jirgas* are highly organized formal events following the tribal code of conduct, the *Pashtunwali*, and are convened to prevent tribal wars.[132] This *jirga* came together at the invitation of the pro-

131 Emma Graham-Harrison, "Afghanistan's Garmsir is a Success for NATO—but its Future Remains Uncertain," *The Guardian*, December 12, 2012.

132 Madeline O. Nosworthy, "Jirga/Shura (Afghanistan)," Global Informality Project, School of Slavonic and East European Studies, updated April 24, 2020.

vincial governor to discuss life in the war after the 2008 battle of Garmsir.

As the only woman present, I stood closer to the back of the mud and concrete courtyard, trying not to draw undue attention or criticism. In these tribally conservative parts of the country, women did not participate in political decisions or share public spaces with men. Nonetheless, I gratefully listened to the discussions, spellbound by hearing the harsh realities of life these communities faced every day. I wondered what stories women would tell if they were invited into these spaces.

One by one, the elders voiced their frustration with the war. Many were middle-aged, although their bodies and faces appeared decades older because of the harsh conditions they faced daily to survive. They were pleased US troops routed out the Taliban, but this hard-fought security did not improve living conditions for their families.[133]

"We have no drinking water in my family compound," one elder said. "No wells, no canals, and no infrastructure."[134]

"We have no jobs," said another. "Our only hope is to survive off the poppy fields."

Afghans here struggled to access basic services and experienced many hardships. Flooding the region with Western troops and Afghan security services did not bring about the

---

133 Kerry, "Afghanistan: Defining the Possibilities," 2009.
134 Ibid.

economic security they desperately needed. Life after the Taliban did not become easier for these villagers, leading many to question supporting the Western-backed Afghan government in the first place. At least the Taliban provided jobs in the poppy fields, guaranteeing an income.

"What are the Americans offering us?" they questioned. "How long do you plan on staying?" With a weak Afghan central government unable to run much of the country, when US troops left Afghanistan, it would leave behind a power vacuum for the Taliban to fill. There was little incentive for villagers to openly defy the Taliban and incur their long-term wrath. No one trusted or expected Americans to stay forever. The Taliban could easily wait us out.

We sat somberly under the October sun listening to the elders describe what their families did every day just to survive. Despite billions of dollars being pumped by the United States and other donors into the country to support development needs, Afghans struggled with everyday necessities like accessing clean water or basic health care. Mothers frequently died in childbirth, orphans filled the crowded and unsanitary bazaars, and men could not provide enough food to feed their families. The Afghan government had little reach into villages and was seen as weak, corrupt, and in the pockets of the West. As man after man spoke in vivid terms, it became clear the United States was failing here in Afghanistan. The price of peace was hunger and illness. Afghans would not be safe and secure without long-term, sustainable investments in their economic and social development.

As we said our farewells to the elders, our delegation reflected on the enormity of the testimony we heard, not in the formal Senate Committee hearing room but under the sun on the dirt floor of an Afghan village courtyard.

> If we can help Afghans dig the wells and dredge the canals asked for by…[the] village elder[s] in Garmsir, then I am convinced together we can marginalize the Taliban across Afghanistan," Senator Kerry reflected: "This is a microcosm of what needs to happen wherever our troops are. It underscores how much we need to strengthen our civilian assistance and develop a coordinated approach that targets our resources on the people and places where we can show measurable successes to the Afghan people.[135]

As the C-130 took off to return us to Kabul that evening, I pondered the role I could play to improve the quality of life in Afghanistan. The men in the *jirga* did not care if we worked on national security, foreign policy, or international development. Everything ended up interconnected on the ground where communities lived. As an SFRC staffer, I exercised jurisdiction over both the State Department and USAID and could exercise authority to hold both agencies to account.

I can do something different here. I don't have to work in a single lane. I know our current strategy is not working. How do I convince others of another way forward? As I considered my options, I filled my spiral notebook with the powerful testimony from Garmsir, ready to help Senator Kerry secure

---

135 Ibid.

long-term peace. I believed strongly in his vision. We could make a real difference here, but we would have to take a multidisciplinary approach here in Afghanistan, in neighboring Pakistan, and throughout the region. We would have to break through the artificial silos separating foreign policy and international development.

That evening, we returned to Kabul, exhausted from an intense day of travel and emotional testimony. After a planned dinner with Massachusetts soldiers, we could finally enjoy our first full night of sleep. I attacked my tray of mac n' cheese, mashed potatoes, corn, and rice, soaking in the carb loading I associated with the US Army cafeterias of Afghanistan. I loathed this diet when I ate it every day during my time working at the embassy in 2007, but after snacking all day on granola bars and dried fruit, this tray was sent from heaven.

Plus, I loved talking to the Beantown troops. As we sat around a long rectangular table, I listened to them share their experiences in their strong Boston accents. A few of them deployed to either Iraq or Afghanistan multiple times, leaving behind a spouse and kids. They struggled to reconcile what they saw on the ground with our official strategy.

"It's like whack-a-mole," one soldier observed. "We clear out one area, and the Taliban just pop up somewhere else."

I cherished these informal meals with troops on the front lines where we could speak openly. Typically, it could be difficult to have unscripted, honest conversations with senior military officials who would not be authorized to stray from their official talking points. But these soldiers were not in charge of the strategy—their bosses with the stars on their shoulders worked on that—while they lived it every day. Their perspectives gave me a new way of looking at the war and considering policy solutions to achieve lasting peace.

Throughout the day in the *jirga* and then over dinner with the troops, we spoke at length about the war. Security and war tended to dominate most of the discussions. Still, as the village elders reminded us, the real fight was not about guns. In Afghanistan, politics and poverty were just as lethal. Development and diplomacy had to go hand in hand if we were ever to secure peace in Afghanistan.

CHAPTER 5

SHUTTLING ACROSS BORDERS
IMPACT OF POLITICAL
DIALOGUE AND FOREIGN AID

- Brilliant diplomacy requires active listening, empathy, and respect for all points of view.
- Conspiracy theories can derail development initiatives if left unchecked.
- Best laid plans can unravel without political support from all sides.
- Being flexible even in stressful situations is a game changer.

ELECTIONS GONE AMOK

As we wrapped up dinner that Friday night on October 16, 2009, Karl Eikenberry, the US Ambassador to Afghanistan and retired US Army lieutenant general, discreetly pulled Senator Kerry aside for an emergency intervention. Ambassador Eikenberry was in the Pentagon when American Airlines flight 77 crashed into it on September 11, 2001, and several of his colleagues were killed. He would spend five of the next ten years in Afghanistan, serving first as an Army general, commander of US troops, and finally as America's top diplomat.[136]

Now at the mess hall, Ambassador Eikenberry informed us Afghanistan's President Hamid Karzai would not accept the results of the recent Afghan presidential election. Despite the long day with our visit to Garmsir, Senator Kerry went to see President Karzai at the presidential palace that night. He returned to the US Embassy somber and grim.

"It [seems] entirely possible that a constitutional crisis [is] unfolding," Senator Kerry relayed to us.[137]

In August 2009, about two months before our visit, Afghanistan held its second set of elections under its present constitution. These elections filled 420 seats for the provincial council and the presidency. From the onset, violence, insecurity, widespread fraud, low voter awareness and turnout, and election intimidation from the Taliban calling for a boycott marred the elections. The controversies threatened to undermine the very concept of a free and fair democracy in the country.

According to human rights groups, dozens of candidates associated with human rights violations and links to illegal armed groups and drug traffickers ran on the ballot. Powerful warlords likely made deals with key voting blocs

136 Karl Eikenberry, interview by Renee Montagne, "Ambassador Eikenberry to Leave Afghanistan," *Morning Edition*, National Public Radio, radio broadcast, July 8, 2011.

137 John F. Kerry, *Every Day is Extra* (New York: Simon & Schuster, 2018), 373.

throughout the country to deliver votes for President Karzai and his rivals.[138] While many Afghans despised the role these warlords and powerbrokers played in cutting deals and evading accountability for gross human rights abuses, they also understood the reality of power and politics in Afghanistan.

The presidential election did not yield a clear-cut winner. Official results took about a month to tabulate, but within a day of vote counting, both President Karzai and his closest rival, former Foreign Minister Abdullah Abdullah, claimed they each obtained a majority of the votes. Media reports declared President Karzai won by a landslide, with almost three-quarters of the votes. These claims, in turn, provoked accusations of vote-rigging and fraud by those supporting Foreign Minister Abdullah.[139]

During our October 2009 visit, the Electoral Complaints Commission (ECC), an independent commission established under Afghanistan's electoral law and backed by the United Nations (UN), prepared to officially declare widespread fraud.[140] President Karzai reacted furiously, accusing the Americans and UN of undermining his victory and suppressing the vote of his ethnic Pashtun voting blocs. As we dined with the Beantown troops, President Karzai prepared to declare victory prematurely against Foreign Minister Abdullah, potentially triggering a major political and security crisis.

---

138 Jon Boone and Peter Beaumont, "Afghanistan Poll Legitimacy Fears as Taliban Violence Keeps Voters Away," *The Guardian*, August 20, 2009.

139 Abubakar Siddique, "Karzai Campaign Declares Victory," *RadioFreeEurope/Radio Liberty*, updated August 21, 2009.

140 Grant Kippen, "Afghanistan: Electoral Complaints Commission—Press Conference 12 May 2009," ReliefWeb, transcript, May 12, 2009.

After consulting with Ambassador Eikenberry, our CODEL worked through the night to clear the senator's weekend schedule so he could spend time with President Karzai. We hoped Senator Kerry could be a trusted power broker in helping negotiate a political solution with both presidential candidates. Tensions were already high between President Karzai and his US counterparts—including Ambassador Eikenberry and Ambassador Richard Holbrooke, President Obama's Special Representative for Afghanistan and Pakistan (SRAP)—due to previous crises and overall disagreements on the war. President Karzai did not want to be seen as an American puppet, ceding his power and authority to the United States and NATO under the pretext of its war against Al Qaeda. Washington, meanwhile, did not want to invest billions of dollars and sacrifice the lives of American troops in a country with corrupt leadership.

Throughout the weekend, Senator Kerry and President Karzai looked for a face-saving way out. In the paradoxical presidential palace, with its large, dark oak-paneled rooms contrasted by its bright, open courtyard gardens, both men shifted seamlessly between formal negotiations at the table and frank discussions in the palace gardens. They debated how to fairly resolve disputes on the elections without undermining Afghanistan's nascent democracy. Senator Kerry dismissed claims of a Western-backed conspiracy to disenfranchise Pashtun votes and insisted no candidate could legitimately declare himself the outright winner. He spoke passionately about building democracy in Afghanistan and putting the needs of the state above individual egos. He empathized with President Karzai's anger and frustrations while urging him to see the bigger picture. Every time we thought we achieved a breakthrough, President Karzai would reverse course, resulting in many circular conversations.

I accompanied Senator Kerry, watching history unfold. Seeing brilliant diplomacy up close in action was one of the most defining moments of my career. Senator Kerry exhibited incredible energy, grace, and humility, actively listening as much as he spoke. His body language signaled respect and honesty. He dismissed the formality of officially prepared talking points to instead understand President Karzai's point of view and the history and context of Pashtun discontent underlying it. He listened. He made eye contact. He exuded patience and empathy while sharing his own vulnerabilities in surviving the politics of Washington. Over endless cups of tea, certainly more than the *Three Cups of Tea* author and controversial philanthropist Greg Mortenson advised for negotiating in Central Asia, he acted as if he had all the time in the world.[141]

"My marathon sessions with Karzai [are] more like three thousand cups of tea," Senator Kerry joked with us later.[142]

President Karzai received tremendous pressure from his constituents and advisors not to cede the election and from the diplomatic community not to endorse an illegitimate outcome. Throughout the weekend, he received a flurry of calls from US Secretary of State Hillary Clinton, Ambassador Holbrooke, and Defense Secretary Robert Gates, who all urged him to take the compromise Senator Kerry

---

141 Kevin Sieff, "Mortenson Returns to Afghanistan, Trying to Move Past His 'Three Cups of Tea' Disgrace," *The Washington Post*, October 12, 2014.
142 Kerry, *Every Day is Extra*, 373.

discussed.[143] British Prime Minister Gordon Brown and UN Secretary-General Ban Ki-moon also spoke with President Karzai and Foreign Minister Abdullah. In Kabul on a visit, French Foreign Minister Bernard Kouchner emphasized the importance of both candidates respecting the UN-backed audit process while former US Ambassador to Afghanistan Zalmay Khalilzad engaged the Kabul political circuit as a private citizen.[144]

When we were not at the palace, we sat on Ambassador Eikenberry's rooftop terrace, meeting with UN and Afghan officials and brainstorming how to help the Afghans move forward and accept the results. We spoke about psychology as much as politics. A proud man, President Karzai viewed himself as a transformative figure in the history of Afghanistan. His legacy was as important to him as his current standing with his people. He would never accept an outcome imposed from the outside that lacked legitimacy with the Afghan public.

By Sunday night, both sides seemed closer to accepting a political compromise for a run-off election. Our CODEL prepared to leave shortly for our planned visit to Pakistan. We wanted to stick to our schedule and return to Washington on time for critical Senate votes. As far as we were concerned, Senator Kerry did his job in moving the diplomatic needle in Kabul. We wished Ambassador Eikenberry and UN Special Representative Kai Eide well on finalizing the

143 Sabrina Tavernise and Mark Landler, "Allies Press Karzai to Accept Election Audit Results," *The New York Times*, October 17, 2009.

144 Associated Press, "Results in Afghan Election Fraud Probe Expected," *WBUR*, October 17, 2009.

way forward. We thanked the US Embassy staff for all their hard work and support for our trip. We were wheels up for Islamabad. At the time, we could not imagine we would be back in Kabul in twenty-four hours.

WHEN MONEY ROUSES SUSPICION

A few hours later on October 18, 2009, we landed in Pakistan's capital, Islamabad, and drove to the US Ambassador's residence in the heavily guarded diplomatic zone where we were staying. We once again traveled through the night, the seeming norm for our pace of travel. I caught a quick catnap and rose as the morning dawn broke through the clouds, keeping the heat and humidity at bay for the time being. Within minutes, I showered, dressed, slapped on some makeup, blow-dried my hair, and searched for a strong cup of chai to clear my head. My brain needed to switch gears from the politics and turmoil of Afghanistan to that of Pakistan.

"Welcome, Fatema. I hope you got some rest," US Ambassador to Pakistan Anne Patterson warmly greeted me in her dining room.

Ambassador Patterson had a special place in my heart from my earlier visit to the country in April 2009. I sought refuge with her when the Pakistani Taliban, a loose alliance of militant groups founded in 2007 by the then-Taliban chief Baitullah Mehsud, came within sixty miles of Islamabad targeting foreign diplomats like me staying in the city.[145] I was

---

145 Barbara Starr, et al., "US 'Extremely Concerned' about Taliban Movements in Pakistan," *CNN*, April 24, 2009.

terrified. When working in the region, I often had nightmares of being captured by either the Afghan or Pakistani Taliban, both fundamentalist Sunni-based groups whose hatred for minority Shia Muslims, including those of my community, was well-known.

During that April visit, I traveled by road with armed convoys twice to Peshawar, the capital of Pakistan's former Northwest Frontier Province. In Peshawar, I saw the danger the Pakistani Taliban posed up close. Just thirty-five miles from the famed Khyber Pass in the formidable Hindu Kush Mountain range bordering Afghanistan, Peshawar was the frontier gateway for various militant groups based along the Pakistan-Afghanistan border. Lawlessness ran rampant. In my mind, Peshawar still resembled what English author Rudyard Kipling described in his nineteenth-century stories and ballads as "a place peopled by tribal warriors, smugglers, soldiers of fortune, spies [and] the playground for the great game of espionage."[146]

The imminent danger of the Pakistani Taliban's proximity to Islamabad frightened me. I felt incredibly grateful when Ambassador Patterson personally moved me from my lightly protected embassy guest house into her heavily fortified residence, extending the full weight of her diplomatic protection and earning my lifelong gratitude in caring for my safety.

"Thanks so much for hosting us in your historic residence, Ambassador," I replied during our October trip as I gratefully

---

146 Rone Tempest, "Afghan Rebel Gateway: Peshawar: Many Lured by Intrigue," *Los Angeles Times*, May 12, 1986.

accepted the delicate china cup filled with steaming tea. "I'm looking forward to making progress here on our bill. We have a lot to accomplish in so little time."

Working in Pakistan was challenging, to say the least. Home to more than 175 million people and with a significant Pashtun population, Pakistan was critical to stability in neighboring Afghanistan and the broader South Asia region.[147] Over the years, US assistance to Pakistan fluctuated with political events, sending mixed messages, and leading most Pakistanis to question American intentions and staying power, especially in neighboring Afghanistan.

Despite President Obama's global popularity in 2009, 64 percent of Pakistanis viewed the United States as an enemy, and only 9 percent described the United States as a partner.[148] Most Pakistanis believed the United States would cut and run when it served American purposes. This belief undermined long-term US efforts to defeat extremists, foster democratic change, and support transparent and accountable institutions promoting security and stability. Without changing this baseline, no pathway existed to dry up popular tolerance for anti-US terrorist groups who enjoyed sanctuary and covert material support to launch attacks from Pakistan into Afghanistan in places like Garmsir.

Just days before our trip, President Obama signed the Enhanced Partnership with Pakistan Act into law, informally

147 PTI. "Security Situation in Afghan Linked with Stability in Pak," *The Economic Times,* updated December 2, 2009.

148 "Pakistani Public Opinion," Pew Research Center's Global Attitudes & Trends Project, August 13, 2009.

known as the Kerry-Lugar-Berman (KLB) bill for its authors Senator Kerry, Senator Richard Lugar, and Representative Howard Berman.[149] While far from a Marshall Plan for the country, the bill, nonetheless, attempted to rebalance the bilateral relationship by focusing on the development needs of the Pakistani people. KLB would triple US foreign assistance to Pakistan to $1.5 billion a year for five years. The money could be spent on education, energy, health, agriculture, infrastructure, and other critical needs in Pakistan. Funds could tackle poverty in the tribal areas bordering Afghanistan in places like Peshawar, a region that was among the poorest parts of the world. The Senate version of the bill passed in September 2009 with unanimous consent, meaning no senator voiced an objection, which rarely happened for significant pieces of legislation.[150] Its historic passage spoke to the legacy and deep respect Senators Kerry and Lugar commanded from their Senate colleagues over decades of service.

The premise underlying KLB rested on a simple thought exercise, as my SFRC colleague Jonah Blank liked to say. Following the 2005 Kashmir earthquake, the United States devoted nearly one billion dollars to relief efforts and reaped a greater reward in popular support than any amount of public diplomacy could generate. The sight of American servicemen and women saving the lives of Pakistani citizens equaled ten times the cost of operating the Chinook helicopters. Senators Kerry and Lugar believed through legislation, the United States could recreate these conditions without

---

149 "Obama Signs Kerry-Lugar Bill into Law," *Dawn*, October 16, 2009.
150 John Kerry and Richard Lugar, "Senate Unanimously Passes Kerry-Lugar Pakistan Aid Package," US Senate Committee on Foreign Relations, press release, September 24, 2009.

waiting for a natural or man-made disaster. Only then would the people of Pakistan see the United States as an ally with shared interests and goals, such as defeating militant extremists who threatened the national security of both countries.[151]

Despite this logic, Pakistan's military and civilian leadership remained deeply suspicious of American motives to invest in civilian assistance. There was substantial backlash and outcry in Pakistan against the KLB bill. Some in Pakistan deemed KLB "less an assistance program than a treaty of surrender." They found the language in the bill conditioning development aid on security conditions offensive. For instance, they argued the bill's terms for Pakistan "ceasing support" for terrorists implied Pakistanis were supporting terrorism in the first place. Further, language on India in an aid bill for Pakistan incensed proud Pakistanis who accused the United States of a perceived bias toward India. Finally, the bill's demands on severing Pakistani ties to nuclear supply networks angered those in Pakistan who resented American accusations of Pakistan's support for nuclear proliferation.[152]

Before the bill's passage in Congress, we scrambled for months to reconcile the milder Senate version of the bill with the stronger House text, which contained the stricter and more offensive provisions setting off the Pakistani storm. It took multiple rounds of negotiations with House Foreign Affairs Committee (HFAC) staff and Representative Berman, the bill's sponsor in the House of Representatives. The talks

---

151 Ibid.
152 Karin von Hippel and Shiza Shahid, "The Politics of Aid: Controversy Surrounds the Pakistan Aid Bill," Center for Strategic & International Studies, October 19, 2009.

were intense, with a periodic breakdown of trust between the Democratic staff of both committees. We fundamentally had different visions of what was possible in Pakistan, making it hard to agree on the way forward.

I remember one such meeting in S-116, the historic Senate Foreign Relations Committee suite in the northeast corner of the Capitol, where Senator Kerry personally tried to repair the damage. The Senate Committee on Patents used to occupy this space in the 1870s. During this time, famed artist Constantino Brumidi executed the fresco of American innovator Robert Fulton above the entrance to the committee room. It was in the majestic lobby outside S-116, known as the Patent Corridor, alongside emblems on the ceiling representing science, agriculture, navigation, and the arts.[153] Over a hundred years later, S-116 was now the official diplomatic symbol of American democracy in the Capitol, and it was where Senator Kerry asked Representative Berman and his staff to meet to resolve the sticking points of the respective Senate and House bills.

The meeting was polite but hard-hitting, with both sides seemingly dug into their respective versions. Senator Kerry observed the dynamic, listening more than talking as the staff aired their arguments in front of their bosses. It did not look like we would be able to compromise. Toward the end of the meeting, Senator Kerry quietly and simply put his hand on Representative Berman's shoulder.

---

153 US Congress, Senate, US Senate Foreign Relations Committee, "The US Senate Foreign Relations Committee Suite," addendum to *The US Senate Foreign Relations Committee Suite* brochure, S. Pub. 115-9, revised April 2018.

"Howard, let's get this thing done," he said. "We have bigger problems to deal with as you know."

"Okay, John," Representative Berman replied. "We will work it out."

With trust at the member levels, within days, we successfully reconciled the Senate and House versions of the bill at the staff levels. Each side painfully conceded some ground allowing the House and Senate to pass their respective bills which then went over to the White House for presidential signature.

Beyond Congressional points of view, negotiations on the bill also involved other stakeholders. Throughout the summer and fall, we coordinated closely with the State Department and USAID on acceptable language, opened channels of dialogue with Pakistani officials in Washington and Islamabad, engaged in diplomacy with the Indian government, and spoke with civil society groups on programming development aid in a challenging security environment. Multiple rounds of development diplomacy took place to arrive at the final language in the bill.

Even with its passage, however, US aid would not be effective in reducing poverty if the Pakistanis rejected US motives underlying the bill. Our trip to Pakistan in October 2009, therefore, could not have been timelier.

A SEARCH THROUGH THE SKIES

On this October 2009 visit to Islamabad, we planned to meet with Pakistani Prime Minister Yousaf Gilani, Foreign Minister Shah Mehmood Qureshi, Finance Minister Shaukat

Tareen, and other Pakistani officials to address their concerns. We would also speak with former Prime Minister Nawaz Sharif, whose opinions carried weight within the ranks of the Pakistani Army.[154] Having witnessed the day before just how little our aid helped the people in Garmsir and realizing we needed to adjust our plan of action, this bill became even more relevant. It promised to be another long, tough day.

But first, the breakfast buffet at Ambassador Patterson's residence filled with scrambled eggs, potatoes, and fresh fruit beckoned. As the first rays of light hit the dining room early on Monday morning, October 19, 2009, I helped myself to generous portions of food, appreciative of the momentary respite from travel, meetings, and diplomatic protocol. It took my tired brain a few moments to realize that our delegation did not eat alone. As I looked around the long, rectangular dining table, I saw Senator Kerry deeply engrossed in a private discussion with a high-ranking US military official.

"Who's he talking to?" I whispered to Greg, who looked as worn out as I felt.

"Petraeus. *The* Petraeus," he replied, stunned.

A four-star Army general, David Petraeus led US Central Command down in Tampa, Florida. He happened to be in the region during our visit and joined us that morning in Ambassador Patterson's dining room. General Petraeus

---

154 "Kerry Meets Gilani," *The Nation*, October 19, 2009.

shared a grim diagnosis. He heard overnight from sources that things were falling apart in Kabul.

"Senator, I think you need to go back right away," he said solemnly as he shared the latest intelligence from Afghanistan.

A subsequent call between Senator Kerry and Ambassador Eikenberry confirmed all hell was breaking loose. President Karzai would not agree to a runoff election. Ambassador Eikenberry urged Senator Kerry to return to Kabul as soon as possible.[155]

"I can see if we can get you the C-21," Ambassador Patterson offered, referring to the planes the United States flew as part of the State Department's Air Wing, normally used for counternarcotics operations.[156]

Despite the generous offer, planning safe transport to Kabul last minute turned out to be quite complicated. Arranging secure travel in and out of an active war zone usually took weeks of preparation, not hours. Nor could we pull down our planned meetings with the Pakistanis without risking significant blowback on the KLB bill.

"Senator, go to your meetings. I'll stay behind and figure out how to get you to Afghanistan later today," Greg offered, outwardly confident and poised while inwardly stressed, as he confided in me later.

---

155 Kerry, *Every Day is Extra*, 374.

156 Joseph Trevithick, "The US State Department Has Its Own Sprawling Air Force, Here's What's in its Inventory," *The Drive*, October 4, 2018.

With Greg's assurance, we wrapped up breakfast and moved into our armored embassy vehicles for the trip down Constitution Avenue, where Prime Minister Gilani and his cabinet waited. Our meetings that day with Pakistan's leadership were cordial, but frank, as we tackled tough issues amid the backdrop of low levels of trust between both countries. The Pakistanis urged us not to make civilian aid conditional on security issues. Senator Kerry emphasized the historic opportunity of investing in the people of Pakistan, not just their security forces, and putting development at the heart of our bilateral relationship.

Our discussions were development diplomacy in action. The pressure in the room to thread the needle and find a way forward to implement the KLB bill steadily grew, matched only by the parallel stress of avoiding a political meltdown in Afghanistan. In between meetings, we kept checking our Blackberries and calling Greg, anxious to see his progress on securing a plane.

"No word yet but stay tuned. When I call, you need to be ready to go," Greg counseled us as we moved into another meeting.

As the hours went by, I kept glancing at Frank Lowenstein, who, as the Chief Counsel, would make the call on pulling the Senator out of his meetings. I wondered if he felt as nervous and stressed as I did. As promised, halfway through one of our afternoon meetings, we received word from Greg.

"I got the plane, but you need to get him out now, Frank," Greg insisted.

"Let me see what I can do," Frank replied. "He's in the middle of tense talks on the bill. The Pakistanis aren't happy with some of the conditions. He's not going to want to leave like that."

Greg waited impatiently. Minutes passed, and nothing. He contacted Frank again.

"Do you want to return? We must leave right now. I'm not kidding, Frank. We're about to run out of crew rest," Greg stressed, referencing the strict rules in place for how many hours military pilots could fly before needing to take a mandatory break.

Somehow, Frank diplomatically managed to extract Senator Kerry from heated discussions without causing a diplomatic rift. We assured the Pakistanis we recognized their concerns and would follow up diligently on the next steps. We got in our cars and raced to the airport with just minutes to spare, all eyes on the clock to see if we could take off before the crew rest kicked in. At the tarmac, we bolted from our cars into the waiting plane.

"Now! Let's go now," the pilot exclaimed as we ran to find our seats and buckled in with not a moment to lose.

We were wheels up in the air before we could fully relax and let go of the stress of the day.

"Frank, don't ever do that to me again," Greg declared.

"You did good, Greg," Senator Kerry said, squeezing his shoulder. "Now, let's figure out what to do about Karzai."

LAST CHANCE AT THE PALACE

A short hour later, we landed in Kabul around dinnertime. Once again, Senator Kerry rushed to the presidential palace for the fourth night of talks. He was tired but determined to end the impasse. Hours later, he returned to the US Embassy, optimistic that he had broken through.

"I think we have a deal," he told us triumphantly.[157]

The confidence was short-lived, however. By the next morning, something dramatically changed once again.

"What happened?" I asked as we picked at our breakfast on the rooftop terrace of the Ambassador's residence under the warm sun, too tired to do justice to the spread. "Seriously, you just saw him last night. What could have gone wrong in just a few hours?"

"President Karzai really deeply believes he…won the election and…the international community [is]…conspiring to push for a different outcome," Senator Kerry replied. "He [has] people within his government, people within the election commission who [feel] they [are] being insulted about putting together a faulty election process."[158]

---

157 Kerry, *Every Day is Extra*, 375.
158 Associated Press, "Afghan President's Political Rival Accepts Runoff," *WBUR*, October 21, 2009.

We assumed some of President Karzai's advisors rushed to the palace overnight to convince him the Americans were not to be trusted. This pattern was consistent with reports we heard concerning President Karzai's indecision and willingness to listen to the last person who spoke to him. We were back to square one, like the movie *Groundhog Day*. Senator Kerry's time was running short, and he needed to return to Washington. He had one last chance to reason with the president.

Once more, we piled into our armored cars and headed for the palace. I did not think anything would change. Afghanistan's history of wars, corruption, poverty, and foreign interference threatened to repeat here through this election drama. How could diplomacy break through this endless cycle? This time, Senator Kerry tried another tactic.

"I am going to try to separate President Karzai from his advisors to make it a one-on-one Hail Mary conversation," he mused as he went to ask the president for a private walk touring the palace gardens.

I watched Senator Kerry from afar, in awe of his diplomatic prowess. This guy refused to give up. Twice my age, he possessed more energy, patience, determination, and optimism than I did.

As Senator Kerry put his arm around President Karzai, he confidently declared, "Mr. President, we're going to find a way to make this work for both of our countries."

He implored the president to consider how history would view both of their legacies. He shared personal stories of his electoral loss to President George W. Bush in 2004 and his decision to put the country's needs ahead of his own as he conceded the race. The senator painted two scenarios—one where Hamid Karzai would be remembered as a respected statesman and democratic leader and another where he led his country down a dark path toward war and dictatorship. President Karzai could write history but had to decide now.[159]

"Okay, I'll do it," President Karzai responded simply. "But I cannot accept the invalidation of 250,000 Pashtun voters."[160]

Senator Kerry reassured him they could work something out if he accepted there would be a runoff. With that, he led the president directly from the gardens to a stage in the palace, making sure none of his advisors could intercept him and convince him to change his mind once again. The foreign and domestic press were already assembled, waiting for days on end for any news of a breakthrough. On the stage, flanked by Senator Kerry, Ambassador Eikenberry, UN Special Representative Kai Eide, and ECC Head Grant Kippen, President Karzai publicly accepted the ECC's findings that neither candidate received more than 50 percent of the vote. He agreed to a second round of voting for the Afghan presidential elections.[161]

Holy crap! He did it! John Kerry just changed the course of world history. The victory felt hard-won. We were exhausted, but a monumental weight lifted from our shoulders. In my

159 Ibid., 375.
160 Ibid., 375-376.
161 Associated Press, "Karzai Endorses Afghan Runoff Election," *WBUR*, October 20, 2009.

mind, I could hear the sigh of collective relief from capitals all around the world. We dodged a major bullet and averted a constitutional crisis that could have spiraled dangerously out of control. Problems in the elections would likely continue, but for now, we sidestepped a massive breakdown.

We said our goodbyes for real this time and returned to our plane for a flight to Dubai. Everyone finally relaxed, the men taking off their suit jackets and rolling up their sleeves. I happily kicked off my heels and threw on a warm, fuzzy pair of socks, finally enjoying a moment of informality and comfort. I turned toward Senator Kerry, listening eagerly to his impressions and reflections of the past days. He was proud of the moment and his role but humbled by how little trust President Karzai placed in our government. As we transited in Dubai from our military plane to a commercial one, the senator fielded calls from the press, eager to hear his version of what happened.

My adrenaline started to crash. Yet despite my exhaustion, I stayed awake during the next plane ride processing the enormity of the moment. Images of our meetings with the troops, village elders, and politicians flooded my mind. I was not naïve. Our trip by itself would not solve the underlying problems of the region. Afghanistan would struggle to hold the second round of elections, combat corruption and bad governance, invest in the needs of its people, and negotiate peace with neighboring Pakistan. The Pakistanis would continue to question our efforts to build a more strategic partnership rooted in economic development and undermine US efforts in Afghanistan. The road ahead promised to be riddled with setbacks.

Still, the visit brought many things into focus. First, the power of diplomacy to avoid crises was on full display. Great diplomacy required multiple skills, such as the emotional intelligence that John Kerry deployed seamlessly. Second, despite our intent to advance development strategies in both countries, security issues and political instability overshadowed everything else. Creating space to focus on sustainable development was challenging and often the third wheel of political priorities. In Garmsir, counterinsurgency strategies focused largely on security, not economic needs. In Kabul, political in-fighting took up all the oxygen, preventing a focus on good governance, anti-corruption, and economic development. In Islamabad, deep-seated political mistrust limited a potentially historic partnership on foreign aid.

The interconnected nature of development, politics, and security was on full display during our travels. In both Afghanistan and Pakistan, no security existed without development, and politics often crowded out everything else. Diplomacy between foreign leaders remained critical to diffusing crises and creating space for political dialogue, particularly when it came to development issues. Success relied on political savvy, emotional intelligence, deep knowledge of the region, and flexibility to respond as the situation required. Development diplomacy was a critical tool but faced limits in such a challenging political and security environment. To advance sustainable development in this complex and volatile region, I needed to think differently about how to leverage the power of development diplomacy. But first, I really had to sleep.

CHAPTER 6

BREAKING INTO PEACE
THE FALLOUT FROM HUMAN RIGHTS INVESTIGATIONS

- Reach across the aisle even when it is politically unpopular to do so.
- Take care of your physical and mental health while managing stressful work conditions.
- Trust your gut instincts when safety and security are at stake.

POLITICS AND STRANGE BEDFELLOWS

On the fourth floor of the Senate Dirksen building a day after returning from our marathon journey to Afghanistan and Pakistan in October 2009, I sighed as I sank into my chair in my office and kicked off my heels. Memos and briefing papers ranging from congressional notifications on USAID funds for Tajikistan and Kyrgyzstan to democracy issues in Bangladesh cluttered my desk, a snapshot of what I was working on before my recent trip.

I slowly massaged my temples and took three deep breaths as I sorted out what to tackle first. Committee life in Washington could be unpredictable, filled with intense days of hearings and briefings on specific issues to quieter days where I determined the pace and scope of work. This wide latitude was one of the things I loved best about Hill jobs; no two days were ever the same. Some days I focused exclusively on Afghanistan and Pakistan; other days, I deliberately carved out time to review the rest of my regional portfolio. Just as I set out to write up the official readout of our recent trip to Kabul and Islamabad, the door opened.

"Oh good, you are finally here," my SFRC colleague Nilmini Rubin exclaimed. "We have a lot to do to finalize the details of our upcoming visit to Sri Lanka."

"That's not for a while though, right? I have to dig out from this Af-Pak trip and everything else I dropped," I responded casually, my mind completely unfocused on Sri Lanka.

"Umm...we are flying out next weekend. Have you forgotten?" Nilmini asked with concern.

"Are you serious? I can't believe it's so soon." *My husband is going to kill me for leaving again on another trip.*

"Well, we need to finalize all the logistics. Grab your purse; we'll get coffee downstairs and talk."

Nilmini Rubin was my Republican SFRC counterpart covering South Asia for Senator Richard Lugar, the lead Republican and ranking member on the Committee. Together in

Washington, we organized committee hearings and briefings on Sri Lanka to acquire as much knowledge as possible. As the Sri Lankan civil war ended in May 2009 and post-war tensions set in, we knew secondhand accounts would not suffice and decided to organize a staff delegation visit to Sri Lanka. We believed the United States could help Sri Lanka navigate a path toward peace but wanted to see conditions on the ground for ourselves. With the extensive support of the US Embassy in Colombo and the Sri Lankan Embassy in Washington, we decided to conduct a week-long fact-finding mission and issue a bipartisan report on US policy options.

Nilmini was one of our leading Sri Lanka policy experts, a fellow South Asian woman, and a mom to young daughters, so I welcomed the opportunity to partner with and learn from her. I enjoyed spending time with someone who looked more like me than most others on the Hill and shared similar parenting experiences. It seemed one of us was always pregnant! We often compared notes on everything from nausea to nursing, from feeling guilty about leaving our kids behind when we hit the road to celebrating our legislative successes when things went right.

As minority women, we struggled at times to be taken seriously by our colleagues, even getting mistaken for each other, but overall, we supported one another and leaned into life on the Hill together despite working on opposite sides of the aisle. Politically, we partnered at a time when bipartisanship on foreign policy began unraveling in earnest. In the aftermath of the controversial 2003 US invasion of Iraq, the rise of the Tea Party movement, and other political tensions dividing Republicans and Democrats, working across the aisle became increasingly taxing (although nowhere as hard as it would become in subsequent years).

"I'm getting a lot of grief from Ken for traveling with you on this trip," Nilmini told me, referring to Senator Lugar's Staff Director, Ken Myers. Unlike the House Foreign Affairs Committee (HFAC), SFRC staff did not need to travel on a bipartisan delegation and usually flew on their own.

"I'm fighting hard with him because I want to work with you on this trip," she relayed. "Plus, with Sinhalese ancestry myself, I don't want to travel alone and risk being perceived as biased."

In Sri Lanka, the Sinhalese represented the dominant ethnic group and the political party in power. For this trip, our backgrounds complemented each other in building trust with ethnic groups, especially minority Tamil and Muslim communities who suffered from many exclusionary policies. In our week abroad, we planned to meet with leaders representing all ethnic groups. We would speak with government officials, opposition party leaders, nongovernmental organizations, a prominent jailed journalist, international donors, foreign diplomats, academics, civil society leaders, businesspeople, internally displaced persons (IDPs), and Sri Lankan citizens in a variety of settings.

In addition to meetings in Colombo, we would travel throughout the island, visiting the IDP camp near Vavuniya in the North, viewing demining activities in Mannar territories in the Northwest, touring schools and areas rebuilt after the December 2004 tsunami and fighting in Vakarai in the East, and speaking with local government officials in the South. As the first official international visitors to the island since the end of the Sri Lankan civil war, we planned on a busy and intense fact-finding mission. We did not expect the drama that followed.

CIVILIANS TRAPPED IN CONFLICT

Sri Lanka stood at a critical juncture in its history. After decades of separatist war, on May 17, 2009, the Sri Lankan army defeated the terrorist Liberation Tamil Tigers of Eelam (LTTE or Tamil Tigers). Two days later, Sri Lankan President Mahinda Rajapaksa declared total victory after government soldiers killed the Tamil Tigers' leader, Velupillai Prabhakaran, and seized control of the entire country for the first time since 1983.

With an estimated 70,000 casualties over the years, this bitter and hard-fought victory represented one of the few instances in modern history where a government defeated a terrorist group militarily. President Rajapaksa framed the victory as part of the global war against terror, declaring in a May 19, 2009 speech before the Parliament, "Ending terrorism in Sri Lanka means a victory for democracy in the world. Sri Lanka has now given a beginning to the ending of terrorism in the world."[162]

The civil war concluded, but peace and reconciliation remained elusive. Thirty years of violence exacted a toll on

---

162 US Congress, Senate, Committee on Foreign Relations, *Sri Lanka: Recharting US Strategy After the War*, 111th Cong., 1st sess., 2009, committee print 111-36, 1.

the majority Sinhalese population and led to a siege mentality toward the ethnic Tamil minority. Tamils and other minority ethnic groups were actively targeted and threatened, an enemy to both the LTTE and the government since they were often associated, rightly or wrongly, with the Tamil Tigers. Sri Lanka also faced multiple challenges like a humanitarian crisis in the north of the country, where much of the infrastructure – roads, schools, and housing – was destroyed from years of war.[163]

The tumultuous conflict resulted in the internal displacement of approximately 800,000 civilians, with hundreds of thousands more fleeing the country and becoming one of the world's largest groups of asylum seekers. During the last phase of the war, approximately 300,000 civilians stayed and moved with the LTTE as the Sri Lankan army pushed the Tigers East. These people lived under LTTE control for years, sustained the Tigers, and provided them with recruits. As a result, the Sri Lankan army suspected the people's loyalty to the government and set up Manik Farm, in addition to other internally displaced persons (IDP) camps, to weed out the LTTE fighters and identify the civilians that comprised the LTTE base. The army converged in Tamil Tiger territory, rounding people up in the guise of safety and security to bring them to the camps. Once there, the army issued government identification for easy tracking when civilians returned to their villages to ensure those same citizens did not help the Tigers mount a comeback.[164]

---

163 Ibid. 1-2.
164 Ibid., 4-5.

Anyone criticizing the government's actions faced tremendous pressure. For instance, Sri Lankan NGOs, especially human rights and political rights activists, experienced constant surveillance and even intimidation in some cases because they advocated for the rights of Tamils trapped in the North. The United Nations (UN) and international NGOs (INGOs) also received criticism for calling out the government on human rights concerns.[165] There was a general feeling, not just on the part of the government but on the part of the Sinhalese public and civil society, that the international community and NGOs did not support the Rajapaksa government.

Consequently, the Sri Lankan army did not permit widespread access to the IDP camps. Tamil and Muslim political leaders, journalists, various NGOs, and the International Committee of the Red Cross (ICRC) were denied entry. The fourteen international relief organizations operating in the camps issued some reporting on the conditions, but overall access and information coming out of the North remained limited.[166]

"The camp management is actually not bad," one international aid official told *The New York Times* in May 2009. "That's not why the government doesn't want to let people inside. They don't want the media to be talking to people about what happened in the conflict zones."[167]

---

165 Taylor Dibbert, "Sri Lanka's NGO Clampdown," *Foreign Policy*, July 25, 2014.
166 "Sri Lanka Ignores Calls by Aid Groups for Better Access to War Refugees," *The New York Times*, May 22, 2009.
167 Ibid.

The government's clampdown on outside observers and restrictions in the North sparked an outcry within the international community, particularly in Washington and New Delhi. The world called for the Sri Lankan government to move faster on rates of return for people detained in the camps, freedom of movement, access to the camps, and compliance with international standards set forth by the UN. While Sri Lankan officials may have been eager to resettle the IDPs, which cost them approximately one million dollars a day, the security challenges of LTTE cadres hiding among the IDPs trumped other short-term considerations for the army.[168]

The United States closely followed events in Sri Lanka. Days before the war ended, President Obama delivered a statement from the Rose Garden urging Sri Lanka to "seek a peace that is secure and lasting, and grounded in respect for all of its citizens." While economic and security relations continued, the US approach heavily focused on humanitarian issues and political reforms.[169] As the leading donor of food and humanitarian assistance to Sri Lanka, with a total USAID budget of $43 million, the United States assisted more than 280,000 IDPs with food rations, water and sanitation facilities, temporary shelters, emergency medical treatment, and mobility aids for the disabled. The Obama administration called for an end to human rights abuses, protection, and rapid resettlement of IDPs, and genuine efforts toward reconciliation. The Treasury Department abstained on the $2.6 billion International Monetary Fund (IMF) loan to Sri Lanka because of humanitarian concerns.

---

168 US Congress, Senate, Committee, *Sri Lanka*, 4.
169 Ibid., 14.

Congress played a critical role in shaping US policy towards Sri Lanka in the aftermath of its civil war. At Congress's behest, the US government continued to suspend military aid to Sri Lanka and issued a report on incidents during the war that may have constituted violations of international humanitarian law.[170] Nilmini and I were determined for SFRC to do its part. Our trip would be a critical input into a report we planned to publish upon our return, laying out options for US policy.

To have complete information, however, we needed access to the camps in the North. Despite considerable effort, we still did not have permission to visit the camps when we landed in Colombo. Before departing Washington, we sought advice from Ambassador Jaliya Wickramasuriya, Sri Lanka's Ambassador to the United States. He told me to call him as soon as I landed on the island. My fingers started dialing his number as I exited the plane's ramp in Colombo.

"You've reached? Good. Call this mobile number; he will help you," Ambassador Wickramasuriya told me cryptically before hanging up.

I called the number as instructed, not knowing who or what to expect. It turned out to be the direct line to Sri Lankan Defense Secretary Gotabaya Rajapaksa, President Mahinda Rajapaksa's brother. He was expecting my call and promised to get us full access to the camps and anything else we needed during our visit, even offering us his private military plane to travel to Manik Farm. He wanted the United States

---

170 Ibid., 14-15.

to see things improving in Sri Lanka under the Rajapaksas' leadership.

I thanked him and prepared to hang up.

"Wait one second," Defense Secretary Rajapaksa interrupted. "Where are you staying in Colombo?"

NIGHTTIME VISITORS

The intense pounding on my hotel room door never seemed to end on that fateful night in November 2009. As my desk lamp flickered, I was on the edge of sleep after a long day of travel.

"Open up! Open the door now!" The booming voices echoed from the hallway causing my heart to beat rapidly.

We returned earlier that day from a trip to Manik Farm in northern Sri Lanka. The images of heartbreaking living conditions symbolized through miles of tarps and tents replayed in my mind. The faces of children surviving through multiple traumas would haunt me for years to come. The IDPs did not look liberated from war; they looked imprisoned by the peace.

As we flew back from Manik Farm to Colombo over mountains and tea plantations, still unsteady from our visit to the camps, our Sri Lankan army plane experienced severe turbulence high up in the clouds. It continued to get worse, and the plane descended prematurely at an alarming speed. For a few terrifying moments, I thought we were going to crash into the mountains as I gripped my seat's armrests tightly.

The sound of the engines filled the plane with a deafening noise as the wings dipped toward the trees on the mountaintops below. *Oh my God, this is just turbulence, right? We are not really going to crash here; I mean, this cannot be how it ends.* As I closed my eyes tightly and tried to breathe deeply, the plane finally found its footing. I cried out in relief alongside others on the plane, relieved to be in the clouds again.

One near-death experience that day was quite enough. I could not stomach any more excitement that night in the hotel room. I quickly scrambled out of the tangled bed sheets and ran to the door as my pulse raced furiously. I squinted through the peephole and saw three huge, ripped guys in tight T-shirts, ready to enter the room by force. I broke out in a cold sweat. On instinct, thanks to the security training I received during my time at the State Department, I scrambled the chain on the door and locked the deadbolt in place while looking for additional objects to jam under the door. My eyes desperately searched the hotel room, zeroing in on the desk. Quickly, I placed the back of the desk chair underneath the door handle, hoping to buy a few extra minutes as the pounding continued.

"Who are you? Why are you here?" I asked desperately, my voice cracking.

"Let us in! We know you are hiding someone," came the reply. "Open up now!"

I ran to the phone and anxiously called Nilmini, who was staying just across the sixteenth-floor hall.

"They're banging on my door too," she cried out. "Whatever you do, do not let them in."

"Not planning to, but they could break down the door," I exclaimed as my mind raced through violent scenarios. "Who are they? And what do they want?"

"Listen to me carefully," she said. "They will white van us if they get the chance." We both knew well the stories about the white vans in Sri Lanka where people would mysteriously get picked up, never to be seen or heard from again.

"Oh my God!" I replied as terror gripped my heart. I fought hard to stay calm and rational as our security trainings taught us. "You call the front desk. I'll call the RSO," I instructed.

The next hour or so turned into a standstill as the US Embassy's Regional Security Officer (RSO) negotiated with the men outside our doors and the hotel's front desk. The thugs turned out to be plainclothes Sri Lankan policemen who received an anonymous tip about a Tamil terrorist in my room. The hotel management and RSO finally convinced them their information was inaccurate and reminded them we were here on official US government business.

Not surprisingly, even after the hallway cleared, I could not fall asleep. If someone meant to scare me, they succeeded. This trip already had its fair share of drama. In addition to these security threats, I was still reeling physically from landing in the hospital just days ago after we arrived.

I ended up getting sick on the plane ride from Washington to Colombo, feverish and frequently vomiting. After a few hours of meetings at the US Embassy on the first day, I knew I needed to see a doctor. The embassy medical clinic recommended I go immediately to the hospital, where the medical staff treated me for exhaustion and fever. I was in the early stages of my second pregnancy, and the nonstop travel, first in Afghanistan and Pakistan and now in Sri Lanka, was taking a toll. (My pregnancy would end in a miscarriage a few weeks later when I returned to Washington, leaving me with longstanding feelings of guilt for pushing myself hard on back-to-back trips for work.)

What started as a fact-finding mission was turning into a week of physical survival. We were the first international delegation visiting Sri Lanka following the end of its civil war. We asked a lot of tough questions about human rights and post-war reconciliation during our meetings that week. Perhaps we did not fully appreciate how our work could incriminate or embarrass senior political and military leaders. It looked as if we had become targets.

The morning after the hotel break-in, Nilmini and I met with Defense Secretary Gotabaya Rajapaksa, who I called when we first landed in Colombo. Patricia A. Butenis, the US Ambassador to Sri Lanka, and Lieutenant Colonel Lawrence Smith III, our embassy's Defense Attaché, joined us. We underscored our concerns about what we witnessed in the North and East, particularly on human rights issues. We highlighted the troubling conditions facing IDPs living in Manik Farm. We stressed the United States wanted to see conditions emerge to support post-conflict reconciliation and reconstruction. Not surprisingly, the meeting was quite tense. Taking on someone twice our age who wielded tremendous power and confidence was not easy.

Secretary Rajapaksa listened to us but quickly dismissed many of our critical findings, regretting that his government was "poor at propaganda" and not doing a good job selling its story to the West, particularly to Americans.[171] He was still euphoric regarding the Sri Lankan army's victory over the Tamil Tigers and could not understand why the United States and other governments cared more about the suffering of the Tamil people than ending the terrorism of the Tigers. US criticism of the treatment of the Tamil population in Manik Farm and other camps made little impression when he sought global recognition and respect for their military victory. According to him, the government was not doing anything wrong but failing to share its side of the story more effectively.

When we pushed back, underscoring the government did not have a public relations problem but rather a human rights problem, the defense secretary refused to concede or engage. He explained the complexities the Sri Lankan government was managing to prevent the LTTE from mounting a comeback and the post-war reconstruction efforts the government was undertaking to improve lives for the Tamils.

We then raised the hotel security incident. To our astonishment, he did not act surprised or remorseful. On the contrary, he knew all about it, taking credit for what happened!

---

171 US Congress, Senate, Committee, *Sri Lanka*, 10.

He personally called the police when he received the tip but did not know it was my room, he said, apologizing for the miscommunication. There were heightened security concerns, and sometimes mistakes happened to protect innocent people on the island. *No hard feelings though.*

He hoped our personal experience and the subsequent report would underscore the fragility and insecurity in the country, thereby justifying steps the government took to protect people at all costs. *He's proud he scared the daylights out of us! No question who has more power here.*

At the time, we could not effectively process the enormity of his confession. We planned to be in the country for another day or two and wanted to be able to leave freely and safely. Without saying anything further on the topic, we ended the meeting and went to see another Rajapaksa brother.

Basil Rajapaksa was President Mahinda Rajapaksa's national security advisor and the de-facto czar of the IDP camps. He wanted to see stronger ties with the United States but criticized us for recent US remarks critical of the Sri Lankan government. Weeks before our trip, the State Department issued a scathing report detailing credible and substantiated allegations of human rights abuses in the final days of the civil war. The report found government forces abducted and killed ethnic Tamil civilians, shelled, and bombed no-fire zones, particularly hospital facilities, and killed senior rebel leaders with whom they brokered a surrender.[172] According

---

172 Daniel Nasaw, "Sri Lanka Blasts US Report on Human Rights Abuses," *The Guardian*, October 22, 2009.

to some estimates, up to 30,000 civilians died in the ensuing combat during the final months of the war, including when the Sri Lankan army cornered the remaining Tigers on a strip of beach in the northeast of the island.[173]

We asked Basil Rajapaksa about these human rights allegations, which the government denied up to this point. He strongly defended the measures taken by the Sri Lankan army in the last days of the war and steps taken since to weed out the remaining Tamil Tigers fighters hiding among civilian refugees.

"I'm not saying we're clean," he told us defiantly that day. "We could not abide by international law; [the civil war] would have gone for centuries, an additional sixty years."[174]

This bombshell admission confirmed our suspicions of human rights abuses from some of the highest levels of the Rajapaksa government. We left the meeting stunned he chose to openly reveal this information.

"Holy smokes," I said later that day to Nilmini. "I feel like we walked into a bad movie."

"For now, let's wrap up this trip and get home in one piece," she replied. "We'll then figure out what this all means."

---

173   Jason Burke, "Former Sri Lankan Army Chief Convicted for War Crimes Claim," *The Guardian*, November 18, 2011.

174   Nilmini Rubin, interview with the author, November 24, 2020.

SOMETHING FOR EVERYONE

Safely home in Washington, we worked furiously to sort through our notes and debated what we should say. I celebrated my thirtieth birthday in December 2009 by calling for a new US strategy with Sri Lanka as SFRC released our bipartisan findings in its committee report, "Sri Lanka: Recharting US Strategy After the War."[175] The report raised human rights concerns, focusing on the conditions faced by Tamils, journalists, and others in civil society. It also recommended taking a broader view of the bilateral relationship to include economic and security dimensions, so the United States did not "lose" Sri Lanka to China. It focused on China's rise in the Indian Ocean, which few at the time discussed.

With Sri Lanka's strategic drift from the West, the Chinese were investing billions of dollars in Sri Lanka through military loans, infrastructure loans, and port development, with none of the conditions attached by Western nations. The report urged the US government to adopt a more multifaceted strategy capitalizing on the economic, trade, and security aspects of the relationship even as the United States prioritized human rights concerns and post-war reconciliation.[176]

The report received widespread media coverage, including in *The New York Times* and major US outlets.[177] It particularly went viral in Sri Lanka, as well as with Sri Lanka watchers in Washington, the Tamil diaspora, and communities that cared deeply about US views on Sri Lanka. We even had

---

175 US Congress, Senate, Committee, *Sri Lanka*.
176 Ibid.
177 Lydia Polgreen, "US Report on Sri Lanka Urges New Approach," *The New York Times*, December 6, 2009.

various Sri Lankan American constituents from across the United States camp out in the hallways of our Senate offices, asking to meet with us to support or contest our findings.

Overnight, our findings became a hot potato, generating incredibly vocal views from its supporters and detractors. We received pushback from some parts of the US administration and Tamil diaspora groups who wanted us to focus solely on human rights issues, which they felt should be the sole lens of the relationship. Others cheered our findings, taking a more holistic, long-term view of the bilateral relationship.

The toughest part of the report concerned what we left out. We deliberately chose not to include the security incidents we faced or confessions we heard from senior officials. We privately shared with the State Department full details of our visit when we returned. Ultimately, we decided to be deferential to the State Department to follow up appropriately with the government through its bilateral channels. If we published first without letting quiet diplomacy do its job, it could affect the administration's ability to negotiate a post-war peace, which we wanted to avoid. Moreover, as committee staff, we did not want to make the report about us, but instead about the situation in Sri Lanka and our forward-leaning recommendations. *Did we do the right thing? Should we have been more publicly transparent when we had the chance? Even if we did, would it have made a difference?*

It was hard to know. We never expected to be at the heart of the broader foreign policy discourse concerning Sri Lanka. Our work looking at the intersections of national security, human rights, economic development, and geopolitics as the country emerged from civil war crossed disciplines and fields. It required thinking across silos and using a broad range of tools. We needed to consider the diversity of views in complex ways and sort through the perspectives of various constituencies, who each felt strongly about their version of the truth. In looking for ways to plan for peace, we had to appreciate what triggered the war. Throughout the trip and its aftermath, we tried to think like development diplomats who could bridge worlds to plant the seeds for a more secure future. We had to rise above the physical and security threats we faced to put the needs of our two countries ahead of our own.

The work to build a post-war peace in Sri Lanka would go on for many years. It would continue to be complex and dangerous. I did not know then I would have another chance to play a significant role in shaping the island's options for economic development just a few years later. My work on development diplomacy in Sri Lanka was not yet over. At the time though, with the war in Afghanistan and neighboring Pakistan raging on with no end in sight, I turned my attention back to those countries. After all, what else could go wrong in Sri Lanka?

CHAPTER 7

PUMPING AND DUMPING IN WAR ZONES
IMPACT OF CONGRESSIONAL OVERSIGHT ON FOREIGN ASSISTANCE

- Speak up about your childcare and caregiving needs in the workplace.
- Pressure to spend foreign aid can quickly undermine effective development.
- Constructive dissent can be a game changer in pushing systemic change.

SQUISHED IN THE BACKSEAT

"Mommy! Baby hungry!" screamed two-and-a-half-year-old Zahra from the top of the stairs as I heated the same stale cup of tea for the fourth time that morning in January 2011. While juggling a newborn and toddler during my maternity leave, I rarely experienced a moment of peace. Sri Lanka, Pakistan, Afghanistan, or any other country was the furthest thing from my mind.

Then I received a call from William Frej. I crossed paths with Bill multiple times in my career when he led USAID Missions in Central Asia and Afghanistan. With his gray hair and wire-rimmed glasses, Bill was one of the kindest and smartest development officials I knew. He always leveled with me, giving honest and timely feedback on our development strategy, being upfront on what was not working.

Bill recently retired from the US government and returned home to his native Santa Fe, New Mexico, where he became the first diplomat in residence at the Santa Fe Institute, the world's leading research center for complex systems science. I loved that a development official was recognized formally in this way as a diplomat. At the Institute, Bill wanted to use data and science to find a way forward in complex crises, such as Afghanistan.

"Fatema, I want to pull together policymakers, academics, development experts, scientists, and Afghan tribal and business leaders. I want you to join this team," Bill wrote. He asked me to join him in Santa Fe in a few weeks to be part of the group developing new ways of thinking and working in conflict-affected countries.

"We are going to learn from each other and listen to presentations in the languages of science, policy, development, and military strategy," Bill explained, the excitement in his voice contagious. As part of this vision, we would stretch our thinking to see the same problem from different lenses. We would be guided by data, not politics, to sort through the complexity and pursue a more innovative approach.

"Bill, I would love to join, but the timing is terrible," I replied. "Let me see what I can do."

I groaned as I hung up the phone, knowing my husband, Nageeb Sumar, would not appreciate me taking off for a work trip at the tail end of my maternity leave. Our newborn daughter Safya refused to take a bottle, making it impossible for me to leave her behind. Traveling solo with a small baby while figuring out childcare logistics for a toddler also sounded exhausting. Yet, the opportunity Bill described felt unique from the usual Washington conferences. *Could I make it all work?*

It took a few rounds of negotiation with my husband and his parents, Salim and Anar Sumar, before a plan took shape. Nageeb would once again hold down the home front, caring for Zahra with support from our nanny. My in-laws would reroute their upcoming vacation in Phoenix, Arizona to Santa Fe to provide an extra set of hands to watch Safya. Despite questioning my sanity in going to such lengths to make this trip come together, my family came through when most needed.

Once at the Santa Fe Institute in February 2011, I juggled work and motherhood. Again. At the conference, I learned about complexity science, studying data from counterinsurgencies, listening to presentations on behavioral change, and examining history to learn from the past. When it was my turn to present, I focused on the foreign policy and development challenges we faced in the region. But I kept a strict eye on the clock the whole time. Every two and a half hours, I quietly ducked out of the conference room and ran to the parking lot where my in-laws waited with Safya. I climbed into the backseat of their rental car and nursed her. When we finished, my in-laws drove her to the hotel before returning a couple of hours later for the next feed.

At the time, it did not even occur to me to ask Bill to use a room at the Institute for childcare. It certainly would have made nursing more comfortable than being squished in the small rental car. My in-laws could have avoided shuttling all day during the cold winter. I now recognize there must have been a better way to handle childcare. During those days, I rarely discussed my personal life with senior colleagues. I worked in a conservative culture where women did not often share their needs as working moms. I did not challenge this norm, instead trying hard to fit into a largely male-dominated field without drawing undue attention. With few female role models who also balanced motherhood and their marriages with intense foreign policy and development careers, it was hard to imagine another way of doing things.

It was why I secretly pumped and dumped breast milk in war zones, covertly nursing in Army tents, Porta-Potties, and makeshift cubicles in the back of military planes without anyone, including senators or four-star military generals, noticing. Sometimes the conditions were downright disgusting and always cramped, but this seemed secondary to the importance of keeping up my milk supply without getting caught on the job.

To be clear, I did not hide having young children in the workplace. My bosses knew of my pregnancies and sent lovely cards and flowers each time I delivered a baby. Fair or not, I felt pressure to keep up with my male colleagues on the Hill. I did not want to be excluded from travel or meetings because people assumed motherhood would slow things down. As a minority woman, I already struggled to be taken seriously in corridors of power and privilege and could never safely assume I would be invited to join senior-level meetings. Typically, younger women on the Hill were viewed as notetakers or secretaries instead of senior policy advisors, and few minority women challenged the status quo of power at the time.

As a Muslim American working in the post-9/11 climate where anti-Muslim sentiments could be found in both US political parties, I also needed to be careful to be seen as trustworthy and reliable. I wanted my firsthand knowledge of Asia and Islam to be viewed as an asset and not a threat. As a result, I worked twice as hard as some of my male colleagues. I had to be strategic in knowing when to use my voice and when to stay silent. I negotiated intensely for each promotion and pay increase, never moving up the food chain easily on the basis of merit.

Given this context, I tried not to add motherhood to the list of things that made me stand apart from my colleagues. Accordingly, in the beginning, I went out of my way to avoid making it obvious that I was a working mom with moments of struggle. As a junior staffer with little power, I had insufficient incentive to openly be a mom at work. Over time as I juggled multiple babies, I realized something would have to change if I was to survive this type of career. Eventually, I followed Anne-Marie Slaughter's advice in her famous 2012 essay in *The Atlantic*, "Why Women Still Can't Have It All."

I mustered the courage to ask to work from home on Fridays. This seemingly small step was a game changer in allowing me to better manage work and care responsibilities.[178,179]

As I rose through the ranks in my career, I realized I could model and empower staff by openly discussing and supporting the needs of working mothers, even if it went against the cultural norms of the time. Today, as a senior manager and leader who has the power to make choices to support working parents, I am always looking for improved ways to balance work-life responsibilities. Unless we actively support the needs of working moms (and dads and other caregivers), we will never make meaningful progress in diversifying the workforce. We need to continue making these conversations more mainstream within the US workforce, especially amid the COVID-19 pandemic, the resulting shutdowns, and the work-from-home environments creating new opportunities to rethink the future and burdens of unpaid care.

In Santa Fe in 2011, I got away with this double life thanks to the incredible support of my in-laws, who spent hours in the rental car so I could travel. My mother and sisters also stepped in on multiple occasions from their home bases in New York and New Jersey to help with the kids when they could. Day to day, I somehow managed to pull off my crazy career, in large part because my husband Nageeb Sumar, was an incredibly supportive and active spouse who moved mountains even though he held down a demanding job of his

---

178 Anne-Marie Slaughter, "Why Women Still Can't Have It All," *The Atlantic*, July/August 2012.

179 Anne-Marie Slaughter, "To Make Big Change, Start Small: Have the Conversation with Your Boss," Linked In, October 3, 2015.

own. With support from Michael Deich, his amazing boss at the Bill and Melinda Gates Foundation, Nageeb successfully shifted his work meetings and travel schedule to help navigate school schedules, daycare pickups and drop-offs, doctor's appointments, and dentist visits.

Together, we spent a good chunk of our salary to cover the costs of nannies and daycare, which could run anywhere from $25,000 to $30,000 a year per child in Washington. We became proficient multitaskers and highly efficient workers since we could not afford the luxury of fully being present in any single facet of our personal or professional lives. We internalized the stress of constantly balancing kids and jobs as we collapsed from exhaustion on too many nights.

We tried hard to carve out time to make sure our marriage stayed strong, but there were some hard weeks and months. It was like running a marathon without the prerequisite physical training. I felt blessed to have family support at times, but since our extended family lived far away, it also raised the stakes to justify so many people rearranging their lives. It meant every trip, including Santa Fe, had to be worth it.

THE FLOODGATES OF FOREIGN AID

When I returned home to Washington, I could not leave Santa Fe behind as my mind processed our discussions, looking for hidden patterns in complex situations. One night, after I finished nursing Safya around two in the morning, I struggled to fall asleep. My brain would not shut down as something kept nagging me. I crept out of bed and turned on my computer. As I squinted against the harsh screen light, a thought began crystalizing. *We are losing the war, and we are losing the peace. We just keep pouring in money and troops into Afghanistan, but it's a mirage with nothing behind the curtain. What are we doing wrong?*

I found the answers later that spring after returning to work, pulling everything I could find from hearings, briefings, interviews, administration documents, newspaper articles, trips, and reports. Without realizing it at the time, I spent two years investigating the war in Afghanistan from both a foreign policy and development lens. I conducted hundreds of interviews and briefings with senior American and Afghan officials, civil society representatives, and foreign policy and development experts. Amid all the noise and complexity of the war, I saw patterns emerging in our foreign aid strategy. Something did not add up.

By 2011, the United States invested more on foreign aid in Afghanistan than in any other country combined, a mind-boggling $320 million a month in Afghanistan alone. From 2002 to 2010, the United States spent nearly nineteen billion dollars in Afghanistan, making the country the largest recipient of US foreign aid.[180] The US government, however, did not measure success by the impact this money had on reducing poverty. Instead, Congress and the US foreign policy community focused largely on how much, and how quickly, money could be pumped and dumped into Afghanistan, even if it fell into the wrong hands.

---

180 US Congress, Senate, Committee on Foreign Relations, *Afghanistan: Right Sizing the Development Footprint*, 112th Cong., 1st sess., 2011, S. Hrg. 112-201 1, 3.

From a very low baseline, Afghanistan's gross domestic product per capita doubled from 2002, with five million people lifted out of a dire state of poverty. Access to basic education and health also expanded dramatically.[181] Despite these often-touted developmental gains, Afghanistan remained one of the poorest countries on earth. This was partly due to international aid being too focused on military goals to counter terrorism, not development goals to end poverty.

During the 2000s, at the height of US wars in Iraq and Afghanistan, counterinsurgency (COIN) strategy dominated military thinking. Unlike conventional warfare, COIN relied on a comprehensive civilian solution alongside massive numbers of troops and a focus on winning the hearts and minds of the population, not just killing the enemy. COIN required a legitimate, functioning government to meet the needs of its people.[182]

For Afghanistan, which met none of these requirements in 2001, it meant constructing a functioning nation from scratch on the American taxpayer's dime. Nation-building required capable Afghan police and security forces, government ministries, courts and legal systems, roads, schools, and farms. These institutions all needed to be created by the international community overnight. Nation-building only worked by neutralizing the Taliban and its sources of income, including the world's largest opium markets.

---

181 Ibid., 9.
182 Bureau of Political Military Affairs, "US Government Counterinsurgency Guide," United States Government Interagency Counterinsurgency Initiative, US Department of State, January 2009.

As a result of the pressures to build a new nation-state and defeat the Taliban, USAID spent roughly 80 percent of its resources in Afghanistan's restive south and east, where the Taliban dominated the landscape. Most of these funds, in turn, were spent on short-term stabilization programs in areas like Garmsir, where the US and coalition troops cleared the areas of Taliban fighters.[183] US aid paid poor farmers to dig irrigation ditches for a few weeks so they would not join the Taliban in the hopes of providing short-term stability at the expense of a comprehensive, long-term development strategy.

Pressure from Congress to achieve rapid results put civilian agencies like the State Department and USAID under enormous strain to spend money quickly. In some places, for instance, the US government could spend a million dollars a day in an impoverished village to buy short-term loyalty with no clear development gain. Contractors needed to spend astronomical sums of money to receive their next installment from USAID. Insecurity, abject poverty, weak indigenous capacity, and widespread corruption created challenges for spending aid money. High staff turnover, imbalances between military and civilian resources, unpredictable funding levels from Congress, and changing US political timelines further complicated efforts for US foreign assistance to Afghanistan.

This enormous cash flow—with insufficient accountability for how funds were spent—resulted in the unintended effects of fueling corruption, distorting labor and goods markets,

---

183 US Congress, Senate, Committee on Foreign Relations, *Evaluating US Foreign Assistance to Afghanistan*, 112th Cong., 1st sess., 2011, committee print 112-21, 2.

and undermining the Afghan government's ability to exert control over resources of the state.[184] Ironically, US aid likely contributed to further insecurity, propping up a counterfeit economy that rewarded the very corrupt power brokers and human rights abusers the United States fought in the first place. These conclusions may be commonplace today, but at the time, they were a bombshell and went against conventional wisdom in Washington.

I decided to pull this information together in one place within a committee report, which I hoped Senator Kerry would support publicly releasing in his name. It could be embarrassing for the Obama administration's Afghan aid strategy to be criticized by a Democratic-controlled Congress. But continuing to spend billions on foreign aid without achieving sustainable development gains for the people of Afghanistan was far worse. I knew putting pen to paper was risky. The Obama administration worked closely with Senator Kerry on the entire region, as demonstrated by the seamless partnership during his October 2009 visit with President Karzai. State Department and USAID officials briefed the committee regularly, and we maintained close working relationships across the legislative and executive branches. Publicly calling out the administration on their foreign aid strategy would win no friends, particularly if the press crucified the White House.

I kept writing anyway, fueled in part by the courage of the younger Senator Kerry, the one who spoke out during the height of the Vietnam War and forced a national reckoning

---

184 Ibid, 2-3.

on the costs of our wars. When he hired me, he said he always wanted to tell the truth to the American people and be on the right side of history. I took his words seriously.

"Doug, I need your help," I said, barging into his fourth-floor office of the Senate Dirksen building in April 2011, visibly stressed out. "I'm on to something here. I think it's the right thing to do, but it's going to be really unpopular and politically stupid."

"Hey, take a deep breath," SFRC Deputy Staff Director Doug Frantz replied, looking at me with concern.

Doug was from the midwestern state of Indiana and thirty years my senior. We shared little in common at first glance. As an award-winning investigative journalist with honors like a Pulitzer Prize for his coverage in the aftermath of 9/11, a former editor at *The Washington Post, Los Angeles Times*, and *The New York Times*, and an author or co-author of more than ten books, Doug was well-known on the committee. His experience reporting from forty countries, living through the Vietnam War, and covering major wars brought him instant star power and fame with Senator Kerry.[185] At first glance, he appeared to be a tough, grumpy older man with little patience for inexperience or incompetence. His crass language could turn off a more sensitive soul.

After spending many hours with him in the war zones of Afghanistan to the battlefields of Capitol Hill, I discovered

---

185 "Douglas Frantz—Participant," The Aspen Institute, accessed June 6, 2021.

Doug was a big softie under a hard outer shell. His brilliance and kindness shone brightly when putting a spotlight on injustice. He took painstaking time to mentor and teach me how to think and write. He pushed me to be brave and say the truth, even when the consequences could be tough to bear. He made me believe in myself. I needed his wisdom at this critical time. He knew writing and political controversy inside and out.

As I fretted in his office, Doug counseled, "Don't worry about politics. That's my job. Put your head down and keep writing. Go after the truth." After a long pause, he added in a serious voice, "And make sure your sources are impeccable. We'll talk to JK; he'll understand why he can't keep silent on this."

True to Doug's word, I briefed Senator Kerry and his senior team on the draft report in May 2011. The timing was less than ideal. US forces recently killed terrorist mastermind Osama bin Laden on a covert mission in Abbottabad, Pakistan, raising the wrath of the Pakistanis for violating Pakistani national sovereignty.[186] President Obama prepared to deliver a major speech on Afghanistan at West Point, where he would announce the drawdown of US troops. Tensions in the region were high, and public critiques of US war strategy in the region could undermine the Obama administration's bargaining power.

---

186 Peter Baker, Helene Cooper, and Mark Mazzetti, "Bin Laden is Dead, Obama Says," *The New York Times*, May 1, 2011.

Senator Kerry patiently listened to my findings but remained noncommittal, his body language hard to read and his hands largely silent, which was never a good sign. He asked tough questions about my sources, data, and conclusions, refusing to be part of any "gotcha" moment with the administration. He wanted to trust the due diligence before agreeing to publish. He planned to hold a few more hearings and return to Afghanistan and Pakistan on another CODEL. Only after would he consider the next steps. I left the meeting feeling defeated.

"Let's use these hearings and the upcoming trip to make sure we're on solid ground," Doug offered when I fretted to him privately that the report would never see the light of day.

"Be patient; these things take time. You can't rush an earthquake."

ABOVE THE FOLD

The next few weeks were intense, like walking on pins and needles. We organized additional committee hearings on numerous angles of the war strategy, including foreign aid. I joined Senator Kerry on his CODEL in Kabul and Herat in northern Afghanistan, peppering US and Afghan officials all the while with questions on our development strategy. When we returned to Washington, I worked with committee colleagues like Andrew Imbrie to finalize our findings and confirm our facts checked out.

"Can we publish, Doug?" I asked impatiently for the fifth time. If so, the committee would print the report, making it part of the official record of the US Senate and available to the public.

"Listen, I just don't know if you will get approval to move forward. You need to be prepared; this report could die quietly," Doug replied candidly, noting the politics involved in a Democratic Senate publicly calling out a Democratic administration.

Frustrated, I nonetheless continued working, determined to give public voice to what so many knew privately was a flawed aid strategy. I refused to let the report disappear. At one point, I almost threatened to quit if the Committee chose not to publish. My colleagues' calls for patience fell on deaf ears.

Then, quietly and without much fanfare, we got the word from Senator Kerry to proceed with publishing our findings. He simply wrote "OK" on top of one our memos, formally giving us the green light. With those two simple but powerful letters, the seeds of change planted in Santa Fe could now start to take root if the politics allowed.

"Get ready," Doug quipped. "You're going to be one unpopular lady."

I could not believe it. I conducted investigations and published findings before, yet this report felt different, larger in scope and scale. *This could be a big deal! I can't believe what is about to happen.*

After consulting with David Wade, Senator Kerry's Chief of Staff, we decided to engage in quiet development diplomacy with the Obama administration before the report went public. We did not want to blindside the administration on our findings. Accordingly, we sent an advance copy to the

State Department and USAID, inviting them to submit a response we would consider publishing alongside the committee's findings.

We worked the phones with senior US officials, particularly those in the White House, to make sure there would be no surprises. Within days, we received responses from USAID Administrator Raj Shah and Deputy Secretary of State Thomas Nides defending the administration's approach on US foreign aid to Afghanistan.[187,188] Senator Kerry then sat down for an exclusive interview with *The Washington Post* national security correspondent Karen DeYoung to walk through the report in detail.

On June 7, 2011, *The Washington Post* ran an exclusive front-page article above the fold with a photo of a chopper and dozens of parachutes under the headline "Afghan nation-building programs not sustainable, report says."[189] The lead paragraph stated:

> The hugely expensive US attempt at nation-building in Afghanistan has had only limited success and may not survive an American withdrawal, according to the findings of a two-year congressional investigation...The report calls on the administration to urgently rethink its assistance programs

187 Rajiv Shah, "Letter from USAID Administrator Rajiv Shah on Evaluating US Foreign Assistance to Afghanistan," US Department of State, June 1, 2011.

188 US Congress, Senate, Committee, *Evaluating US Foreign Assistance to Afghanistan*, 39.

189 Karen DeYoung, "Afghan Nation-Building Programs Not Sustainable, Report Says," *The Washington Post*, June 7, 2011.

as President Obama prepares to begin drawing down the number of US troops in Afghanistan this summer.[190]

The following day, the committee officially released the report "Evaluating US Foreign Assistance to Afghanistan," with Senator Kerry announcing it during a committee hearing considering Ryan Crocker's nomination to be US Ambassador to Afghanistan.[191] Senator Kerry highlighted the report's central argument: US aid should be necessary, achievable, and sustainable. Over the next few weeks, the report garnered thousands of media hits, earning placement as a lead story on the major US television networks and widespread interest in key Afghanistan policy circles.

"Anthony Weiner should thank you," a member of the committee press team joked with me. "You knocked him off the front pages for a second," referring to Representative Anthony Weiner's first sexting scandal breaking in public that June.[192]

Predictably, the report received a mixed public response from the administration. Privately, some US government officials told me they were upset we went public. "I thought we were partners," one of the State Department Deputy SRAP officials told me. "You threw us under the bus."

---

190 Ibid.

191 John Kerry, "Chairman Kerry Opening Statement at Nomination Hearing for Ambassador to Afghanistan," US Senate Committee on Foreign Relations, press release, June 8, 2011.

192 Eli Rosenberg, "Key Moments in the Downfall of Anthony Weiner," *The New York Times*, October 28, 2016.

Others, such as senior officials in USAID and diplomats in Kabul, felt relieved the problems with our aid strategy were finally all out in the open so we could fix a broken approach. Secretary Clinton weighed in as well. "I think that the recommendations that the committee made are ones that we are very, very seriously looking at," she testified before the committee on June 23, 2011.[193] She went on at length to address some of the report's main points:

> We need to focus on the sustainability of our programs so that the Afghans can continue them. We're looking at that as well. So, we don't agree with all the recommendations or all the conclusions of the committee report…[But] we've learned a lot from this, and we will do our very best to try to implement those lessons. I certainly, working with our team and Raj Shah over at AID, have been trying to wrestle to the ground how we get more accountability and more measurable outcomes from our assistance. So, we're going to be changing in light of the military changes, but also in light of the lessons we've learned.[194]

USAID's Raj Shah told reporters, "The Senate report has some misperceptions of the overall effort," but he did not dispute its central conclusions according to the *LA Times*.[195] By

---

193 US Congress, Senate, Committee on Foreign Relations, *Evaluating Goals and Progress in Afghanistan and Pakistan,* 112th Cong., 1st sess., 2011, S. Hrg 112-103, 33.

194 Ibid.

195 Ken Dilanian, "US Risks Wasting Billions More in Afghanistan Aid, Report Says," *Los Angeles Times,* June 17, 2011.

August 2011, USAID announced new "Sustainability Guidance for Afghanistan." Consistent with the report's recommendations, the new guidance focused on the conditions required "for a successful, sustainable, Afghan-led transition, including achieving basic levels of security and stability, and building the confidence of the Afghan people so that there is a positive movement toward capable, inclusive, and pluralistic governance."[196]

According to Alex Thier, USAID's Director of the Office of Afghanistan and Pakistan Affairs, this new guidance would "increase the focus on sustainability in assistance efforts and [address] growing concerns about how the Afghan economy (and therefore Afghan stability) [would] weather the drawdown in international resources over the next four years."[197] In other words, USAID would focus on long-term development sustainability, not short-term tactical stability in programming its foreign aid to Afghanistan.

On September 8, 2011, the State Department's Deputy SRAP Daniel Feldman shared with the committee additional steps the administration would take in a hearing on the report's recommendations:

> As the transition process advances, we will be shifting our civilian efforts from short-term stabilization projects, largely as part of the military strategy, to longer-term sustainable development that focuses on spurring growth, building Afghan

196 Alex Thier, "Sustainable Assistance for Afghanistan," *US Agency for International Development Impact Blog*, August 1, 2011.
197 Ibid.

Government capacity in critical areas, and integrating Afghanistan into South Central Asia's economy. This approach is consistent with this committee's recommendation...that we focus on increasingly implemented projects that are necessary, achievable, and sustainable.[198]

Within a few short months, the report led to a significant shift in thinking within the Obama administration to focus more on long-term sustainability for development gains in Afghanistan. Going public resulted in media and advocacy pressure on the Obama administration to be held accountable for billions of dollars of US development aid. I celebrated the administration's willingness to seriously consider our findings and commit to tangible changes in its development strategy, even though I was realistic about the challenges ahead.

It would take time to jumpstart investments in Afghan-led, sustainable development initiatives. Turning the engines of US aid contracting, procurement, and staffing could not be done overnight. Similar problems existed with other donors to Afghanistan beyond the United States. Security challenges, political instability, corruption, weak governance, limited capacity, and regional tensions further complicated efforts to spend development dollars responsibly throughout Afghanistan and neighboring Pakistan.

Although I was proud to use the committee's high profile to challenge failed development approaches, I was under no illusion that anything would change quickly from our efforts

---

198 US Congress, Senate, Committee, *Afghanistan*, 4-5.

to reform US development approaches in either Afghanistan through this committee report or Pakistan through the Kerry-Lugar-Berman bill. Long-term sustainable development needed a meaningful and strategic political commitment over decades, not years, which was challenging to achieve in short-term US political cycles dominated by security concerns. My unease only grew over the years as I watched subsequent failed development efforts in the region.

FLAWED THEORY OF CHANGE

By spring 2021, despite twenty years of an American war and more than two trillion dollars in US war-time spending, including more than twenty-four billion on economic development and thirty billion on humanitarian and reconstruction aid, the Taliban controlled 22 percent of districts and contested another 51 percent.[199,200] According to the IMF, Afghanistan was the seventh poorest country in the world in terms of GDP per capita, with some of the highest rates of maternal mortality and lowest rates of life expectancy.[201] The UN Office for the Coordination of Humanitarian Affairs raised the alarm in spring 2021:

> Forty years of war, recurrent natural disasters, chronic poverty, and the COVID-19 pandemic continue to be a deadly combination for people in

---

199 Sarah AlMukhtar and Rod Nordland, "What Did the US Get for $2 Trillion in Afghanistan?" *The New York Times*, December 9, 2019.

200 Annie Pforzheimer, "Protecting Wider US Interests after a Troop Withdrawal," Center for Strategic and International Studies, May 26, 2021.

201 Avery Koop, "Mapped: The 25 Poorest Countries in the World," Insider, April 22, 2021.

Afghanistan. Nearly half of the population (some 18.4 million people) are in need of humanitarian and protection assistance in 2021. More than one-third of people are facing crisis or emergency levels of food insecurity, and nearly half of all children under five are expected to face acute malnutrition in 2021. Needs are being further compounded by emerging threats such as drought conditions and escalation of conflict, with some 13.2 million people anticipated to have immediate needs during the spring alone. Protection and safety risks to civilians, particularly women, children, and people with a disability, are also on the rise.[202]

According to the World Bank, Afghanistan's economy continues to be shaped by fragility and aid dependence with grants financing around 75 percent of public spending.[203] Afghanistan never transitioned from a satellite state dependent on foreign aid to a self-functioning economy with private-sector-led growth and strong institutions capable of effectively delivering services to its people.

Many of the underlying issues affecting its economic growth in 2021 are the same problems raised a decade earlier in the SFRC committee report. This grim reality is a stunning indictment of a fundamentally flawed theory of change on what it would take to successfully invest in sustainable and

202 "The Cost of Inaction Afghanistan Humanitarian Crisis," UN Office for the Coordination of Humanitarian Affairs, updated on reliefweb.int on May 25, 2021.

203 Habiburahman Sahibzada et al., "Afghanistan Development Update: Setting Course to Recovery," The World Bank, April 2021.

inclusive development in Afghanistan. From the onset, US development efforts in Afghanistan were in service of a larger political and security mission to defeat the Taliban through COIN and nation-building. This strategy, naively coined as "reconstruction," was implemented in short-term political cycles and annual budgets in select geographies of the country dictated by security needs and not by the needs of the poor. It was not an Afghan-driven, bottom-up development strategy tailored to the needs of the local population but rather a western-imposed vision of nation-building out of sync with the cultural, geopolitical, and financial realities of the region.

As I look back, I believe the United States should have worked from the beginning with international donors to support local, Afghan-led development efforts instead of Western-imposed solutions. Women, particularly Afghan women, should have been at the heart of the leadership making key decisions on where, what, and how to spend funds in ways that were locally and culturally sustainable. Rather than flooding the country with money during a short number of years, more US funds could have been invested in long-term accounts, such as the World Bank's Afghanistan Reconstruction Trust Fund, to be spent as needed over a longer range of time. The political pressure in Washington and western capitals to spend money quickly undermined long-term, inclusive, and sustainable development efforts, creating perverse incentives for a wartime economy where corrupt actors, both in Afghanistan and in the West, wielded undue influence.

If the United States – across both Republican and Democratic administrations – wanted to make a long-term commitment to Afghanistan in order to sustainably achieve security and stability, it should have pursued evidence-based development approaches focused on impact, investing in the highest areas of need not tied solely to a political and security agenda. Spending money through international and Afghan civil society instead of large, US-based contractors or the "Beltway Bandits" could have also been a game changer by putting funds in the hands of those closest to the ground instead of corporate entities profiting from the war.

With the U.S. withdrawal from Afghanistan completed on August 31, 2021 and many questions being asked about how we got here, policymakers should fully consider the costly development choices and mistakes made over twenty years. Afghanistan continues to be one of the poorest countries in the world despite billions of American taxpayer dollars spent to improve the quality of life for Afghans. Women and girls face the most dangerous consequences of the American withdrawal, with more women and children already killed and wounded in Afghanistan in the first half of 2021 than the same period in any other year since 2009, according to the UN.[204] Without human security in Afghanistan, there can be no political security for its people, neighbors, and the world at large. No political deal will last if it does not invest in the real needs of the Afghan people, especially its women and those across the country who are the most vulnerable.

Senator Kerry spoke truth to power on these very issues during his time as chairman of the Senate Foreign Relations

---

204 Susannah George, "Civilian Casualties in Afghanistan Hit Record Highs as U.S. Forces Withdraw, U.N. Mission Reports," *The Washington Post*, July 26, 2021.

Committee. While one congressional report or bill alone could not alter the course of US development aid in South Asia, legislative oversight shaped US foreign policy and aid in important ways. My time on the Hill showed me both the power and limitations of development diplomacy.

Taken together, the experiences highlighted in Part II underscore how hard and complex it is to fight poverty in some of the most dangerous and poorest parts of the world. Congress has a critical role to play in advancing a pro-poor global agenda and considering the intersection of politics, security, human rights, and economic development in some of the toughest parts of the world. Political negotiations, legislation, reports, investigations, media pressure, and attention from political stakeholders are all tools that Congress can use to advance development diplomacy. Failure is commonplace, making success even more valuable when a breakthrough is achieved. Development diplomats who understand how to use the power of Congress to advance key development initiatives are better positioned to achieve transformative results to fight poverty at scale.

PART III

THE ART OF A DEVELOPMENT DEAL IN GOVERNMENT

*Most of our... activities have been born from the grass roots
of developing countries, reflecting their aspirations and
their fragilities. Through the years, of course, this landscape
has changed fundamentally, with the creation of new states
like Bangladesh, the horrors of ethnic cleansing in Uganda,
the collapse of the Soviet empire and the emergence of new
countries...such as Tajikistan. More recently, of course, we
have faced the conflicts in Afghanistan and Syria.*

*Our work has always been people-driven. It grows out of
the age-old Islamic ethic, committed to goals with universal
relevance: the elimination of poverty, access to education,
and social peace in a pluralist environment... Amongst the
great common denominators of the human race is a shared
aspiration, a common hope, for a better quality of life.*

—His Highness the Aga Khan[205]

---

205 His Highness the Aga Khan, "Address to Both Houses of the Parliament of
Canada in the House of Commons Chamber," February 27, 2014, Special
Joint Session of Canadian Parliament, Ottawa, Canada, speech transcript.

CHAPTER 8

BRIDGING A REGIONAL ENERGY MARKET
FINDING MONEY FOR INFRASTRUCTURE DEALS

- Take calculated risks in your career.
- Leverage political and financial moments with active leadership.
- When Plan A fails, start on Plan B.

RETURN TO FOGGY BOTTOM

As the cool wind whipped up on the banks of the Amu Darya River in March 2014, I swiftly zipped up my black fleece, grateful for the layered warmth. Shielding my eyes from the sun, I peered from my vantage point on the Friendship Bridge across the muddy river separating southern Uzbekistan's fertile oasis and northern Afghanistan's harsh desert landscapes, the yin and yang of Central Asia's diverse topography.

"It's like being in two worlds but in the same place," I commented off-handedly to some of my US Embassy Tashkent colleagues traveling with me.

In some ways, it mirrored my career, shifting between the executive and legislative branches of the US government and covering Asia from unique vantage points. The past year brought big changes to my professional life, starting when President Obama appointed Senator Kerry as Secretary of State in December 2012. When your boss on the Hill leaves his or her perch, it can have huge ripple effects for the entire staff, with colleagues departing either by choice or demand. While many Senate Foreign Relations Committee (SFRC) staffers joined now-Secretary Kerry at the State Department, through much of 2013, I initially stayed on the Committee.

The truth was I loved life on the Hill; working on a congressional committee may be one of the best jobs around for those passionate about public policy. I had a high-profile perch to influence US national security and foreign policy choices without any of the bureaucracy of working in the executive branch. Conducting oversight of US foreign policy and foreign assistance from the Hill provided me a unique point of view to see the big picture of how policy, money, and politics intersected.

I interacted with many senior US and foreign officials—US Ambassadors, foreign embassies, heads of state, and foreign ministers—all eager to make sure their policies lined up with Congress. I also learned about international development on the Hill. Through committee hearings, nominations, legislation, travel, reports, and meetings, I learned how *not* to spend money even as I appreciated the critical role strategic development efforts played to lift people out of poverty and promote stability and prosperity.

Life on the Hill also allowed me to be a mom in many ways. During congressional recess periods, members of the Senate and House of Representatives left Washington to return to their home districts or travel overseas. This provided me needed personal respite to focus on household chores and the kids. I came to love recess, frantically scheduling pediatrician appointments and other mommy tasks during these times if I was not traveling myself for work. I was reluctant to give up this lifestyle, especially with three children under the age of five following the birth of my youngest daughter, Insiya. I wanted to be an active part of Insiya's life, soaking in each of her "first" life experiences since she would likely be my last child.

Fortunately, Senator Robert Menendez, who assumed the SFRC Chairmanship following Senator Kerry's departure, asked me to stay on the committee staff.[206] While I did not know Senator Menendez before working for him, I hoped he would keep me on the Committee staff when he took over and not let me go, which can happen when there is a change of leadership. We were both from New Jersey and being from the same geographic state or region can be an advantage in securing jobs with Congressional Members.

---

206 Robert Menendez, "Chairman Menendez Meets with President Karzai to Discuss Afghanistan's Future," US Senate Foreign Relations Committee, press release, February 20, 2013.

But what probably helped more is spending time with him during his first overseas trip as Chairman to Afghanistan and Pakistan in February 2013.[207] I was on maternity leave at the time of his trip but lobbied his staff to join him on the CODEL, nonetheless. Despite the personal hardships of leaving baby Insiya and the mad rush to once again secure childcare, I wanted to seize the opportunity to shape Senator Menendez's thinking on the region and get to know him and his staff so I could remain on the Committee doing what I loved.

The February 2013 visit provided an opportunity to introduce Senator Menendez to the politics, culture, and even cuisine of the region firsthand. In addition to meetings with Afghan and Pakistani leaders, we toured the Mangla Dam in Pakistan, where USAID supported the work to modernize the dam by increasing its power supply by one hundred megawatts (MW) to cover an additional 226,000 households in Pakistan.[208]

We even went carpet shopping when we found an hour of downtime! The journey home, unfortunately, took a figurative nosedive when our US military plane from Islamabad was diverted due to wartime needs in neighboring Afghanistan. The delays added long hours to our travel and included unplanned stops at US military bases in Afghanistan to secure safe transport to the Middle East and finally to Washington. Even these more difficult moments of travel, though, provided an opportunity to get to know my new boss.

---

207 Robert Menendez, "Chairman Menendez Meets with President Karzai to Discuss Afghanistan's Future," US Senate Foreign Relations Committee, press release, February 20, 2013.

208 Robert Menendez, "Chairman Menendez Meets with Pakistani President Zardari on Counter-Terrorism and Bilateral Cooperation," US Senate Foreign Relations Committee, press release, February 22, 2013.

Life on the Committee looked promising despite the change in leadership. I thought I was all set! Then, halfway through 2013, Secretary Kerry's senior staff contacted me about joining him at the State Department. While I initially hesitated, his offer to be appointed a Deputy Assistant Secretary (DAS), a senior role in the US government, overseeing the State Department's regional South and Central Asia (SCA) portfolio was hard to pass up. The appointment was a huge career opportunity, as I would report to the SCA Assistant Secretary (A/S) and be responsible for leading on all regional issues, including economic and energy connectivity, security assistance, women's rights, and people-to-people connections.

Should I take the job? It means going back to an exhausting schedule and tons of bureaucracy. I would be years younger than my peers and subordinates. Will career senior foreign service officials such as Ambassadors take me seriously? Will the hectic pace of travel and long working hours affect raising the kids? Will my marriage survive the intensity of the job?

Despite a lot of qualms and after lengthy discussions with family and close friends, I ultimately decided to rejoin the executive branch and accepted the offer. I believed strongly in Secretary Kerry's leadership and vision. I wanted to help him advance President Obama's priorities in a region I loved dearly. I now had the rank and the title to move mountains if the political will existed to make real change. In many ways, the opportunity to return to the same regional bureau where I began my career as an intern and junior officer was like a homecoming, with many friendly faces and familiar bureaucratic processes and jargon.

The shift from being a staffer behind the scenes to becoming a principal externally representing the US government was a bit jarring and took some time to adjust. I was easily startled whenever staff formally addressed me as "DAS Sumar" or stood up when I entered a room. Predictably, the hours were brutal and the travel nonstop, but the mandate to connect the least economically integrated parts of the world could not have been more vital.

Six months later, in March 2014, I was on the banks of the Amu Darya River, trying to figure out just how to promote regional connectivity in the least connected region of the world. I shivered as the wind picked up speed on that brisk spring day, wishing I packed gloves or at least a hat. The enormity of the moment was not lost on me, standing on a spot well-trodden over thousands of years as I pondered how to influence the region's future. *The Friendship Bridge...not sure if that's iconic or ironic given all its history.* Closing my eyes, I thought of all the things that happened on the Amu Darya.

A NEW SILK ROAD

On February 15, 1989, the last Soviet troops departed Afghanistan via the very bridge where I stood, following the "last hot conflict of the Cold War" with the end of the Soviet-Afghan war. [209,210] I could see these troops defiantly waving their banners and flags as they marched into the Uzbek Soviet Socialist

---

209 Editors of Encyclopedia Britannica, "Soviet invasion of Afghanistan," *Encyclopedia Britannica*, May 11, 2020.

210 Thomas Ruttig, "Crossing the Bridge: The 25th Anniversary of the Soviet Withdrawal from Afghanistan," Afghan Analysts Network, February 15, 2014.

Republic from Afghanistan. The Soviets seemed certain history would write them as the victors of the war when, in fact, the opposite was true. On that fateful February day, Boris Vsevolodovich Gromov, the last commander of the 40th Army, led the Soviets across the bridge without looking at the wreckage they left behind. Afghan analyst Thomas Ruttig captured this moment in his writings:

> When Gromov reached the middle of the iron bridge, he climbed down from the tank and went the last meters calmly on foot. From the Soviet side, his teenage son walked toward him, handed him a bouquet of red carnations. "Turn around!" I thought. "Turn around and show the Afghans a sign of apology or at least of respect!" But Gromov walked on, with his son's arm tucked under his, toward a Soviet TV crew and did not turn. Then the live [Afghan TV] broadcast ended.[211]

So much for friendship between the Afghans and Soviets, I thought as I considered Gromov's departure. *History seems destined to keep repeating itself here.*

Despite its friendly name, the bridge stood on a spot that historically witnessed conflict and conquest across empires. The ancient Bactrian Empire recognized the crossing's strategic importance 2,500 years ago. Alexander the Great conquered this point in the year 329 BC, giving rise to the city known then as Demetrius and today as Termez, on the northern side of the river in present-day Uzbekistan. It was a key crossing point for travelers along the Great Silk Road

---

211 Ibid.

and a thriving center of Buddhism, and later Islam, before being destroyed by the Mongols in the twelfth century. By the nineteenth century, Imperial Russia built a military base and river port. The area became a border outpost of the Russian Empire before the Soviets built the Friendship Bridge in 1982 to supply their troops based in Afghanistan during the Soviet-Afghan War.[212]

Twenty-five years and another conflict later with the onset of the US war in Afghanistan, the bridge now connected Termez on the Uzbek side with the Afghan city of Hairatan via a two-lane road and a single rail track, carrying essential food, goods, and supplies for the war. During my visit that March, I met with Uzbek officials responsible for the bridge and rail operations to assess possibilities for greater trade and transport between Central Asia and Afghanistan beyond just military logistics. Could this spot on the Amu Darya River, which for thousands of years connected ancient civilizations, now be a commercial lifeline for this landlocked part of the world? More broadly, could Central Asia economically integrate with Afghanistan and the rest of South Asia to lift millions of its people out of poverty? As the newly appointed SCA DAS, it was my job to find out.

Central Asia, which is made up of the former Soviet countries of Kazakhstan, Kyrgyzstan, Tajikistan, Turkmenistan, and Uzbekistan, borders Afghanistan to the north. While these landlocked countries share historic, economic, and political ties, such as the ancient Silk Road and involvement in

---

212 "Day 18: Afghanistan-Uzbekistan Friendship Bridge," *Intentionally International* (blog), June 11, 2018, accessed February 18, 2021.

the Soviet Empire, the united front crumbles at the tensions around ethnicity, culture, and language.[213] Despite their similarities and shared history, including the Mongol Khanate and Mughal, Persian, and Soviet Empires, there is great variation in how each country views itself and each other. This tension extends to differences among the countries in who is proud to have ties to Genghis Khan and who bemoans the lost Persian Empire. Afghanistan sits at the intersection of Central and South Asia.

This fascinating mix of both regions and contexts is why, historically, Afghanistan has been critical to the region's success, but also the center of occupation, wars, and grand bargains by external powers. Mistrust and political rivalries run deep within the psyche of Central Asia, with many of its leaders viewing regional cooperation as a zero-sum game. As a result, Central Asian countries remain largely isolated from one another, resulting in one of the least economically developed and integrated parts of the world, connected largely by flows of militant groups and illicit narcotics.

Like other former communist Central and Eastern European countries that were part of the Soviet empire, Central Asia experienced similar economic fallouts from the breakup of the Soviet Union. Skyrocketing inflation, partial de-industrialization, and the collapse of Soviet-type welfare systems were common throughout the region.[214] While Central Asian

---

213 US Congress, Senate, Committee on Foreign Relations, *Central Asia and the Transition in Afghanistan*, 112th Cong., 1st sess., 2011, committee print, 1, 4.

214 Uuriintuya Batsaikhan and Marek Dabrowski, "Central Asia Twenty-five Years after the Breakup of the USSR," *Russian Journal of Economic* 3, no.

countries initially achieved significant development gains in the early 2000s, with the poverty rate dropping to nearly 20 percent in Kyrgyzstan and from 70 percent to almost 25 percent in Tajikistan, they stalled on further progress with few significant economic reforms. Rural and remote areas were poverty hotspots, especially in parts of Tajikistan and the Kyrgyz Republic, where more than 40 percent of its population lived under the poverty line.[215]

Secretary of State Hillary Clinton believed the United States could bring greater economic and political stability to Afghanistan by connecting the economies of the region. In a historic speech in New Delhi, India in 2011, she announced US policy toward Afghanistan would focus on encouraging:

> [S]tronger economic ties through South and Central Asia so that goods, capital, and people can flow more easily across borders...As we look to the future of this region, let us take this precedent [of a past Silk Road] as inspiration for a long-term vision for Afghanistan and its neighbors. Let us set our sights on a new Silk Road—a web of economic and transit connections that will bind together a region too long torn apart by conflict and division... Turkmen gas fields could help meet both Pakistan's and India's growing energy needs and provide significant transit revenues for both Afghanistan and

---

3 (2017): 296-320.

215 The World Bank, "Poverty Continues to Decline, but Pace of Poverty Reduction is Slowing in Central Asia," press release 2020/ECA/17, October 17, 2019.

Pakistan. Tajik cotton could be turned into Indian linens. Furniture and fruit from Afghanistan could find their way to the markets of Astana or Mumbai and beyond.[216]

In other words, the United States wanted to build a New Silk Road. Just as Genghis Khan's Mongol empire connected distant lands and people, creating new marketplaces where goods and ideas could be exchanged, a New Silk Road could revitalize this part of the modern world. The idea sounded intriguing to me when I first heard her speak in 2011. *How would we accomplish this? What type of development would we need to break down deep-seated political and economic barriers throughout the region?*

I wrote up some initial policy ideas in an SFRC report I co-authored with my colleague Andrew Imbrie in December 2011 titled "Central Asia and the Transition in Afghanistan."[217] But I never expected to be put in charge of executing the New Silk Road vision for the Obama administration. After spending five years writing reports, legislation, and recommendations for US foreign policy and development aid in an oversight capacity on the Hill, I now needed to execute and implement the very policies I championed. It started with a thousand-year-old economic vision.

---

216 Jim Nichol, "Central Asia: Regional Developments and Implications for US Interests," Congressional Research Service, March 21, 2014, 45-46.

217 US Congress, Senate, Committee, *Central Asia and the Transition in Afghanistan.*

POWER IN ROOM 6243

"We should pony up the money if we're serious," I appealed to my new boss, SCA Assistant Secretary (A/S) Nisha Biswal, as she sat across her wide oak desk in her distinguished sixth-floor office in fall 2013. We shared many similarities, such as being the first South Asian women to hold these senior positions in the bureau. Like me, Nisha straddled both the international development and foreign policy spaces, having worked at USAID, the House of Representatives, and the American Red Cross. To top it off, we both had young daughters named Safya.

The sixth floor was a far cry from where I began my career years ago, a few floors down. As a junior officer, I needed an appointment to have a meeting like this with the A/S. Now, I just popped in unannounced from my swanky office next door, overlooking views of the majestic Lincoln Memorial. However, I paid little heed to my surroundings that day, bypassing the beautiful paintings and displays of Asian and American art in her office. Instead, I paced the floor, burning holes in the soft carpets under my feet, determined to make my case.

"Are you sure this project, CASA-1000, is a good investment? The World Bank has been talking about it for years, and not much has happened," Nisha noted. "We can't throw good money after bad."

Following her Senate confirmation two months earlier, Nisha hit the ground running in leading the bureau as a strategic thinker and savvy leader. I knew she would be careful in where she invested her political capital and resources.

"I agree, but I'm telling you we can make this real. The World Bank needs US leadership to move this forward. I promise you we can turn the lights on in the region," I replied with conviction. "Give me a chance. Give CASA-1000 a chance."

The concept of creating a Central Asia South Asia (CASA) regional energy market (CASAREM) first originated under the Soviets and gained steam with the independence of the Central Asian republics. The basic premise linked Central Asia's surplus energy resources with South Asia's energy shortages and growing demand for energy. During the summer months when Kyrgyzstan and Tajikistan experienced a surplus flow of water from the snowmelt of the Tien Shan mountain range, they could convert this surplus to hydropower potential by selling 1,300 megawatts (MW) to energy-starved Afghanistan and Pakistan.[218] This project, known as CASA-1000 for the 1,000 MW that would eventually reach Pakistan, could be a significant opportunity to invest in the region's economic potential and develop a nascent regional energy market benefiting sixteen million Pakistanis. It would boost desperately needed income and economic diversification for the entire region while simultaneously promoting clean energy.[219]

All four countries shared crippling economic challenges. Landlocked Kyrgyzstan and Tajikistan were the poorest of the Central Asian republics, with their gross national income (GNI) per capita below US $1,000. This amount was in stark

---

218 "Secretariat for CASA-1000 Power Transmission Project Fact Sheet," US Agency of Development, updated September 14, 2020.

219 "US Support for the New Silk Road," US Department of State Archived Content 2009 to 2017, accessed May 15, 2021.

contrast to India's GNI, which was more than double.[220],[221] Afghanistan needed to find sustainable sources of long-term inclusive growth outside of wartime foreign aid, for which a well-functioning energy sector remained critical. Finally, Pakistan faced one of the worst energy crises in its history, resulting in massive blackouts and economic losses.

In my first few months on the job in fall 2013, I struggled to find tangible development projects to make the New Silk Road vision a reality. My staff informed me CASA-1000 could be one of our signature investments if we could breathe some life into it. Development experts talked about its potential for years, but the project lacked the political momentum or diplomatic leadership to make it happen across the four countries. CASA-1000 could be the opportunity to boost economic prosperity in one of the poorest parts of the world while bringing greater regional stability. Its payoff could be enormous.

Unlike many other major energy investments, this project did not require building any new power plants. Instead, it would support the construction of 1,200 kilometers of transmission lines at a price of just over a billion US dollars, a mere fraction of the cost of building new power plants or dams.[222] The Asian Development Bank (ADB) and World Bank completed the feasibility work, meaning the project technically

---

220 "CASA-1000 Central Asia South Asia Electricity Transmission and Trade Project Regional Environmental Assessment," Central Asia South Asia Electricity Transmission and Trade Project, February 2014, 14.

221 "GNI per capita, Atlas method (current US$)," The World Bank, accessed February 18, 2021.

222 Sabena Siddiqui, "CASA Project and Energy Dynamics across Central, South Asia," Al Arabiya, updated May 20, 2020.

looked ready to go. USAID funded the CASA-1000 Secretariat, which coordinated the procurement, construction, and establishment of power transmission infrastructure, as well as commercial and institutional arrangements, to facilitate regional and cross-border electricity trade between Central and South Asia.[223] Now, CASA-1000 needed a major political and financial diplomatic push to make it real. I seized the opportunity to move forward a development project that could have stayed dormant by pulling all levers of the US government. I could sense the power and potential of development diplomacy.

"SHOW ME THE MONEY"

The first step required US leadership to support CASA-1000 in tangible ways. In addition to speeches such as the one Secretary Clinton delivered in India in 2011, we needed to break the political logjams and fill the massive financing gaps facing Tajikistan and Kyrgyzstan. I remained convinced that if the US government could offer grant financing, it could unlock funding from others, particularly multilateral institutions such as the World Bank and Islamic Development Bank (IDB) and bilateral development agencies. Project financing for complex infrastructure projects in developing countries remained a significant challenge for multiple reasons, such as lack of access to finance for concessional lending and grants, inability to develop projects to required levels of bankability, lack of know-how on complex project management and execution, and political and security risks in the region.

---

223 "Secretariat for CASA-1000," USAID, September 14, 2020.

When the United States backed a major development project, it could leverage precious grant dollars for multilateral financing and signal an acceptable level of political risk. This support paved the way for reluctant investors, whether they be bilateral donors or development banks, to come online. As the largest shareholder of the World Bank, the United States played a pivotal leadership role in influencing and shaping global development priorities. Investing US funds in the project would send strong support for the Bank's International Development Association (IDA), which provided low-interest loans and grants to the world's poorest countries for the four CASA countries.[224]

I knew it would be hard to find funds within the State Department or USAID for CASA-1000 since most development funding showed up in bilateral country budgets earmarked for a specific country, not accounts tagged for a region. Historically, funding for regional projects was limited. Country teams set aside their budgets for priorities years in advance, making it near impossible to secure last-minute funding for expensive regional projects. Moreover, Tajikistan and Kyrgyzstan received only a tiny fraction of the development funds Afghanistan and Pakistan received, given the US war in Afghanistan. Most of the available US development funds sat in the Afghanistan and Pakistan accounts managed by the State Department's Special Representative for Afghanistan and Pakistan (SRAP) and USAID's Office of Afghanistan and Pakistan (OAPA). The SCA bureaus at the State Department and USAID did

---

224 "The World Bank in the United States: Overview," The World Bank, updated December 1, 2020.

not have access to these funds and managed substantially smaller budgets for Central Asia.

As a result, I first lobbied my SRAP and OAPA colleagues to invest funds from their "Af/Pak" budgets for CASA-1000. My goal was to convince them this project would not be a white elephant, an expensive endeavor that ultimately fails. Successful lobbying required a political plan for bringing the four countries together on the same timeline, a daunting prospect given the lack of trust and cooperation between the region's political leaders. There was no proof of concept the region could work together on something so massive, having never accomplished anything on this scale. The economics of the project needed to make sense, especially when the project required building over a thousand kilometers of transmission lines in an active war zone. With many volatile variables to consider, no one wanted to waste time or money on the wrong development investment.

After weeks of internally making a case for CASA-1000 within the halls of both the State Department and USAID, I realized I would not succeed.

"It's just not going to happen," one SRAP advisor told me privately. "The funds will not be released even though the project could be a win-win."

In addition to the challenging regional context, SRAP and OAPA were reluctant to fill the funding gap for countries outside of their mandate. Sharing bilateral resources for regional projects was complicated given how budgets were set up and approved, a lengthy multi-year process requiring approvals from the State Department, the White House Office of Management and Budget (OMB), and Congress. It could also raise problematic questions in Congress. On a personal level, some ill-will may have lingered in SRAP over my role on the SFRC Afghan aid report a few years earlier, which criticized how US development funds were spent in Afghanistan, although no one admitted so. While disappointed, I was not deterred. Time for a Plan B, which brought me to Nisha's desk that fall day.

"Where will you get the money since SRAP is saying no?" Nisha probed, a good sign she would not immediately reject my proposal.

"I'm going to sweep the Central Asia Regional Affairs budget, which I manage, for funds," I replied. "It means investing in one big bet, so it's a calculated risk, but I think we should take it."

Investing most of the regional budget for one project meant turning down other worthy opportunities. None of these smaller projects, however, could reach as many people at scale the way CASA-1000 could across four countries. By investing a few million dollars this way, the United States could leverage over a billion dollars of project finance, generating a massive return on investment for millions of people. Nisha gave me the green light. Weeks later, in December 2013, the State Department announced the United States would commit fifteen million dollars in financing toward CASA-1000.

"We believe CASA-1000 can be a potentially transformative project, helping create a regional energy grid that connects Central and South Asia for the first time," stated the press release, which I helped draft. "We hope US financial support for CASA-1000 will help leverage other donors to support the project and encourage the World Bank to present the project to its Board of Directors for final approval next year."[225]

Contributing US financing changed the political momentum going into 2014 on the entire project. Overnight, the four CASA countries and our European allies paid closer attention to CASA-1000. Something must be going on if the Americans were supporting it. The move to contribute even a symbolic amount of funding was a significant win for development diplomacy. American financing typically unlocked, incentivized, and crowded-in multilateral financing from others. Achieving this outcome required seeing past structural barriers, strategically using regional funds, and looking for creative solutions to work in new ways within the US bureaucracy.

"The United States signaling its financial and political support for CASA-1000 is a game changer," Saroj Kumar Jha, the World Bank's Regional Director for Central Asia, told me. "It means the Americans are serious in their commitment to the project. When the United States puts money on a big multilateral project like this, it helps unlock a lot of the challenges that we often may have in accessing multilateral financing."

---

225 US Department of State, "US Announces $15 Million in Funding for CASA-1000 Electricity Project," US Department of State Archived Content 2009 to 2017, media note, December 11, 2013.

We succeeded in generating political interest, but I knew we still had a long way to go. Regional politics remained deeply polarized. Nothing in this region happened easily. For every step forward, we always took two steps sideways or backward.

"Now let's see if we can get the Tajiks, Kyrgyz, Afghans, and Pakistanis to agree to move forward," Nisha told me. "We'll need a breakthrough…and a miracle."

"Don't worry; we'll haggle them on the deal until they give in," I replied, only half-joking. "Seriously, we're on it."

CHAPTER 9

NEGOTIATING A DEAL IN THE BAZAAR
SECURING COUNTRY BUY-IN FOR DEVELOPMENT

- Never underestimate the power and value of face-to-face diplomacy in critical negotiations.
- Regional projects can fail if one neighboring country remains strongly opposed.
- Create conditions for political trust to translate into economic gains.

THE ART OF BARGAINING

"Don't walk away, ma'am. You won't get a better deal anywhere else on an Afghan rug," the Kabul shopkeeper begged as I threatened to leave his stall upon hearing his outrageous price in the spring of 2007.

Having shopped in the great bazaars of Cairo, Aleppo, Marrakesh, Istanbul, and Samarkand, among others, I was no stranger to the art of bargaining in Central Asia. The rules are simple. The buyer should not show too much interest in a particular item and pretend to just be looking. After the merchant reveals his initial price, the buyer should act offended and threaten to walk away. The merchant responds by acting insulted, invoking *Allah*, and daring his potential purchaser to walk away. In turn, the buyer demands a lower price, although he or she is willing to pay much more. The merchant, in turn, starts complaining about how much he is losing just by having this conversation even as his initial price starts coming down dramatically. Finally, the buyer profusely thanks the merchant for honoring him or her with such a good price. By the end, they are both friends for life as they exchange business cards, all hard words and threats forgotten.

"Okay, but let's be serious then. Give me a good price, and I'll tell all my friends to do business with you," I responded in my broken Dari language, hoping to snag a beautiful item for a bargain.

Having grown up in a South Asian culture where the art of the deal was as important as procuring the product, I took inspiration from watching my dad haggle his way through running his own small business in central New Jersey, an Ace Hardware store. Bargaining was in my blood. I knew the art of bargaining worked for buying carpets but did not know if similar rules of business also applied to complex development deals in Central Asia such as CASA-1000. It turns out before we could get the four CASA countries to trade electricity with each other, we needed to get them to shop at the same bazaar.

PLANES, TRAINS, AND AUTOMOBILES

Throughout 2014, my State Department and USAID colleagues and I worked closely together with the World Bank and our Central Asian partners to make CASA-1000 a reality. We made significant progress in fall 2013 by securing US grant financing for the deal. Now, with a narrow political window to make progress, we needed to secure formal approval from the World Bank, fill the rest of the financing gap, and have all four countries agree on the pricing for electricity trade.

"Work the phones, set up meetings, and get out cables," I instructed my teams across the State Department and USAID as we looked for ways to get CASA-1000 moving. Cables summarized in writing confidential messages between a diplomatic mission, such as an embassy or a consulate, and the headquarters of a foreign ministry, such as the State Department. They could be powerful tools to share information and coordinate diplomatic strategies between Washington and foreign capitals.

"And let's get on planes if we need to. Let's get this done," I said energetically, committed to pulling a Central Asian energy rabbit out of our diplomatic hat.

Despite the considerable stress of leaving my kids behind again, I traveled to London, Brussels, Berlin, Moscow, Tashkent, Termez, Ashgabat, Baku, Almaty, Dushanbe, Kathmandu, Muscat, and Istanbul that year to advance diplomatic negotiations on the project and other regional initiatives. I also focused on development diplomacy in Washington. The first order of business required convincing the State

Department to raise CASA-1000 as a top economic priority in the region.

"Robin, I need your help," I said, drumming my fingers on the table in the State Department cafeteria, where the real discussions often happened.

"Well, let's see what we can do here," she replied cheerfully as she blew steam off her Dunkin' Donut's coffee. "It's a good project...but then good things often die in this region, as you know well."

Intelligent, politically savvy, and extraordinarily kind, Ambassador Robin Raphel was a US diplomatic legend in the world of South Asia. She worked in Iran and Pakistan and had expertise throughout the region, fluency in Urdu, working knowledge of South Asian politics and people, and extensive relationships with the region's political and military ruling elite. President Bill Clinton appointed her as the first Assistant Secretary of State for the newly created South and Central Asian Affairs Bureau in 1993. She then served as the US Ambassador to Tunisia and held several South Asia-related diplomatic posts before retiring from the Foreign Service in 2005. Ambassador Richard Holbrooke convinced her to rejoin the State Department in 2009 to coordinate non-military assistance to Pakistan.[226]

I spent significant time with Robin when I was a Senate staffer overseeing the implementation of the Kerry-Lugar-Berman bill. I always enjoyed working with her and the USAID teams

---

226 Richard Leiby, "Who is Robin Raphel, the State Department Veteran Caught Up in Pakistan Intrigue?" *The Washington Post*, December 16, 2014.

in Islamabad, greatly valuing her partnership and mentorship on the overall development agenda.

Throughout 2014, Robin and I worked with our respective SRAP and SCA teams to send cables to US embassies in the region, "demarching" or tasking them to highlight CASA-1000 as our signature regional development priority in their bilateral meetings with regional governments. We asked our British friends to do the same in their diplomacy since they also supported the project. In due course, US and British Ambassadors and their teams, alongside senior World Bank officials in Dushanbe, Bishkek, Kabul, and Islamabad, repeatedly raised CASA-1000 in their meetings with regional leaders, encouraging them to move forward.

We could see political momentum in the region growing. While hosting a special international Nowruz festival in Kabul to mark the Persian New Year in March 2014, for instance, Afghan President Karzai raised CASA-1000 in his discussions with Pakistan and Tajikistan's leaders.[227] Just a few months later, during his June 2014 visit to Dushanbe, Pakistani Prime Minister Nawaz Shariff followed up on CASA-1000 with Tajikistan's President Emomali Rahmon.[228] In Washington, the World Bank secured a major milestone when its board approved the project in March 2014, committing over half a billion dollars in IDA financing.[229]

227 "Kabul Hosts International Nowruz Festival," *ToloNews*, updated March 28, 2014.

228 "Prime Minister, Muhammad Nawaz Sharif Arrived in Dushanbe, Tajikistan for Two Day Official Visit," Office of the Prime Minister, Islamic Republic of Pakistan, June 17, 2014.

229 "World Bank Group Invests in Energy Trade between Central Asia and South Asia," The World Bank, March 27, 2014.

Still, finding another half of a billion dollars to pay for the entire project remained a significant obstacle. Even as the United States committed fifteen million dollars, we needed other partners to come forward and plug the remaining financing gap. With unyielding persistence, our teams worked the phones and arranged meetings with potential funders, particularly multilateral banks like the European Investment Bank and Islamic Development Bank (IDB), that could afford these levels of project finance.

"Let's call Jedda, Saudi Arabia again and ask the IDB for a meeting when they come to Washington," I told my team, refusing to give up when cables and emails did not do the trick in getting the Saudi-based bank to commit financing.

I decided to take a few pages from John Kerry's diplomatic playbook, especially as I witnessed firsthand the power of face-to-face diplomacy during my time in the Senate with him. It worked! We collectively cheered later that year after a coordinated diplomatic effort from many partners across multiple governments and development banks— the Islamic Development Bank, the UK government, and others—committed the remaining funding to close the financing gap.

Another thorny issue involved neighboring Uzbekistan's opposition to the project. The Uzbeks initially viewed CASA-1000 as a backdoor way for the Tajiks to build the massive Rogun Dam. The Uzbeks were long opposed to the Tajiks going forward with Rogun, fearing the dam would divert their shared river away from its agricultural fields.[230] Bilateral relations between the two countries remained tense, with little trust between their political leadership. Realistically, it would be difficult to proceed on a regional project of this magnitude if one of the neighbors outright opposed it. Uzbek President Islam Karimov reportedly hinted divisions of water allocation in the region could result in "wars."[231]

World Bank leadership worked nonstop to diplomatically defuse tensions in the region, and I knew the United States could also help. We worked closely with US Ambassador to Uzbekistan George Krol, US Ambassador to Tajikistan Susan M. Elliott, and US Ambassador to the Kyrgyz Republic Pamela Spratlen and tried hard to successfully address Uzbekistan's technical and political concerns regarding diversion of water flow in the region. Development diplomacy included engaging the Uzbeks in dialogue through meetings and conferences in Washington and Tashkent, Uzbekistan's capital. Reducing tensions with Uzbekistan could also help rebuild trust with the Asian Development Bank (ADB) on CASA-1000. While the ADB originally participated actively on CASA-1000, it suspended its involvement in early 2009, likely due to pressure from the Uzbeks. As the ADB's largest client in the region, ADB leadership did not want to support a development project the Uzbeks opposed.

One way we could build greater trust with both the Uzbeks and ADB included supporting another electricity line in the region called TUTAP, sponsored by the ADB. This project

---

230 Casey Michel, "What Happens to Uzbek Opposition to CASA-1000 if Karimov is Dead?" *The Diplomat*, September 2, 2016.
231 Ibid.

looked to export electricity from Turkmenistan, Uzbekistan, and Tajikistan to Afghanistan and Pakistan.[232] TUTAP also needed political support and leadership to advance beyond technical feasibility studies. Given the dearth of energy in the region, each viable power project contributed an added benefit, and I saw no reason why the United States could not champion both projects simultaneously since they were complementary.

As a result, we announced US support for both projects and worked hard with both ADB and World Bank leadership on a broader vision for a thriving regional energy market.[233] While it would take an additional four years for the Uzbek government to publicly support CASA-1000, working closely with the Uzbeks in 2014 to defuse tensions helped lay the groundwork for regional energy cooperation.[234]

SEAL THE DEAL WITH A PHOTO OP!

The last major hurdle involved getting the four CASA countries to come together and agree on pricing for the electricity trade.

"Let's roll out the red carpet for them when they come to Washington next month for the Bank/Fund meetings," I

---

232 "Power Interconnection Project to Strengthen Power Trade Between Afghanistan, Turkmenistan, Pakistan," *Asian Development Bank*, February 28, 2018.

233 Fatema Z. Sumar, "A Transformation: Afghanistan Beyond 2014," US Department of State Archived Content 2009 to 2017, April 30, 2014.

234 "Uzbekistan Supports CASA-1000 Project—Kamilov," *The Tashkent Times*, November 29, 2018.

brainstormed with my State Department teams. "Let's ask Cathy to host."

On the margins of the World Bank and International Monetary Fund (IMF) fall 2014 meetings, Catherine Novelli, the State Department's Under Secretary for Economic Growth, Energy, and the Environment, graciously agreed to sponsor a lunch for the CASA-1000 finance ministers. During this meeting, Under Secretary Novelli stressed the historic opportunity for regional leaders to connect their energy markets. The fact these four countries' leaders kept meeting to find ways to make CASA-1000 work was transformative in and of itself and challenged the prevailing narrative of conflict and distrust constantly dividing the region. The effort to come together created the foundation for other promising pathways toward shared stability and prosperity across Central and South Asia.

The State Department luncheon complimented another meeting the World Bank arranged at the Georgetown Four Seasons Hotel for the finance ministers to agree on a trade price for electricity. Together, these conversations set the scene for productive discussions occurring weeks later when the CASA countries gathered in Istanbul for a meeting of the CASA-1000 Joint Working Group and Inter-Governmental Council. The body language, tone, and sentiments in these sessions led us to be cautiously optimistic we were on the verge of a historic breakthrough. Just like negotiating in a bazaar, though, the buyer and seller could appear far apart and threaten to prematurely end the negotiation, thereby aborting the entire regional deal. Could the four countries agree on a price for electricity trade?

When the four CASA countries gathered in the fall of 2014 in Washington to negotiate the price of electricity trade in the region, the sellers—the Tajiks and Kyrgyz—asked for more money than what the economics suggested made sense. While only a fraction of a cent higher than the recommended technical price, the difference could be enough to unravel the entire deal for the buyers—the Pakistanis.

Pakistanis were price sensitive since they faced a balance of payments and financial crisis whereby the nation was unable to pay for essential imports or service its external debt repayments. Even tiny increases in the price could make the entire deal financially unviable for them. Emotions ran high. At one point, the Pakistanis threatened to walk out and exit the deal. Just like at the bazaar, all sides acted offended and exchanged heated words. The stakes here, however, were much higher, with the economic livelihoods of millions of people depending on the outcome. We could not afford for any country to feel insulted and seriously leave the table.

"I think we need to divide and conquer here," I said to the three S's—Salman Zaheer, Sunil Khosla, and Saroj Kumar Jha, the World Bank's negotiating leads on the deal. They each decisively moved CASA-1000 forward in their respective roles as the World Bank's South Asia Director for Regional Integration, Lead Energy Specialist, and Regional Director for Central Asia. Alongside many other colleagues, especially those at the CASA-1000 Secretariat, the four of us spent countless hours on development diplomacy among the four CASA countries by acting as neutral and trusted intermediaries across borders, boardrooms, and bureaucracies.

"Let's bring down the temperature," Sunil said during one meeting as we went off to find the Pakistani minister who just left the room, speaking to him in his native Punjabi to calm him down.

"The Kyrgyz need to understand what's at stake," noted Salman as he tried to negotiate a lower price with the Kyrgyz delegation.

The Kyrgyz had the impression the Tajiks, Afghans, and Pakistanis negotiated a pricing deal without them in March 2014 during Afghan President Karzai's Nowruz gathering in Kabul. Suspicion and distrust dominated politics in the region, and the Kyrgyz likely wanted to save face.

"I'll speak with the Tajiks," said Saroj.

He recently met with Tajik President Rahmon in Dushanbe and did not want the Tajik delegation overshooting their asking price during these negotiations. Technically speaking, there was little room to change the price from the economic modeling for the overall deal to make financial sense. Political games and brinksmanship could derail a sound economic model. After multiple rounds of discussions with each country delegation individually and then collectively, we finally reached a deal in our electricity bazaar. We found a way to lower the price while keeping it above the original asking price, offering a face-saving compromise for each country.

"Let's lock it in before they leave," I urged my World Bank colleagues after the Afghans and Pakistanis reached a deal on the transit price during the Washington meetings. "Can we put together a fancy signing deal to commemorate this moment?"

Our teams scrambled overnight to put together a historic signing ceremony formally announcing the deal. On a rainy and cold Saturday morning on October 11, 2014, I left my daughters playing in their pajamas at home to drive downtown to the World Bank's headquarters on 17th Street NW in Washington to join dozens of others who worked tirelessly on the project for years, some starting in the 1990s and 2000s. Together, we clapped loudly when Pakistani Finance Minister Dar and Afghan Finance Minister Zakhilwar signed an agreement on the CASA-1000 electricity transit fees in front of the World Bank President Jim Kim.[235]

It was an emotional moment for so many across bilateral, regional, and multilateral spaces who worked for years on CASA-1000. Milestones such as these were not business as usual for the South and Central Asia region. Each signing and project agreement became part of history, the first time these four countries peacefully worked together on their collective economic development. It took countless people across multiple governments and multilateral institutions working together on the technical, financial, political, and regional aspects of the deal for the project to start becoming a reality. It took development diplomacy to break bureaucratic silos, fill a billion-dollar financing gap, and create conditions for political trust in the region to translate into economic gains.

---

235 "CASA-1000: Pakistan, Afghanistan Agree Electricity Transit Fee," *The Express Tribune*, October 11, 2014.

There were still many issues to work through and finalize in the coming years for CASA-1000 to come together. The political winds, though, now turned. Construction on the transmission lines began a few years later. Before the Taliban takeover of Afghanistan in August 2021, the lights were scheduled to turn on in 2022.

CHAPTER 10

POWERING THROUGH EARTHQUAKES
DESIGNING A DEVELOPMENT DEAL

- Do not get blinded by the present; look ahead to the future.
- Change up how you work with partners to increase transparency and trust.
- When measuring progress, be prepared to take one step forward, backward, and sideways.

THE POWER OF WATER

As the helicopter wound its way through the spectacular peaks and narrow valleys of the Himalayan ranges northeast of Kathmandu in February 2015, I stared out of the window, mesmerized by Nepal's stunning contrasts. Tucked away between China and India, its thirty million people lived life on all terrains from the high plateaus of Tibet to the dense Kathmandu Valley, from the tropical jungles in Chitwan to the fertile plains of the Ganges.

Directly across from my eye line, I came face to face with terraced steps carved intricately into the mountains, an agricultural practice going back centuries for smallholder farmers eking out daily survival in tough conditions. The beautiful symmetry of these steps high on the mountain slopes mocked gravity. The land hinted at the physical challenges of living in the world's remotest places with no roads, power, or basic infrastructure, things I took for granted every day in the United States.

"Life is so isolated up here. Think about the hardships people endure daily just to survive," I said into my headset to Dana Hyde.

As the chief executive officer (CEO) of the Millennium Challenge Corporation (MCC), a US government foreign aid agency focused on reducing poverty through economic growth, Dana was on her first trip to Nepal to consider a transformative development investment in the country.[236] She asked me to join her delegation given my role in regional South Asian economic and energy issues at the State Department.

"I can't even imagine," Dana responded as the helicopter dipped suddenly to the right, descending alongside the spectacular Bhote Koshi River with its deep gorges roaring down from Tibet.

"Bhote Koshi" aptly translates into the "River from Tibet," with the border crossing into Nepal marked by the Friendship

---

236 Prithvi Man Shrestha, "Nepal, US Expected to Sign Pact Within a Year," *The Kathmandu Post*, February 13, 2015.

Bridge (yes, another Friendship Bridge). The mighty Bhote Koshi joins the Narayani River and the Karnali River as the major river systems providing the economic backbone for Nepal's agrarian economy, eventually meeting up with the Ganges River, which connects Nepal to India in many ways beyond physical geography. Together, these rivers overflow their banks during the summer monsoon season, irrigating the countryside while splitting the country into distinct regional parts, largely isolated from one another.[237]

After safely landing on a site by the river about seventy miles northeast of Kathmandu, we piled into cars waiting by the helicopter landing site to drive the rest of the way to the Bhote Koshi hydropower plant. Upon arrival, we gladly stretched our stiff legs in the wide-open expanse, grateful for the respite from cramped spaces as our lungs inhaled the fresh mountain air. We then donned hard hats, posing for quick selfies we would tweet out later as we prepared to tour the plant and appreciate the technology that harnessed the river's mighty power into electricity.

"What you are going to see here represents the future of Nepal," Himesh Dhungel, MCC's Energy Lead, explained to our multi-agency delegation, which included USAID Nepal's Mission Director Beth Dunford in addition to Dana and me.

As Nepal's first independent power producer, built with US and Nepalese investment and still partly owned by a US company, the Bhote Koshi forty megawatt (MW) run-of-the-river

---

237 Michael Buckley, *Meltdown in Tibet: China's Reckless Destruction of Ecosystems from the Highlands of Tibet to the Deltas of Asia* (New York: St. Martin's Press, 2014), 88, 206-210.

power plant produced enough electricity annually for about a tenth of Nepal's citizens.[238] The plant experienced its fair share of natural disasters, including severe flooding in 2014 and a series of devastating earthquakes and aftershocks in 2015, but was still standing on its feet during our visit. (Note: As of 2021, the Bhote Koshi power plant was not operating due to the devastation caused by the Glacial Lake Outburst Flood in 2016, requiring substantial rebuilding of the plant).[239]

"I don't get it," I responded as I stood on a platform overlooking the river. "I mean, look around us. We are standing at the foothills of the mighty Himalayas, and it's great this plant is doing well. But you're telling me Bhote Koshi represents only 5 percent or so of the country's total installed hydropower capacity of 758 MW.[240] That total amount for the country is nothing; it could be one small dam alone in India. What am I missing?"

"You're thinking too small, Fatema. Consider what Bhote Koshi's success is telling us," Himesh counseled. "This plant is proof private-sector-led hydropower development is possible in Nepal. If Nepal can sustainably develop its hydropower potential, it could fuel the entire Nepali economy and ensure all Nepalis have energy access. In the long term, any surplus energy could be sold to whoever wants to buy it in the region, countries like India or even Bangladesh."

238 Fatema Z. Sumar, "Helping Nepal Develop New Sources of Energy," *US State Department DipNote* (blog), March 27, 2015.

239 Himesh Dhungel, email message to author, May 1, 2021.

240 Sumar, "Helping Nepal Develop New Sources of Energy," 2015.

"How big are we talking, Himesh?"

"Twenty Hoover Dams...Twenty Hoover Dams!" he replied passionately. "We are talking about the potential to transform Nepal into the engine of clean energy for all of South Asia. This could be the game changer for the entire region!"

GOOD HOUSEKEEPING SEAL OF APPROVAL

Nepal is one of the poorest countries in Asia, with nearly half of the country living on less than three dollars a day.[241] Its GDP per capita hovers among the lowest in South Asia, comparable to Afghanistan.[242] Most Nepalis live in rural areas such as isolated villages high in the mountains, far from any roads or power lines. High transportation costs and an inadequate supply of electricity combined with decades of social and political upheaval contribute to Nepal's stunted economic growth. About a quarter of the population has no access to electricity at all, whether on-grid or off-grid. With few economic opportunities at home, almost half a million people leave the country each year to look for jobs abroad.[243]

With a long history of friendship and strong bilateral ties, the United States wanted to help Nepal make transformative investments to spur economic growth, create jobs, and lift millions out of poverty through one of its development agencies, the Millennium Challenge Corporation (MCC).

241 Fatema Z. Sumar, "Opinion: MCC has engaged in a $500 million compact with Nepal. Here's why," *Devex*, February 15, 2018.
242 "Afghanistan vs Nepal: Economic Indicators Comparison," Georank, accessed May 25, 2021.
243 Sumar, "Helping Nepal Develop New Sources of Energy," 2015.

MCC was created in 2004 by President George W. Bush to deliver smart foreign assistance by focusing on good policies and country ownership. MCC reduces poverty around the world through grant financing. It is one of the few US agencies that build large-scale infrastructure, institutionalizes policy reforms, crowds in the private sector, and tackles a country's binding constraints to economic growth.

MCC is governed by a board of directors, a mix of public and private sector members, including the US Secretary of State, the US Secretary of the Treasury, the US Trade Representative, the USAID Administrator, and the MCC CEO. While part of the overall US foreign policy toolkit, MCC exercises unique independence as a quasi-governmental development agency with a focus on data-driven and evidence-based investments focused on poverty reduction.[244]

Many developing countries aggressively seek to be selected for an MCC investment known as a compact, or MCC's signature grant investment vehicle, to reduce poverty through economic growth. The size of an average compact hovers around $350 million, an incredible amount of grant money not available to lower-income countries in almost any other way.[245] Typically, developing countries would have to take out concessional loans or structure other public financing deals to pay for large-scale infrastructure and development projects. The unique opportunity to finance these types

---

244 Nick M. Brown, "Millennium Challenge Corporation: Overview and Issues," Congressional Research Service, updated October 3, 2019, 1-3.
245 Sarah Rose and Franck Wiebe, "An Overview of the Millennium Challenge Corporation," Center for Global Development, January 27, 2015.

of projects 100 percent through grants makes it especially attractive to countries that are eligible for assistance.

MCC never invested in a compact in South Asia. Nepal would be the first country in the region to pass the scorecard and accept the US offer of bilateral assistance. Getting selected for an MCC compact represented a good housekeeping seal of approval for developing countries like Nepal, especially those seeking to attract large-scale private-sector investment. Only countries that passed a scorecard demonstrating their commitment to good governance, economic freedom, and investing in their citizens could be selected for a compact.

When Nepal was chosen in December 2014 by the MCC Board of Directors, it was a historic moment for the country. The selection affirmed the progress Nepal made in good governance and democratic norms, particularly after a ten-year-long Maoist insurgency.[246] Now we had a unique opportunity in Nepal to develop an MCC compact. We kicked off the process in early 2015 with this trip to Bhote Koshi to see firsthand some of the opportunities and challenges facing the country's economy. As my mind processed all we saw on the helicopter ride to Kathmandu later that day, I could not contain my excitement.

"Dana, we could make a groundbreaking investment here that could transform the entire region," I exclaimed as I paced the courtyard of our historic hotel, The Dwarika's, one of my favorite places to stay in Kathmandu. Amid the backdrop of

---

246 "Readout of MCC CEO's Trip to Nepal," US Millennium Challenge Corporation, February 20, 2015.

the hotel's stunning terracotta designs reviving fifteenth-century artistic traditions of Kathmandu Valley, I felt the power of the past, present, and future intertwine themselves seamlessly.[247] "This is a once-in-a-lifetime opportunity to reduce poverty at scale in one of the poorest parts of the world."

"Absolutely," she replied with her characteristic charm, a smile spreading across her face. "Help us make sure it gets done."

"I would love to," I responded enthusiastically.

I pondered how best to do so. After the past few years working on the Central Asian CASA-1000 regional energy project and working closely with USAID on development in South and Central Asia, I loved the idea of building a major program from the ground up. At this point in my career, I wanted to be part of project development and implementation, not just project oversight or foreign policy. Having worked on development from the diplomatic side, I wanted to apply diplomacy from the development perch.

Timing is everything, and it just so happened MCC needed a Deputy Vice President to manage its non-Africa portfolio. It was a dream job. My main hesitation concerned the pace of travel and work meetings, which already felt intense at the State Department. Balancing three young girls with these jobs was already overwhelming. A typical day crammed in ten to twelve hours of work meetings, phone calls, and diplomatic receptions. On top of that, I added in early morning

---

247 Anil Blon, "Dwarika's Hotel Kathmandu," Hotels in Nepal, Responsible Nepal Tours, May 14, 2020.

routines to get the kids ready for school and daycare, cooking and preparing three meals a day, and undertaking a massive clean-up at night after the kids went to sleep. The term "work-life balance" was not in my vocabulary.

"Well, MCC can't be worse than the pace at the State Department," I said to my husband Nageeb when I returned to Washington and debriefed him on the trip and the possibility of once again switching jobs.

"We're not going for worse or the same," he reminded me. "We're going for better, much better."

"Hopefully, I can manage the travel. I'll make tough choices and say no more. How can this job be harder than the State Department?"

Despite serious qualms on work-life balance issues, after a lot of deliberation, I ended up taking the job at MCC in the spring of 2015. It was hard to turn down this type of leadership opportunity to manage billions of dollars of US development aid and work in so many countries ranging from Nepal to the Philippines to Moldova to El Salvador. I had not anticipated I would end up traveling two and half times more at MCC than at the State Department as I chased development diplomacy on our compacts around the world.

Complex development projects, particularly those involving infrastructure and policy reforms, need political will for sustainable development investments to move forward. Political buy-in depends on a shared agenda for inclusive economic growth between governments, which requires building trust, ironing out differences, and working through multiple rounds of negotiations. For better or worse, development needs diplomacy to succeed. This investment takes time, energy, and resources in Washington and capitals around the world. With my diverse background in policy and politics, development, and diplomacy, I felt confident I could add value to MCC and help reduce poverty for millions globally, starting here in Nepal.

GEOLOGICAL AND POLITICAL EARTHQUAKES

"I'm concerned about how long this is all taking," US Ambassador to Nepal Alaina Teplitz said to me candidly in her Kathmandu office during my hours-long visit to the country in October 2016. "We have been talking to the Nepalis for years now. We need to show progress."

"I understand, Ambassador," I replied emphatically. "It took some time in the aftermath of the earthquakes and political upheavals, but we have a plan. We are authorizing up to ten million dollars in Nepal to start the feasibility work on select electric transmission lines to inform our selection of the final projects. I know patience is wearing thin on all sides. I need your help with the Nepali government."

Progress on the MCC compact moved at a glacial pace in 2015. In April 2015, Nepal experienced a massive 7.8 magnitude earthquake and strong aftershocks, killing over 9,000 people and destroying much of the country's housing and infrastructure. By one estimate, over half a million homes were destroyed, and reconstruction would cost around seven billion US dollars.[248] I toured devastated villages and schools up close in June 2015 when I participated in an international donor conference in Kathmandu to help Nepal rebuild. Images of mudslides and rubble where housing and shops once stood still haunted me from previous site visits.

The situation became even worse in September 2015. The passage of Nepal's new constitution effectively transitioned the country from a 240-year-old monarchy to a democracy. It created a decentralized federal republic and divided the country into seven provinces with a proportional electoral system to elect federal and state officials.[249] These decisions were controversial, with violent protests occurring in the Terai, the lowland region in southern Nepal bordering northern India, killing an estimated forty-five people.[250]

The ensuing power struggle between the Madhesi and Tharu people of the Terai and the Pahadia people who traditionally held power in Nepal wreaked havoc on the country. Strikes by the Madhesi and police curfews in the Terai significantly restricted trade across the border with India, resulting in severe fuel shortages while sparking other humanitarian crises when oil and other essential supplies from India were halted. Although India denied imposing a blockade on the border, Kathmandu blamed New Delhi for the border blockages. From the Nepali government's perspective, India blocked the border to pressure Nepal to make changes to

248 Bruce Vaughn, "Nepal: Political Developments and US Relations," Congressional Research Service, updated December 4, 2015, 1.
249 "Nepal Adopts Secular Constitution Amid Violent Protests," International Justice Resource Center, September 30, 2015.
250 Vaughn, "Nepal," Congressional Research Service, 2015, 1.

its constitution on terms more favorable to the Madhesi, who traditionally enjoyed closer ties to India.[251] Amid this upheaval, my teams worked painstakingly with their Nepali government counterparts to advance the technical elements of the compact where they could. Domestic and regional politics, however, kept getting in the way.

"Ambassador Teplitz, I just arrived after meetings in New Delhi to look at the options around regional energy trade," I said, trying to mask my exhaustion from the grueling pace of shuttle diplomacy on this October 2016 visit to the region. Between planes, airports, and conference rooms across multiple time zones, I had not slept in a bed for more than a few hours a night in the past week. "Everyone there understands the urgent energy needs here and the potential for Nepal to build a second cross-border transmission line to bring more power to Nepal to address the current short-ages. Here is what the MCC technical teams are thinking big picture to support the power sector," I explained as I sketched out a game plan we devised with our Nepali partners before my trip.

With the ambassador's support of our overall plan, we made the diplomatic rounds in Kathmandu, meeting with govern-ment officials and political party leaders discussing critical next steps. We spoke with Nepali leaders starting with the Prime Minister, Minister of Energy, Minister of Physical Infrastructure and Transport, and other government offi-cials alongside opposition party leaders. We consulted all major political stakeholders in the country since the compact

---

251 Ibid.

ultimately was for the people of Nepal and not a political tool for any government or any one political party. We reviewed some of the bottlenecks holding up progress to date and identified a way forward on key issues such as funding or timelines.[252]

On the energy side, we discussed potentially adding new transmission lines and substations. We underscored the need for any infrastructure investments to be complemented by critical energy sector reforms, potentially considering the creation of a stand-alone national transmission company, an independent system operator, and an independent power sector regulator. Institutional capacity building to improve coordination, efficiency, and social inclusiveness of Nepal's electrification policy would be key to success. Yet, pushing for structural reforms could be difficult because such politically sensitive issues often meant disrupting rent-seeking behaviors and dealing with labor unions.

We also spoke about how, in the short term, Nepal could meet some of its energy needs by expanding cross-border trade with India. Despite strained political tensions between Nepal and India in the aftermath of the 2015 constitution, India remained the largest economic market in South Asia. By building additional cross-border transmission infrastructure, Nepalis could benefit in the near term while laying the groundwork to be able to export any surplus energy to the region in the long run.

---

252 US Embassy Kathmandu, "Millennium Challenge Corporation Discusses Next Steps with Government of Nepal," US Embassy in Nepal, press release, October 7, 2016.

To this end, I spent many hours triangulating diplomacy in the region to explore a strategic partnership acceptable to all sides that would foster regional cooperation. Development diplomacy involved countless meetings, phone calls, email exchanges, and visits between all countries and required strategic patience to navigate the political currents in each country's external relationships.

On the transport side, inadequate road maintenance in hilly, land-locked Nepal made travel and transportation of goods and people challenging and expensive. To address the high cost of transit, we encouraged the government to invest in maintaining road quality across the strategic road network to prevent further deterioration, a significantly cheaper option and better investment than building expensive new roads. We discussed the idea of creating an incentive-matching fund to encourage the expansion of Nepal's road maintenance budget, in addition to the periodic maintenance of up to 305 kilometers of the country's strategic road network.

Making progress on these visits could be challenging. Line ministries did not always agree on our way of doing things or our deadlines. Some lobbied us to choose geographic areas benefiting their political constituents irrespective of whether those investments made economic sense for the country. Other government officials voiced opposition to our recommended reforms. Opposition party leaders, who I always tried to connect with to ensure longer-term support for the compact, wanted to make sure the compact benefited all Nepalis, not just the ruling party. My job included making sense of all the high-level technical and political feedback to help our teams identify tangible next steps in developing the compact. The compact had to work for Nepal on its terms. My teams and I had to navigate the politics of development without letting politics dictate development outcomes.

"I think we have a way forward," I said to Ambassador Teplitz before taking off that night for Washington.

"I think so, too. Let's stay in close touch on the progress we are making on the USG side," she said, referencing the work we were doing within the US government to make sure all US agencies were on the same page.

Working effectively to coordinate strategy, funding, time-lines, and priorities across the US government required strong interagency communication and teamwork. When things worked well, the results could be life-changing for those we served. When communication broke down, it could lead to delays on projects and breakdowns of trust between agencies. We needed to partner strategically across MCC, the State Department, and USAID in both Kathmandu and Washington to have a shared vision, timeline, and bench-marks of progress. Since this compact was MCC's first in South Asia, the three agencies never worked together in these ways before in Nepal. My teams needed to help State Department and USAID Nepal teams understand how the MCC process worked and avoid or fix miscommunications that could break down trust among some colleagues, which naturally happened from time to time.

Having worked in the State Department South Asia shop before coming to MCC, I knew many of the diplomats we needed to work with in the region. I could appreciate their starting point on the compact differed from my MCC colleagues. The State Department focused on US foreign policy and advancing the overall bilateral relationship while USAID wanted to ensure all development priorities fit within a broader US development strategy. MCC's sole concern was to reduce poverty through inclusive and sustainable economic growth. All three agencies wanted to help the Nepali people through their different mandates so the trick was making sure we were all coordinated and aligned on the same timelines, deliverables, and policy positions.

I looked for new ways to bring together our colleagues across US government agencies. As a result, we launched our first tri-agency coordination effort with senior-level and technical expert meetings in both Washington and Kathmandu to ensure strategic coherence and information sharing. This coordination resulted in increased transparency and trust among our teams, bridging the cultural divides that could otherwise separate our agencies.

I also made it a point to start issuing front-channel cables, or official dispatches, after my travels to foreign capitals detailing each of my high-level meetings. While this was standard practice for the State Department, development agencies like MCC did not often consistently utilize this tool. Cables could be accessed throughout the US government by any agency interested in the compact, which increased transparency and accountability. Slowly but surely, our efforts to shore up US interagency support were paying off.

PROGRESS AND SETBACKS

A year later in September 2017, I could not contain my excitement as the elevator whisked me up to the elegant Treaty Rooms on the seventh floor of the State Department. Among some of the most beautiful diplomatic reception rooms in the world, the elliptical Treaty Room with its Corinthian columns incorporating the Great Seal of the United States and carvings of native American leaves and flowers witnessed some of history's biggest moments like the signing of treaties and trade agreements, summit negotiations, and swearing-in ceremonies. On this day, it would mark another milestone, the signing of a $630 million MCC compact—$500 million from the United States and $130 million from Nepal—to reduce poverty in Nepal.[253]

After many rounds of negotiations, due diligence, and persistent development diplomacy from so many team members, the United States and Nepal would sign the single largest development investment in the history of both countries. It took years to put together, spanning multiple political parties and governments in Nepal, against the backdrop of the devastating effects of the 2015 earthquakes. Success also required triangulating development diplomacy in the region.

"It's finally happening; we did it!" I said to my colleague Jonathan Nash, MCC's Acting CEO. Jonathan and I worked closely on the negotiations along with so many others on both country teams. It was truly a whole-of-government effort as the Nepali Finance Minister Gyanendra Bahadur

---

253 "US and Nepal Sign $500 Million Compact," US Millennium Challenge Corporation, press release, September 14, 2017.

Karki, US Deputy Secretary of State John J. Sullivan, and Ambassador Teplitz joined together at the podium to commemorate the event. In his speech[254], Jonathan remarked:

> This compact is a recognition of the progress Nepal made in establishing the rule of law, democratic institutions, and investments in its people. It's an opportunity to help the country build its own capacity to deliver services to its own people to benefit the economy, regional security, and the broader global community.

Just two years prior, we struggled to make tangible progress. By prioritizing development diplomacy and working in new ways within the US government and with regional government partners, we successfully changed the world of possibilities. Now that both countries signed the compact, Nepal could work on the next steps toward the ratification of the compact. Implementation would still take years to move forward following ratification, and the work was far from over. If things went right, the investment could benefit twenty-three million people, about 80 percent of Nepal's population.[255]

The ball was now in Nepal's court to ratify the compact, so it had the force of a legal treaty according to the laws on Nepal. If Nepal could move quickly, both countries could lay the groundwork to start the five-year implementation period involving the major infrastructure works. If not, the

---

254 Adva Saldinger, "MCC Signs $500M Compact with Nepal to Improve Power, Roads," *Devex*, September 15, 2017.
255 "US and Nepal Sign $500 Million Compact," MCC, 2017.

country would be passing up a unique chance to invest in transformative economic growth and significantly reduce poverty for its people, who face up to eighteen hours a day of power shortages.

As of this book's publication in 2021, Nepal has yet to ratify the MCC compact despite the signing over four years prior given ongoing political paralysis, politicization of the compact by rival parties and factions, and regional geopolitics.[256] During this time, politics bulldozed smart development, but hope remains Nepal will move to seize this historic opportunity as soon as possible.

---

256 "Power Politics Delays MCC in Nepal," *Nepali Times*, May 8, 2021.

CHAPTER 11

NAILING THE COMPACT COFFIN
CONFRONTING THE POLITICIZATION OF DEVELOPMENT

- Political economy analysis is critical to sustainable and inclusive economic growth.
- Be a bridge builder to break bureaucratic silos.
- Failure can be sombering.

SECOND CHANCES

I am going to faint. I better catch my breath. I repeatedly reminded myself to breathe as I stepped off the airplane and onto the jet bridge as dawn broke through the clouds at Colombo's Bandaranaike airport in January 2017. It was a long, twenty-four-hour journey, but the real cause of my anxiety had little to do with the transatlantic flights. Instead, memories of my last visit to the island in 2009 kept flashing back, forcing me to relive the trauma I faced as a young Congressional staffer on a fact-finding mission.

Even though I continued to work on Sri Lankan issues safely from Washington, up until now, I successfully managed to avoid returning to the country. I needed to shake off the bad memories and mentally reset for the mission ahead. With only two hours to get to my hotel, shower, and get dressed before arriving at the US Ambassador's residence for breakfast and then a full day of official meetings, I could not indulge a walk down memory lane. It was time to clear the cobwebs and focus on the task at hand.

Many changes occurred in the country since my previous visit in 2009. Perhaps most significantly, the government changed hands through elections in 2015, restoring the country's image as one of Asia's oldest and most resilient democracies. The Rajapaksas no longer ruled the country. In a startling upset in Sri Lanka's January 2015 presidential election, President Mahinda Rajapaksa lost to former Health Minister and general secretary of the Sri Lanka Freedom Party (SLFP) Maithripala Sirisena. The defeat was remarkable given that Mr. Rajapaksa looked certain to win when he called the early election in November 2014.[257]

> Amending the Constitution to eliminate term limits and dismissing a Supreme Court justice who resisted his changes. He did so under favorable circumstances, riding a wave of popularity among majority Sinhalese after crushing a long-running Tamil insurgency in the north in 2009.

---

257 Associated Press, "AP Explains: The Latest in Sri Lanka's Political Crisis," *The Astorian*, updated November 12, 2018.

When longtime loyalist Maithripala Sirisena defected from Mr. Rajapaksa's own party, others followed and focused their campaigns on allegations of corruption, misgovernance, and authoritarianism.[258]

Upon taking office in 2015, President Sirisena promised an era of clean government and formed a national unity government with Prime Minister Ranil Wickremesinghe's United National Party (UNP) to pursue economic and political reforms. Harsha de Silva, UNP's economic affairs spokesman, said the new government would review all significant infrastructure projects, particularly those considered "white elephant" projects, and have a more balanced approach between India and China, unlike the Rajapaksa regime, "which was antagonizing India almost by its closeness to China."[259] This shift away from China also created new opportunities for the United States to support economic growth on the island, hence the purpose of my visit.

Although the US government first selected Sri Lanka for an MCC compact in 2004, civil war politics took over, preventing its development at that time. Only countries that scored well on the MCC scorecard, committing to just and democratic governance, investing in people, and economic freedom, could be considered by the United States for these sizable grant investments to reduce poverty.[260]

---

258 Ellen Barry and Dharisha Bastians, "Sri Lankan President Concedes Defeat After Startling Upset," *The New York Times*, January 8, 2015.

259 Ibid.

260 "Selection Process," US Millennium Challenge Corporation, accessed March 19, 2021.

Under the Rajapaksa regime that followed, Sri Lanka failed to pass the scorecard due to concerns about human rights and democratic freedoms. After the end of the civil war in the post-Rajapaksa period, Sri Lanka made considerable gains in democratic rights, making it eligible once again. MCC invited Sri Lanka to begin developing a new investment in December 2016, kicking off with my visit to the country in January 2017.[261]

Well, here goes nothing, I thought, as the US Embassy vehicle pulled up to my hotel. *It's a new day in Sri Lanka, so let's see what we can do here.*

PROCESS VS. POLITICS

"We need to move quickly given the political situation," US Ambassador Atul Keshap urged me over breakfast at his residence on the first day of my visit to Colombo in January 2017. "If we pick the right projects as soon as possible, we can make a huge difference by creating economic opportunities for impoverished Sri Lankans. But we need to move fast."

Atul and I worked closely together when we were both Deputy Assistant Secretaries for South and Central Asia at the State Department under the leadership of Assistant Secretary Nisha Biswal. Like most foreign policy careers, our paths now crossed again.

---

261 US Millennium Challenge Corporation, "Millennium Challenge Corporation Board of Directors Selects Burkina Faso, Sri Lanka, Tunisia for New Compacts," press release, December 14, 2016.

"I agree; this opportunity can be historic for the country," I replied as I picked up my steaming cup of Ceylon tea, inhaling its fragrance. The famous tea, like Sri Lanka's other big export commodities of sugar cane, coffee, and pepper, was named after the teardrop island's former name, Ceylon. Its meaning was originally derived over a thousand years ago from the Arabic word *saheelan*, or the land of flowing waters.[262]

I held the warm cup in my hands, considering how to best respond to Atul's political timeline points. It was true the coalition government was fragile and needed to show the Sri Lankan people it could quickly deliver economic results. Though they were formally out of power, the Rajapaksa family and their loyal supporters were waiting to return to office, ready to pounce on any failures of the national unity government. Yet, we did not want to politicize our development work and pick political winners or losers in the country. After all, these projects would take a decade to design and implement and go through several political cycles.

"Here's the thing," I explained. "Designing a complex investment to systematically reduce poverty will take time, longer than you may like. It typically takes us a few years to develop projects with our host country partners. The development timing may not align with the politics here." I proceeded to describe the steps involved in putting together an MCC compact, starting with partnering with the country's economists to analyze the binding constraints to growth. From this analysis, we could look at specific sectors, projects, and

---

262 Asiff Hussein, "The Jewels of Sarandib—Sri Lanka as Seen through Arabian Eyes," *Roar Media*, November 13, 2017.

policy reforms that would unlock economic growth and create conditions to reduce systemic poverty.

"I respect the process, but I also know this country. Let's make sure we move with the urgency the politics here require," Atul responded as we prepared to meet with the prime minister and his team to discuss compact development.[263]

Throughout my visit and subsequent meetings with the Sri Lankan government, civil society, and the private sector, people were initially excited about the MCC compact and the impact it could have in reducing poverty. Our interlocutors wanted to seize the moment and think creatively about how to jumpstart the economy, create jobs, and position Sri Lanka to be more globally competitive. There were many positive signs in the economy: new investments in infrastructure, the highest literacy rate in all of Asia at 92 percent, and progress on digitization.

Still, challenges remained, particularly a widening gender gap, a far cry from the heights of the 1960s when Sri Lanka elected the world's first democratically chosen female prime minister. Sri Lanka also faced a rapidly urbanizing population and post-conflict reconstruction and reconciliation.[264] Significant inequalities in income, opportunity, and living standards persisted, particularly along geographical and gender-based lines with concentrations of poverty in the

---

263 "US Millennium Challenge Corporation Partners with Sri Lanka to Promote Economic Opportunity," *The Daily FT*, January 31, 2017.

264 Anna Bruce-Lockhart, "5 Things to Know About Sri Lanka's Economy," World Economic Forum, August 17, 2015.

northern and eastern parts of the island and among those engaged in low-productivity estate farming.

We can do big things here. I returned to Washington somber about the challenges, but excited about the possibilities of the compact. This moment could result in transformative economic growth and yield an important breakthrough in post-war Sri Lanka. *What could go wrong?*

A KISS IN ACTION

At around half a billion dollars, an MCC compact in Sri Lanka would be the largest single development grant contribution from the United States in the island nation's history. To put this amount in context, the United States delivered more than two billion dollars total in development assistance to Sri Lanka since its independence in 1948. The funds included significant aid for recovery and reconstruction efforts following the devastating tsunami in 2004.[265] Smartly investing this much MCC money involved many steps over multiple years, starting with an economic analysis of the binding constraints to Sri Lanka's economic growth. In other words, what was preventing the Sri Lankan economy from taking off and crowding in private sector growth for the poor?

Our joint American and Sri Lankan teams worked closely throughout 2017 to identify the major bottlenecks: (1) inadequate transport infrastructure and planning and (2) the lack of access to land for productive investment. We consulted government ministries and agencies responsible for transport

---

265 "Policy & History," US Embassy in Sri Lanka, accessed June 5, 2021.

and land administration to identify and refine activities addressing these root causes. We tried hard to balance the need to invest in transport infrastructure in urban areas, where there were large concentrations of poor people, with the need to also target underserved, less populated rural areas of the country.

Our teams only short-listed projects that met our agreed-upon investment criteria, especially projects that generated an economic rate of return of at least 10 percent for the populations served. We relied on data and evidence in making recommendations to reduce poverty for as many people as possible regardless of where they lived or their political leanings. This economic discipline helped reduce the potential politicization of project selection.

Fighting poverty, however, does not happen in an economic bubble. Chilean economist and politician Alejandro Foxley once said, "Economists must not only know their economic models but also understand politics, interests, conflicts, passions, [and] the essence of collective life. For a brief period of time, you could make changes by decree; but to let them persist, you have to build coalitions and bring people around. You have to be a politician."[266]

In other words, understanding political economy—the interdisciplinary branch of the social sciences that focuses on intersecting relationships between people, governments, and public policy—is critical in fighting poverty. In a country as

---

266 John Williamson ed., "What is Political Economy?" in *The Political Economy of Policy Reform* (Washington: Peterson Institute for International Economics, 1994), 3.

politically volatile as Sri Lanka, sustainable and inclusive economic growth depends on political and popular support. No one development agency can act alone. We needed to partner with both the Sri Lankan and American governments, other donors, the private sector, and civil society to ensure meaningful buy-in and support for our work. On the US government side, this meant working beyond development agencies like USAID and partnering actively with the State Department and US Embassy Colombo to appreciate and navigate the complex political environment. We needed to practice development diplomacy.

Each US agency brought its lens to the table in analyzing the proposed MCC investments. The State Department, for instance, wanted to make sure MCC activities would be visible to the Sri Lankan people and move as quickly as possible through all the necessary steps. USAID analyzed potential project selection to make sure the projects resonated within a broader foreign aid strategy. US Embassy Colombo looked to avoid projects that could be politically irrelevant even if they were economically sound. Coordination across our interagency teams was vital but went through ups and downs.

"Let's remember the KISS principle here," Ambassador Keshap remarked in one meeting with MCC teams in Washington in 2017, referring to the acronym for "Keep it simple, stupid."

The KISS design principle was associated with aircraft engineer Kelly Johnson and noted by the US Navy in 1960. It emphasized the importance of simplicity and not making things overcomplicated.[267] In Sri Lanka's case, "kissing" meant making the projects easy to understand and sell to political stakeholders and the general population.

Given my previous work at the State Department and in Congress on South Asia issues, I could see why each agency viewed the compact differently. There were legitimate considerations to consider in putting together an economically sound, politically viable half-a-billion-dollar investment that could survive the fragile post-conflict environment in Colombo. We needed to find ways to hear alternative points of view and coordinate in common cause. As a result, we actively reached out to the State Department, USAID, and US Embassy Colombo to find new ways of working together to advance our shared mission. This outreach included multiple visits to Colombo to work through steps of project analysis and selection.

I saw my role as being a bridge between MCC, which focuses on economic growth largely agnostic of politics, and the State Department, where diplomats viewed development through the lens of advancing foreign policy and political stability. We needed to talk to each other in the same language without second-guessing each other's expertise or ending up in zero-sum negotiations.

The active dialogue paid off. Within a year, we made significant progress. The American and Sri Lankan teams worked not just within their technical silos but across agencies and disciplines to design transformative investments for the

---

267 Ben R. Rich, *Clarence Leonard (Kelly) Johnson 1910–1990: A Biographical Memoir* (Washington, DC: National Academies Press, 1995), 13.

people of Sri Lanka. Patience sometimes frayed, and the work could be frustrating, uncomfortable, and taxing. Nonetheless, by keeping the focus on the north star of reducing poverty in Sri Lanka, we pursued win-win negotiations and demonstrated the value and power of development diplomacy.

CONSPIRACY THEORIES TAKEOVER

In February 2018, I resigned from MCC.[268] Leaving the US government doing work I loved was a hard choice, but morally, I did not share the values of the Trump administration and did not want to represent President Trump around the world. Even though I was no longer at MCC, I felt incredibly proud of the staff in both countries who worked tirelessly to put together the Sri Lanka compact. In April 2019, the MCC Board of Directors approved the compact, committing $480 million of grant assistance to Sri Lanka with the potential to benefit eleven million Sri Lankans, marking a historic breakthrough for both countries.[269]

Despite this incredible progress, the compact fell apart amid dramatic political, social, and economic developments, which permanently ruptured the 2015 national unity government. Two separate events in 2018 created shockwaves in the country. In April 2018, the relative peace the island enjoyed since the end of the civil war in 2009 evaporated when terrorists attacked and killed at least 253 people at churches and hotels

---

268 Fatema Z. Sumar, "Congress Should Decrease Politicization at the Millennium Challenge Corporation," *The Hill*, September 8, 2018.

269 "Millennium Challenge Corporation Approves $480 Million Grant to Sri Lanka to Expand Economic Opportunities and Reduce Poverty," *Colombo Page*, April 26, 2019.

across the country on Easter Sunday.[270] The attacks openly laid bare the political hostility between President Sirisena and Prime Minister Wickremasinghe and "led to deepening mistrust of a government already unpopular for constant policy instability and low economic growth."[271] In October 2018, Sri Lanka plummeted into a constitutional crisis when the president ousted the prime minister in a surprise move, replacing Ranil Wickremesinghe with Mahinda Rajapaksa.[272] The Rajapaksas returned to power in national elections in November 2019, with their supporters openly campaigning against the MCC compact. Rajapaksa supporters, who were known to be pro-Chinese and anti-American, denounced the MCC compact, claiming the loss of national economic sovereignty.[273]

Incoming President Gotabaya Rajapaksa, the former defense secretary I interacted with in 2009, prevaricated on his commitment to MCC by appointing a committee to review the compact and analyze its potential costs and benefits, thereby delaying his endorsement. Media disinformation campaigns voiced conspiracy theories that the compact represented an American proxy war against China being played out in Sri Lanka.

Despite efforts to counter this misinformation, the compact became politicized and held hostage to nationalist politics

270 "Sri Lanka Attacks: What We Know about the Easter Bombings," *BBC News*, April 28, 2019.

271 Kithmina Hewage, "Year in Review: Sri Lanka's Road to Recovery in 2019," Stimson Center South Asian Voices, January 3, 2020.

272 Michael Igoe, "In Sri Lanka, with 'Great Power Competition' comes Great Headaches for MCC," *Devex*, August 5, 2020.

273 Igoe, "Great Power Competition," *Devex*, 2020.

fueled by information warfare.[274] Against this backdrop, the conditions did not exist for MCC to successfully implement a transformative investment to reduce poverty in Sri Lanka. Development diplomacy on the compact between the two sides broke down, perhaps irreparably.

In December 2020, the MCC Board voted to discontinue its partnership with Sri Lanka, the last nail in the coffin.[275] It was a tragic ending to a significant attempt to fight poverty and a warning shot to other countries about how greatly politics and local leadership matter to development outcomes. The MCC compact was never designed to work without country ownership. Without strong political champions to defend the aid and appreciate the opportunity to reduce poverty through the compact, the US government would not invest the funds. Unfortunately, in this particularly extreme case, we could not thread the political needle for transformative development. Development diplomacy could only take us so far. It was a somber experience and example of how intertwined foreign policy, international development, and domestic politics can be.

274 Ibid.
275 US Embassy Colombo, "Statement on Decision of Millennium Challenge Corporation Board," US Embassy in Sri Lanka, December 17, 2020.

CHAPTER 12

NOT JUST A PIPE DREAM
`INVESTING AT LOCAL AND NATIONAL LEVELS

- Invest in women and girls as the ultimate change agents for fighting poverty.
- Even small-scale investments can have profound impacts on changing lives.
- Country ownership is critical for sustainable development to take hold.
- Plant seeds for others to water.

THE SLOW DRIP OF WATER POVERTY

"I just have one dream," Ra'eda proudly exclaimed during my visit to Jordan in October 2015. "Acquiring my own plumbing shop and hiring some women to join my team."[276]

In Jordan, Ra'eda Abu Hallawab defied expectations of what women could do in her culturally conservative city of

---

276 Claudia Pirela, "Women Plumbers Aid Jordan's Water Conservation Effort," US Millennium Challenge Corporation, February 22, 2017.

Zarqa, fifteen miles northeast of the capital Amman. With her *hijab* beautifully wrapped around her face and neck to cover her hair, she sat among a dozen or so other female plumbers.

"Ra'eda, I love your uniform," I said as she proudly showed off her blue vest emblazoned with my organization's logo along with a tool belt swung around her hips.

"See my wrench?" she asked me in Arabic. "Do you know how to use one?"

"Not really, no," I replied honestly. "If I ever need help to fix my house, I am going to call you."

"Anytime, you are welcome," she replied with innate confidence and a sense of purpose that belied the challenges facing many women like her.

Something about Ra'eda's confidence was infectious. I believed in her. It was hard not to be swept away by her passion and determination. Even though our lives were very different, her spunk and perseverance reminded me of so many strong women, including my mother, who fought every day to provide for their families. On this trip, I came to appreciate the challenges many Jordanian women faced and how their stories mirrored women all around the world. For female plumbers in Jordan, their hopes and aspirations represented more than just pipe dreams.

In this dusty part of the globe, good plumbing is lifesaving. Dripping faucets, rusted water tanks, and leaky pipes can be the difference between having safe water or going without. With Jordan being the second most water-poor country in the world, water scarcity threatens human survival here.[277] Every last drop of water counts. Jordanian plumbers are mostly men, but in this conservative country, they face challenges working in their customers' homes during the daytime if no male household members are around. In Jordan, like in many parts of the Middle East, members of the opposite sex do not meet each other outside of their families. Women, therefore, could fill a unique market role and serve a broader customer base than their male colleagues. As Ra'eda pointed out, women know "best how water is being used in the home and how to conserve it."[278]

I knew from years of development work that partnering with women represented one of the most effective and efficient ways to reduce poverty and boost economic growth. Women and girls spend 90 percent of their earned income on their families, while men spend only 30 to 40 percent. Creating economic opportunities for women improves not just their lives but the lives of their families for generations to come.[279] Since gender inequality is one of the oldest and most pervasive forms of inequality in the world, investing in women and girls, therefore, is transformative.[280]

277 Hana Namrouqa, "Jordan World's Second Water-poorest Country," *The Jordan Times*, October 22, 2104.
278 Pirela, "Women Plumbers Aid Jordan," 2017.
279 "Empowering Women & Girls," Clinton Global Initiative, accessed June 5, 2021.
280 "Why the Majority of the World's Poor are Women," Oxfam International, accessed March 8, 2021.

Discrimination against women's workplace rights is a universal issue, with 104 countries restricting women's access to employment. Eighteen countries still require women to receive their husband's permission to work outside the home.[281] As a result, women's voices and work are not economically or politically valued, from the household to the national and global levels. This imbalance costs women in developing countries nine trillion dollars a year in lost income. It also costs countries trillions of dollars in economic growth and the global economy around 15 percent of GDP.[282]

Despite considerable progress throughout the globe in recent decades, women fail to achieve economic equality with men in any country. COVID-19 set back progress by another generation. The UN estimates the pandemic will push an additional ninety-six million people into extreme poverty, forty-seven million of whom are women and girls. This surge of poverty will widen the gender poverty gap so that more women will experience extreme poverty than men, particularly those between twenty-five and thirty-four years old and at the height of their productive and family formation period.[283]

"For the last twenty-two years, extreme poverty globally had been declining. Then came COVID-19, and with it, massive job losses, shrinking of economies and loss of livelihoods, particularly for women. Weakened social protection systems

281 "Women's Workplace Equality Index," Council on Foreign Relations, accessed June 5, 2021.
282 "Facts and Figures: Economic Empowerment," UN Women, updated July 2018.
283 "COVID-19 and its Economic Toll on Women: The Story Behind the Numbers," UN Women, September 16, 2020.

have left many of the poorest in society unprotected, with no safeguards to weather the storm," said Ginette Azcona, lead author of UN Women's report *From Insights to Action* and UN Women's Senior Research and Data Specialist.[284]

Women particularly face the brunt of economic inequality in developing countries since poverty is not gender neutral. Unexplained gender differences—things non-rationalizable due to differences in age, education, life events, having children, working for pay, or other household characteristics—affect young women and girls up to age thirty disproportionately. These differences, called the poverty penalty, account for about five million more women living in extreme poverty across the world, particularly in South Asia and Sub-Saharan Africa.[285]

In Jordan, about one-third of the population experience poverty during at least one quarter of the year, according to the World Bank, due to transient and seasonal poverty. The poor tend to live in large households with low education levels and multiple young dependents. Compounding the problem, a large influx of Syrian refugees, whose poverty profile reflects those of Jordan's poor, exacerbate living conditions in Jordan. The swelling population strains infrastructure in the water, sanitation, electricity, solid waste management, health, and education sectors.

---

284 Ginette Azcona et al., "From Insights to Action: Gender Equality in the Wake of COVID-19," UN Women, 2020.

285 Carolina Sánchez-Páramo and Ana Maria Munoz-Boudet, "No, 70% of the World's Poor aren't Women, but that Doesn't Mean Poverty Isn't Sexist," *Let's Talk Development, World Bank Blogs,* March 8, 2018.

By 2016, Jordan hosted more than 650,000 registered Syrian refugees, 80 percent of whom lived in host communities in cities such as Zarqa. The refugee population represented about 10 percent of Jordan's overall population and created scarcity and competition over jobs and downward pressure on wages, leading to negative impacts on social cohesion. Demand for water alone increased by 40 percent during the compact period.[286]

Creating new economic opportunities, therefore, was critical in places like Jordan, particularly for women like Ra'eda. MCC decided to train thirty Jordanian women to be the first female plumbers in Jordan. While this investment represented just a small part of an outreach effort on water conservation and infrastructure repairs across poor households, it changed their lives.

POWER OF PARTNERSHIPS

By the time I started working on MCC's Jordan compact, we were more than halfway through the implementation of the five-year, $275 million investment focused on transforming Jordan's access to clean water and sanitation.[287] Most of the hard work had been done. Projects were designed and approved, contracts moved forward, and our economic partnership with the Jordanians remained strong. My role focused on successfully finishing the compact, sharing learnings from

---

286 World Bank Group, *Country Partnership Framework for Hashemite Kingdom of Jordan for the Period FY17-FY22*, World Bank Group, Report No. 102746-JO, 2016, 4, 8.

287 "Closed Compact Report: Jordan Compact," US Millennium Challenge Corporation, September 2018.

Jordan for our work around the world, and negotiating any potential next steps with the Jordanian government. This position provided a unique perch not to problem solve complex crises but to take a more bird's eye view and appreciate how development diplomacy worked from a big picture lens on one of the most complex urban investments MCC ever made.

Designed to benefit over three million people or about one-third of the country's population, the compact concentrated on increasing the supply of water to households and businesses through improvements in the efficiency of water delivery, the extension of wastewater collection, and the expansion of wastewater treatment. The compact constructed 1,160 kilometers of new water and wastewater pipelines, bringing water to citizens and businesses in the Zarqa Governorate east of the capital Amman, and reducing water loss from leaky pipes. These investments were coordinated with USAID and responded to Jordan's request for more long-term support to the country's water and wastewater infrastructure.[288]

One of the compact's signature projects successfully expanded the As-Samra Wastewater Treatment Plant, which USAID originally supported in 2008 to replace the highly polluting waste stabilization pond system outside Amman. As the primary facility for treatment in the Amman and Zarqa Governorates, where much of the country lives, As-Samra desperately required expansion to meet the population's growing demands. Otherwise, according to MCC, "the plant would be overloaded, its ability to treat wastewater would deteriorate, and downstream agricultural areas that rely on

288 Ibid.

treated water for irrigation would face serious food safety risks and the loss of markets for agricultural products."[289]

Under a project finance public-private partnership (PPP) supported by MCC, the plant underwent an expansion and technological upgrades. PPPs involve a collaboration between governments and the private sector to finance, build, and operate public infrastructure such as roads, hospitals, water, and wastewater facilities. Years of development diplomacy between the US and Jordanian governments and negotiations with the private sector laid the groundwork for a successful PPP to expand As-Samra. MCC teams worked closely with Jordanian government agencies such as the Ministry of Water and Irrigation and the Ministry of Planning and International Cooperation to negotiate the terms of the investment and ensure project completion on time and within budget. The US Embassy coordinated closely with the Ministry of Foreign Affairs and other government counterparts. The Millennium Challenge Account Jordan team, a Jordanian government entity set up to run the compact, drove local country ownership of the compact and resolved issues across all parties and both governments.

There were setbacks and challenges, especially in working out the details for the PPP deal on As-Samra to ensure acceptability on all sides. Participating in a PPP slowed the compact development process due to the complexity of the negotiations. To ensure a full commitment of the As-Samra expansion, MCC required that all parties to the agreement complete their negotiations and reach financial close before implementation.[290]

---

289 Ibid.
290 Ibid.

Negotiations and commitment from the Jordanian government to sign the PPP, however, took longer to conclude than anticipated. The delays extended the development process by months, costing money and political angst. MCC took a calculated risk in implementing the five-year program anyway, using development diplomacy to put pressure on parties to sign the deal in time to build As-Samra within the compact timelines.[291]

The bet paid off. The compact expanded a world-class wastewater treatment facility guaranteed to sustainably operate for twenty-five years, as I explained to the US House of Representatives when I testified during a hearing in 2016.[292] The PPP allowed MCC's investment of $93 million dollars to mobilize an additional $110 million from the private sector. MCC's role in providing what is referred to as "viability gap funding" contributed to As-Samra's success as MCC's first large-scale PPP.

The As-Samra plant now treats 70 percent of Jordan's wastewater and frees up 133 million cubic meters of high-quality treated water per year—equivalent to over 10 percent of Jordan's entire annual water resources—for irrigation in the Jordan Valley.[293] According to the Suez Group, "What was once heavily polluted water just a few years ago has now become one of the cleanest rivers in Jordan!"[294]

291 Alex Russin, email to the author, May 10, 2021.
292 Fatema Z. Sumar, "Testimony for House Foreign Affairs Committee Hearing 'Jordan: A Key US Partner,'" US Millennium Challenge Corporation, 2016.
293 Ibid.
294 "Nearly Energy Self-Sufficient Treatment and Recycling of Wastewater in the Region of Amman, Jordan," Suez Group, accessed June 6, 2021.

As a byproduct, the plant also provides bio-solids for potential reuse in fertilizer and fuel, producing nearly thirteen megawatts of energy, or 80 percent of its own energy needs, from biogas and hydropower. The contributions to reducing greenhouse gasses are significant, with 300,000 tons of carbon dioxide saved per year and 230,000 kilowatts per hour of green energy produced per day. The benefits for Jordanians are tangible, especially controlled recycling water for irrigation in the Jordan Valley, jobs for Jordanians, transfer of skills and know-how, and tariff affordability.[295]

Development diplomacy resulted in one of the most complex project-financing deals that is now transforming Jordan's economy. The As-Samra plant won international awards like the "Water and Energy Exchange International Award for Innovative Financing" and the "Best Water Project Award" by World Finance Magazine.[296] The compact also created the space for smaller, non-capital investments to take root, like training the first crop of female plumbers.

FROM 0 TO 100S

On my last trip to Jordan in February 2017, I represented the United States in celebrating the completion of the compact.[297] I flew to Amman, excited but also a bit nervous, about standing up and speaking in front of hundreds of our partners and official dignitaries gathered in a downtown hotel ballroom. During my remarks in front of the Minister of Water

---

295 Ibid.
296 "Closed Compact Report," US Millennium Challenge Corporation, 2018.
297 "Fakhoury Urges MCC to Continue Support for Jordan after 'Successful' Projects," *The Jordan Times*, February 23, 2017.

and Irrigation, Dr. Hazim El-Nasser, and US Ambassador to Jordan, Alice Wells, I stressed the real reason our work in Jordan succeeded: country ownership. Although the United States worked behind the scenes to support negotiations and key milestones, the Jordanians determined the problems we should address and provided answers on how to structure the projects to make them work in their cultural context. Country ownership contributed to the long-term sustainability of the investment, both on large-scale capital infrastructure projects and on smaller projects like investing in the livelihood of its citizens.

After the speeches, I ran into Ra'eda and some of her fellow plumbers, who took time off work to join the festivities. Now, they were trailblazers in their communities. As we gave each other a giant group hug, one of them leaned in to say, "We may be the first, but we will not be the last. The compact did not just build pipes and treatment plants; it built a new community of women. This is what we created together."

She was so right.

When I resigned from the US government and joined the anti-poverty humanitarian organization Oxfam in 2018, I assumed I left Ra'eda and the Jordan compact behind. After all, that was a one-time US government investment. I did not realize her story became so inspirational that vibrant women's networks, NGOs like Oxfam, and other governments, including Canada and Germany, wanted to continue investing in female plumbers in Jordan, picking up where

MCC left off.[298,299] MCC's original investment in the first thirty female plumbers paved the way for hundreds more to be trained in Amman, Irbid, and beyond. This success gave me a tremendous sense of confidence that MCC's work could be scaled up and replicated by other organizations.

Today, Ra'eda is joined by hundreds of other Jordanian female plumbers who received support and training. They are redefining what is possible in terms of women's equality in Jordan. One of these plumbers is Fatima Mousa Moham-med Dabouh. Married off at fourteen, Fatima is now in her mid-forties, divorced, and financially independent for the first time in her life, thanks to the income she brings in as a plumber. She stood up to her family and her community to be accepted in this profession, a risky undertaking requiring changing conservative cultural norms. Even the community partner organization originally hesitated to train her because she wore a *niqab* (a veil worn by some Muslim women cov-ering the entire face outside of their eyes).[300]

Fatima recounted the story of how she tried to work on her father's new house.

"I asked him if I could do the plumbing. He refused and hired a male plumber, but he did everything wrong and messed it all up. Secretly, I went and fixed everything and then I told my father what I had done. Now, they all believe me." Fatima

---

298 "More than a Pipe Dream," Oxfam, December 11, 2019.
299 "Water Sector in Jordan: More Women being Trained as Skilled Workers," GIZ, accessed June 5, 2021.
300 "Pipe Dream," Oxfam, December 11, 2019.

has since gone on to build two businesses from scratch and is planning more.[301]

Fatima and Ra'eda's stories have stayed close to my heart because they show the power of what is possible when sustainable and inclusive development takes place. I observed in Jordan the tipping point of change that resulted from critical investments made in local communities in Zarqa, not only in the pipes and plants but also in the women who lived there. Local ownership led to projects that could be sustained at world-class levels like the As-Samra treatment plant and scaled up after the initial investment closed, as in the case of the female plumbers.

Working across government agencies, private sector partners, and civil society organizations required intense diplomatic discussions on compact design and implementation. Patience could be tested at times, especially when deadlines came and went in negotiating the PPP. Ultimately, development diplomacy prevailed, leading to transformative results in reducing poverty in Jordan in the water sector.

Development diplomacy does not guarantee success in reducing poverty, but the experiences shared here in Part III underscore the critical role development diplomacy plays for transformative investments to have a chance. By working across foreign policy and international development, reaching within and across bureaucracies to bring all parties to the table, development diplomacy laid the groundwork for pro-poor investments in many cases. Whether it was bringing

---

301 Ibid.

four countries who historically did not trust each other to work together for the first time in Central and South Asia or providing clean water in Jordan, success required building diplomatic bridges to find new ways to come together to solve development challenges. The job involved hundreds of people on multiple teams over many years to take an idea and make it a reality. It took passion, dedication, and optimism to see it through. The work of development to make people's lives better, reduce poverty, increase opportunity, and afford all people common dignity embodied the very spirit of public service. It made me proud to be a public servant.

PART IV

INVESTING IN THE NEXT GENERATION OF DEVELOPMENT DIPLOMATS: 21 RECOMMENDATIONS

If we are lucky enough to be in a position of power, if our voice and our actions can mobilize change, don't we have a special obligation? Being an ally can't just be about nodding when someone says something we agree with— important as that is. It must also be about action. It's our job to stand up for those who are not at the table where life-altering decisions are made. Not just those people who look like us. Not just those who need what we need. Not just those who have gained an audience with us. Our duty is to improve the human condition—in every way we can, for everyone who needs it.

—*Kamala Harris*[302]

---

302 Kamala Harris, *The Truths We Hold* (New York: Penguin Publishing Group, 2019), 267-268.

CHAPTER 13

RIDING A NEW HORSE
BREAKING DOWN MONEY, BUREAUCRACY, AND POLITICS

SURVIVAL OF THE FITTEST

We lost the GPS connection and wireless service the minute we left the paved roads of southern Mongolia and drove straight into the desert. For hours now, my MCC colleagues and I kept pushing through the sand under the bluest, cloudless skies with no distinguishing landmarks to make sense of our location somewhere in the Gobi Desert. In May 2015, this was my first trip to Mongolia. I looked at my driver with trepidation and confusion. Gobi is translated "waterless place" in the Mongolian language, and the desert spanned over 1,000 miles across China and Mongolia; it was not somewhere I wanted to get lost.

"How do you know where you are going?" I asked him, my voice bobbing up and down as we hit the sand dunes, which only covered about 5 percent of the entire desert.

"No worries, ma'am. We just follow the sun," he replied confidently. "This is how we traveled for hundreds of years. I promise you will arrive where you want to go."

"Tell me honestly. Do you know where you are going? I usually travel by road."

"Ma'am, do not worry. Here we do things differently. Just look at our horses. They are why we conquered the world," he exclaimed, turning up the volume on the CD player and effectively ending my inquisition.

I leaned into my seat, my mind wandering as I blindly trusted I would reach Ömnögovi Province in southern Mongolia. After all, the nomadic peoples of Mongolia displayed an uncanny sense of direction without technology or modern tools. Before cars, they relied on their legendary horses, which were physically small, almost pony-like, but extraordinarily strong animals. Over thousands of years of ruthless natural selection, these horses adapted to survive in the harsh climate of the steppes. They contributed in no small part to Genghis Khan's successful global conquest and the rise of the Mongol Empire.[303]

If the Mongols conquered the world by riding a unique animal, could we change the world today by breeding a different horse? Are we stuck in our ways of working by always riding the same horse?

---

303 Morris Rossabi, "All the Khan's Horses," *Natural History*, October 1994.

"HARD" SKILLS FOR DEVELOPMENT DIPLOMATS

The world is changing at a rapid clip. Whether confronting global pandemics like COVID-19, climate change, or extreme inequality, we are struggling to keep up and adapt. It is time to take a hard look at how we can work to urgently meet these existential challenges. We cannot keep doing business as usual. We must pursue change at scale if we are to meet these challenges and our commitment to achieve the Sustainable Development Goals (SDGs) to end poverty by 2030. The clock is ticking, and like Mongolian horses, we need to adapt to survive.

After working in dozens of countries from 2006 to 2018 for the US government, my overarching recommendation is we intentionally invest in "development diplomacy." Done smartly, development diplomacy successfully navigates political waters to create conditions for sustainable and inclusive economic opportunities to take root. These diplomats manage the critical role of political actors within the development agenda and gauge how their cooperation or antagonism can contribute directly to the success or failure of large-scale development initiatives. Development diplomacy bridges foreign policy and international development, navigating foreign policy and political challenges to explicitly achieve development goals. Development diplomacy does not aim to politicize foreign aid, but rather, ensure the political and policy ecosystems exist for development investments to succeed in the long term.

Development diplomacy is not public diplomacy, although public diplomacy can successfully highlight successful development work. Public diplomacy requires convincing people to support the foreign policy agenda of a certain government by using soft power tools like cultural or educational exchanges or foreign aid projects to showcase the benefits of that government. For instance, the State Department may tout its exchange programs like the Fulbright Program or the Peace Corps as examples of the best and brightest talent America has to offer the world. It may highlight USAID emergency response in humanitarian disasters—like the 2004 Indian Ocean tsunami or the 2021 global COVID-19 pandemic—as ways Americans care about the fate of the world. Public diplomacy may showcase development programs with meaningful outcomes in saving lives. The purpose of public diplomacy, however, is to shore up the image of the host country for political purposes and not for the goal of poverty reduction.

By contrast, development diplomacy is first and foremost about reducing poverty. Development diplomacy leverages the power of diplomacy while managing and minimizing political interference. It is not about public relations or putting a spin on foreign aid. It is not about using development to advance foreign policy goals, although development done right can, of course, achieve shared foreign policy objectives and result in positive political, economic, and social security outcomes. Development diplomacy is about achieving sustainable and inclusive development as an end. It accomplishes this objective through a more sophisticated partnership with nondevelopment actors whose buy-in is critical for a program's success.

An effective development diplomat will strategically know how to work with the foreign policy community to further shared development goals such as meeting the SDGs by 2030, tackling climate change, and helping the world recover from the COVID-19 pandemic. Development diplomats can work together to advance pro-poor policy agendas and support the needs of women, girls, and marginalized communities by partnering in new ways across traditional silos.

This mindset requires savvier ways of working across bureaucratic silos that separate foreign policy and international development. On the foreign policy side, it demands a new appreciation for the power of data and evidence to drive decision-making on development projects. On the development side, it requires greater consideration of the politics and political economies that influence development outcomes. Success means creating more shared knowledge and methods of working between professionals across fields to speak the same language and partnering across numerous institutional perspectives to pursue win-win outcomes.

What can development diplomats do to better fight poverty? How can they do it? This chapter considers the "hard" skills needed for development diplomats focused on money, bureaucracy, politics, and security. The following chapter considers the "soft" skills needed to train development diplomats to succeed. Together, Part IV offers twenty-one recommendations to collectively reimagine the fields of foreign policy and international development, working more intentionally together rather than apart.

MONEY

As the world recovers from the COVID-19 pandemic in 2021 and beyond, its economic impact will surpass that of the 2008 global financial crisis. Poor people around the world, including those living in rich countries, will continue to feel the brunt of the economic pain, setting back our poverty-fighting efforts for years. Developing countries will be unable to afford the recovery and stimulus packages developed economies are enacting as their fiscal space shrinks and the fallout from capital flight takes hold.

Just as President Roosevelt planned for peace in 1941 before entering a war, today's global leaders fighting a war of poverty and inequality must also plan for a new world order that prioritizes equality and opportunity for all. Money alone will not solve the problem. Resources must be spent in line with sound aid effectiveness principles to have the intended impact.

Consider the SDG financing gap could increase 70 percent from pre-COVID levels to $4.2 trillion.[304] As the international development community rallies for governments to increase levels of official development assistance (ODA), expand access to concessional financing and debt relief, and offer emergency public relief packages to developing economies in the wake of COVID-19, development diplomats can help spend scarce resources more effectively.

1. **Development diplomats must realize** *how* **money is spent is just as important as** *how much* **is spent.** The success of our aid should not be measured by how much we spend, but rather the impact the money has on the most vulnerable. This lesson can be seen clearly in the case of Afghanistan. Despite

---

304 Organization for Economic Cooperation and Development, *Global Outlook on Financing for Sustainable Development 2021* (Paris: OECD Publishing, November 9, 2020), report.

the United States investing $35 billion in Afghanistan from 2002 to 2009 for the war, the Afghanistan Living Conditions Survey showed the national poverty rate rising from 38 percent in 2011–2012 to 55 percent in 2016-2017. According to the Brookings Institution Afghanistan Index, the poverty rate increased as the economy and gross domestic product (GDP) per capita stalled and the Taliban insurgency spread. As a result, more than half of the population lived on less than a dollar a day by 2018 despite all the money spent.[305]

Development diplomats should be guided by the Accra Agenda for Action and other aid effectiveness principles that reaffirm the criticality of country ownership when determining their own development strategies.[306] Development diplomats should prioritize inclusive partnerships in which all partners at country and local levels participate fully and not just major donors in western capitals. Civil society actors, particularly women-led organizations, can be critical partners in designing, implementing, and/or overseeing aid programs. Investing in locally owned projects with realistic timelines and funding to support local leadership will best deliver results with measurable impacts in the long term.

2. **Development diplomats should leverage a range of development financing options.** Money to fight poverty is scarce. More creativity is needed to fill the SDG financing gap and leverage resources across governments, the private

305 Sam Gollob and Michael E. O'Hanlon, "Afghanistan Index: Tracking Variables of Reconstruction and Security in Post-9/11 Afghanistan," Brookings Institution, August 2020, 27.

306 "The Accra Agenda for Action," Organization for Economic Cooperation and Development, accessed June 5, 2021.

sector, and civil society. Financing options can include grants, equity, loans, public-private partnerships, blended finance, and other partnership-based collaborations. This approach can be particularly effective for public finance, which provides around 90 percent of infrastructure investments in developing countries and can be cheaper than other complex financial instruments.[307]

I saw the success of these partnerships in looking for ways to address the financing gap of transmission lines in the case of CASA-1000 or building a state-of-the-art wastewater treatment system in Jordan. Pursuing partnerships within or across governments and with external actors can be complicated and time consuming. Development diplomats need to work through the complexities of bureaucracies, legislative mandates, and ways of working across sectors. They would benefit from career experience across multiple organizations to help break down organizational barriers to entry.

3. **Development diplomats should plan for long-term, sustainable, and inclusive growth.** As the world undid 25 years of progress fighting poverty in 25 weeks due to the COVID-19 pandemic, the economic outlook for developing countries as they emerge from the pandemic will be telling. Economists like Homi Kharas predict "COVID-19 will accentuate the long-term concentration of poverty in countries that are middle-income, fragile, and conflict-affected, and located in

---

307 "Financing for Development in the Era of COVID-19 and Beyond: Menu of Options for the Consideration of Heads of State and Government Part II," United Nations, September 2020, 4.

Africa," while the World Bank finds South Asia now accounts for around 60 percent of the new poor.[308] [309]

An equitable and long-term recovery will need development diplomats to pursue sustainable and inclusive economic growth strategies, which will be the largest drivers of poverty reduction. Sustainable growth, in turn, requires multi-year, long-term planning and investments that avoid the traps of annual funding cycles and include clear metrics and benchmarks to independently evaluate foreign aid. Imagine if the United States invested the $4.1 billion it allocated for Afghanistan foreign assistance in fiscal year 2009 to be spent out over a decade rather than a single year and to fight poverty nationwide instead of in support of a counterinsurgency strategy fighting terrorists and drug lords in select geographic areas![310] Development diplomats should consider analytical tools to link development budgets and project proposals with outcome-based evidence metrics, ensuring foreign aid more smartly achieves its intended impact.

4. **Development diplomats must invest resources seriously in women and girls.** Gender equality is one of the most effective and efficient ways to reduce poverty and boost inclusive economic growth. To fulfill SDG five—achieving gender equality and empowering all women and girls—every major development investment needs to put the unique needs of

308 Homi Kharas and Meagan Dooley, "Long-run Impacts of COVID-19 on Extreme Poverty," Brookings Institution, June 2, 2021.

309 Christoph Lakner et al., "Updated Estimates of the Impact of COVID-19 on Global Poverty: Looking Back at 2020 and the Outlook for 2021," *World Bank Blogs*, January 11, 2021.

310 US Congress, Senate, Committee, *Evaluating US Foreign Assistance to Afghanistan*, 2.

women and girls at the heart of its work by addressing the systemic and structural barriers that prevent gender equality. As we saw in the case of female plumbers in Jordan, women's equality and empowerment are integral to all dimensions of inclusive and sustainable development; without it, the other sixteen SDGs fail.

The number of women and children living in poverty is likely much higher than current data-gathering techniques would suggest, given that data collection on poverty is typically conducted at the household level. This calculation assumes resources are evenly distributed to all family members even when we know that is not the case.[311] Given the sizable gender data gap permeating our systems, as the book, *Invisible Women,* powerfully shows, it will take new ways of working across the foreign policy and development divide to transform our policy commitments into tangible outcomes.[312] Development diplomats can lead the way in championing gender equality in every dimension of their work. Every power plant, highway project, and inclusive value chain project has different effects—positive and negative—on women than on men. We need gender integration across all programming to increase women's economic and political access and potential.

---

311 Ana Maria Munoz Boudet et al, "Gender Differences in Poverty and Household Composition through the Life-cycle: A Global Perspective," World Bank Group, Policy Research Working Paper 8360, March 2018.

312 Carolina Criado Perez, *Invisible Women: Data Bias in a World Designed for Men* (New York: Abrams Books), 2019.

BUREAUCRACY

There is a certain irony in that our most pressing development challenges require regional or global cooperation, and yet most of our institutions are set up to work bilaterally. Most development work is not organized or funded regionally across multiple countries. For regional projects, jurisdiction may sit in multiple places in bureaucracies with different chains of commands and budgeting authorities. The staff may have little incentive or authorization to work across borders if it means giving up resources or spending authority targeted at an individual country. Money is power, after all, and the organization of bureaucracy can shape results.

5. **Development diplomats should organize and think regionally, even on bilateral projects.** Development diplomats can help institutions work regionally, not just bilaterally, as I saw in the case of the US New Silk Road initiative from 2013 to 2015. Success requires building political support and financing for regional initiatives, working across multiple countries, donors, and development banks. Internally, within a donor government, the work of development diplomacy may involve coordinating among agencies, bureaus, posts, and missions, all demanding intense shuttle diplomacy and lobbying to find the necessary resources and political support to align development priorities in the region.[313]

Bureaucratic structures, incentives, and ways of working can make it complicated to translate global or regional visions into reality. This organization can lead to political

---

313 Larry Sampler and Jonathan Stivers, "Building the Bridges of the New Silk Road," *US Agency for International Development Impact Blog*, February 13, 2015.

prioritization of the work, conflicting funding mechanisms, insufficient sharing of learnings across countries, and competing sets of priorities. As a result, opportunities to strategically connect the dots on development projects across countries get missed. Development diplomats can be a bridge within and between institutions to help governments and donors plan regionally, not just bilaterally. Greater exposure to multiple country and donor systems can help development diplomats break down organizational barriers and think more creatively in reorganizing bureaucratic architecture for regional investments and partnerships.

6. **Development diplomats can work across bureaucratic silos to connect the dots on shared development priorities.** Development diplomats can break down the artificial silos within bureaucracies by actively connecting people in different offices to the same agenda. Too often within a government, for instance, multiple agencies may focus on one issue or country, but from various angles. As described in the case of Nepal, bilateral investments in the energy sector faced limited success without strategic cooperation from India on a cross-border energy line. Initially, limited engagement across economic and energy teams within these governments made it more complicated to collaborate before teams successfully worked together on a common road map.[314]

Development diplomats can intentionally connect people and agencies within and across governments and other parties to agree on shared priorities. They can create new

---

314 "Millennium Challenge Corporation, India Ministry of External Affairs Announce Cooperation to Promote Economic Growth," US Millennium Challenge Corporation, press release, January 13, 2017.

working groups or convene meetings bringing together people and institutions that may not ordinarily engage with each other. Within the US government, development diplomats can issue front-channel cables, communicating development priorities in a transparent manner to reach wider audiences.

7. **Development diplomats must rise above bureaucratic turf wars.** Protecting one's turf or domain is very common in large bureaucracies and can be either helpful or disruptive, depending on the situation. Turf wars can slow down the collaboration and cooperation needed to successfully implement development priorities. In a large bureaucracy, people gain or lose power through the resources they control. Bureaucrats may be reluctant or unable to transfer their resources even if it could lead to strategic win-win solutions. Without incentives to share budgets, personnel, or resources, collaboration on complex development projects—particularly those that cross borders like the CASA-1000 or TUTAP energy projects—can be challenging to implement.

Understanding these positions both at a bureaucratic and personal level is key. Development diplomats can help minimize turf wars by working within and across agencies to create allies and stakeholders who see the value of the work from a development, foreign policy, or political lens. Successfully navigating bureaucracy requires knowing how it works and seeing the spaces for creative partnership. With time, patience, and some luck, development diplomats can help structure positive negotiations that help grow the pie instead of zero-sum negotiations.

POLITICS

Development does not happen in a vacuum but rather within a political ecosystem that can determine the ultimate success or failure of a development initiative. Sustainable development relies on securing political buy-in, which may involve political leaders, foreign affairs ministries, and opposition political parties. Each of these actors could come to power in numerous election cycles and determine the outcome of a major development initiative. Working more intentionally in a deeply political space requires a unique set of skills to fight poverty without allowing foreign aid to be used for political purposes. Sustainable development efforts ultimately need political support from governments and local populations to succeed.

8. **Development diplomats must navigate political waters for long-term buy-in on development priorities.** Development initiatives involving significant amounts of money, infrastructure, or policy and institutional reforms can take years for policymakers, engineers, economists, project managers, procurement specialists, and finance teams to put together. The work can involve design and feasibility studies, policy and legislative reforms, and political lobbying for resources as described with MCC compacts in Nepal, Sri Lanka, Mongolia, and Jordan.

During this time, governments can come and go with varying political agendas influencing the outcome of development priorities. Development diplomats need to work not just on the design of their projects but on the broader enabling environment to make sure they have political buy-in and support to succeed in the long term. The economics of the project are essential, but so are the politics. Development diplomats should avoid designing initiatives that are politically tone-deaf or hard to successfully implement if the political will does not exist. Political economy analysis can be critical to understanding the conditions for success.

9. **Development diplomats may need to create political momentum to advance development projects.** Because large-scale development projects take years to come together, they may lack sustained attention from stakeholders over time. This means the political will may not be there when the project is technically ready to move forward. Development diplomats can play a critical role in generating political attention to advance key development initiatives.

I saw this take place from 2013 to 2015 on regional electricity transmission lines connecting Central to South Asia when American, British, and World Bank diplomats rallied political stakeholders in the region to commit resources to CASA-1000. Similarly, development diplomats should seize opportunities to rally political stakeholders to support key development initiatives. Development diplomats can take advantage of upcoming summits, meetings, or other key dates on a shared agenda, for instance, to generate political momentum on key projects.

10. **Development diplomats can help countries prioritize competing development demands.** Developing countries face competing development priorities from donors, partners, and their governments. These countries often lack the resources, technical capacity, and staff to simultaneously invest in the development of multiple complex initiatives.

They need to decide on the best investments upon which to place their bets. Development diplomats can help sort through the noise and help partners prioritize development accordingly. When development partners hear a coordinated chorus of voices advocate for certain projects and provide the necessary financial and political incentives to make them a reality, they may be more likely to focus their attention and resources accordingly.

When American, British, and World Bank senior officials started working together in a coordinated way on regional energy projects in 2013, the collective work of diplomatic engagements in Kabul, Islamabad, Dushanbe, and Bishkek helped cut through the chaos for regional governments to effectively prioritize development initiatives such as CASA-1000. This coordination ensured projects received the political and technical support to advance.

11. **Development diplomats must engage with those in power today and consider those who could be in power tomorrow.** Large-scale development projects take years to design and implement, sometimes longer than the life cycle of a single political administration. Getting buy-in from those in power is essential, but long-term success also depends on engaging with those who may come to power in the future. Effective political engagement can be tricky for development officials to get right, which is why a strong partnership with the diplomatic community is essential.

Successful development diplomacy can navigate today's political climate while planning for future political scenarios. This was the case in Nepal from 2015 to 2018 when MCC worked closely with the US Embassy and the Nepali Embassy in Washington on a political road map to engage political parties in Kathmandu on development priorities. By increasing the diplomatic footprint, not just with technical counterparts in the government but also with numerous political bedfellows, MCC built support for the development agenda among a wider range of stakeholders leading to the signing of the compact.

12. Development diplomats may fail in one context but can apply the learnings elsewhere. Development diplomacy does not always succeed. In the case of the Kerry-Lugar-Berman bill tripling US aid to Pakistan, it took repeated negotiations with American and Pakistani diplomats to build the political space necessary for development efforts to even have a chance to succeed. Even then, anti-American sentiment and weak Pakistani institutional capacity made spending US foreign aid challenging, minimizing the intended impact of the assistance.

When the Rajapaksas returned to power in Sri Lanka, anti-American sentiment fueled by media disinformation campaigns created unworkable conditions for major development projects to succeed. Nonetheless, lessons from both experiences helped inform the execution of projects in other politically fragile contexts to improve the next generation of project development. Development diplomats must learn and lean into failure as much as understanding what leads to success.

Taken together, these insights on money, bureaucracy, and politics offer the start of a road map for how we can think about investing in development diplomacy. Building out these capacities and skills means intentionally breeding a different type of horse, one that can survive and thrive in a new landscape.[315] What will it take to train the next generation of development diplomats? How should we start?

"Follow the sun," offered my Mongolian driver. "It will get you where you need to go."

---

315 Paige Williams, "The Remarkable Comeback of Przewalski's Horse," *Smithsonian Magazine*, December 2016.

CHAPTER 14

SPORTING DIFFERENT VIEWS
IMPORTANCE OF LANGUAGE, EMOTIONAL INTELLIGENCE, AND DIVERSITY

THE BOYS AT THE BAR

Amid the muted noise of McGettigan's Irish pub in Dubai airport's Terminal 1 in 2009, three pairs of eyes looked at me with raised eyebrows as I interjected into their conversation about the world of sports.

"Well, I wonder if David Ortiz's potent offense will be able to power the Red Sox through," I said half-convincingly, not even sure of what I was saying.

It must have shown, as Senator Kerry and my SFRC colleagues looked at me oddly. I wondered if I mixed up the Boston sports teams again. Twenty-four hours earlier, my husband, Nageeb Sumar, had given me another crash course on sports to help me for this very moment.

"Remember the Red Sox finally beat the curse in 2003–04 when we lived in Boston, but it's not clear they can sustain a deep playoff run now in 2009 against their archnemesis," Nageeb explained for the third time, his patience wearing thin.

"Against the Mets, right?" I questioned indifferently, preoccupied with folding the girls' clothes into neat piles on the floor. Onesies in this pile, pants and shirts over here, and tiny socks in neat little bundles on the side. I thought about the meals I still needed to cook for the family before I left for another overseas trip. *How many casserole dishes and curries could I make in the next few hours? Did I have enough breast milk in the freezer? I better call the nanny one more time and ask her if she could stay late to help in the evenings.*

"The Yankees! Are you kidding? The Yankees!" Nageeb exploded. The lesson was not going well. "Are you listening to anything I am saying?"

"All right, all right, at least I knew it involved a New York team. Calm down. Is this really such a big deal?"

"Oh my God, he is going to look at you like you're crazy and fire you on the spot," he replied, only half kidding. "Stick with the Celtics; they won the NBA Championship last year. Or better yet, ask him if he's betting on Zdeno Chara, Marc Savard, or Tim Thomas to pull through in the All-Star Game for the Bruins."

"Right, got it...What are those names again?"

Without further ado, Nageeb gave up and made his way upstairs.

Now here I was in Dubai, having arrived after a long transatlantic flight from Washington. With a couple of hours to kill before our onward flight to Doha, Qatar, from where we would board a US military plane to Kabul, Afghanistan, I was determined to make a good impression on Senator Kerry. I always struggled to get time with him in Washington, our communication largely via paper given his busy schedule. In theory, traveling with him provided a unique opportunity to develop our professional relationship if I could get a word in edgewise.

Once more, I felt as if I came from a completely different world than the senator and most of his staff. Nonetheless, I mustered my inner confidence to break into the sports-dominated discussion. As a first-generation South Asian American woman, I did not know the Boston Brahmin world or have familiarity with conversations from the men's locker room. As the only female in the traveling party and the shortest member of the group by a foot, I constantly adapted to the group norms. It was not unusual to see me running in heels through airport corridors and congressional hallways to keep up with my male colleagues' lanky strides and coded conversations.

My technical knowledge of Asia by itself would not guarantee me a seat at the table if I could not also prove my worth as a trusted advisor. I needed to connect on a more informal level. Even though I did not drink alcohol, follow sports, or know much about what guys talked about when they hung out, I decided to try again at the Dubai airport bar.

"Well, I'm from Jersey. Is the Bruins' rivalry with the Devils as deep and bitter as the one with the New York Rangers or Montreal Canadiens?" I asked in one last attempt to contribute.

"Let me tell you about the Devils." Senator Kerry brightened, looking at me with pleasant surprise before going on to explain his prediction of how the hockey season would play out.

Thank God that worked, as I relaxed while he went on about some player or another. I would give him three more minutes before I somehow brilliantly pivoted the discussion to the situation in Afghanistan.

"SOFT" SKILLS FOR DEVELOPMENT DIPLOMATS

Relying on emotional intelligence to build trust is critical to opening doors for dialogue. These types of "soft" skills are more important than ever as the world emerges from the COVID-19 pandemic, protests over racial injustice and white supremacy, soaring rates of unemployment and food insecurity, an increasingly searing hot planet, and exploding global inequality and instability. With crisis comes an opportunity to build back better, including investing in a new generation of development diplomats equipped to solve complex and multidisciplinary global crises. Leaders should consider the "soft" skills outlined in this chapter to support creative, out-of-the-box thinking, rebuild diplomatic and development relationships, and foster trust between teams.

Investing in development diplomacy can be a huge opportunity to remake government bureaucracies. It means rethinking how we train development and diplomatic professionals across foreign policy, economic policy, and development fields starting in graduate schools and professional training institutes along with ongoing professional training and exchanges throughout their careers. It may require creating new interagency working groups and cultural norms for ways of working, breaking traditional silos artificially separating foreign policy and international development. It will rely on new incentives to reward cross-agency collaboration and recognize those who successfully work as bridge builders.

What type of skills do development diplomats need? Development diplomats will succeed by prioritizing language, emotional intelligence, and diversity.

LANGUAGE

In undergraduate and graduate schools, many students interested in an international career tend to spend years studying a foreign language so they can successfully live and work overseas with cultural fluency. With over seven thousand languages spoken in the world today, languages such as French, Spanish, Arabic, Portuguese, and others are critical for development experts and diplomats alike in communicating with local officials and communities throughout the world. Linguistics, however, are not the only type of language development diplomats should learn.

13. **Development diplomats should learn the language of both foreign policy and international development.** In many of today's US training institutes and international public policy schools, students are asked to pick between two tracks: 1) foreign policy or international relations and 2) international development or development economics (or some variations therein).

The first stream focuses on relations with other nations, foreign policy, and issues of national and international security. The second track examines issues of globalization, development economics, and developing countries' pathways to growth. There may be little mandatory cross-over between the two, resulting in generations of public policy graduates only trained in narrow disciplines despite the interconnectedness of the two fields. Most development experts coming out of school cannot speak the language of foreign policy, and most diplomats do not understand the language of development as I experienced with my own education. This educational gap at the onset of international careers must be rectified to successfully train the next generation of development diplomats.

14. **Development diplomats must learn to speak the language of others.** Bridging the silos of agencies, bureaucracies, and cultures to support development diplomacy is not easy. It may require speaking multiple bureaucratic languages and translating between expert cultures that focus on different aspects of the same mission. One way to accelerate these types of exchanges is to create mid-level and senior-level rotation programs across agencies, resulting in more career opportunities for experts to be in others' shoes. Another way

is to create incentives, like awards or performance bonuses, for officials who successfully work across silos or agencies.

Success depends on partners sitting in many agencies and countries working together in more creative ways to achieve win-win solutions. Development diplomats can help parts of bureaucracy work in new ways in common cause, as I witnessed in working with the State Department, USAID, and MCC on multiple development projects. In some cases, success required taking the Rubik's cube and turning the sides in various combinations to find a winning solution.

15. **Development diplomats can voice constructive dissent from time to time.** Many bureaucracies suffer from groupthink. It is often easier to go along with mainstream views than break ranks by challenging a commonly held viewpoint, which can slow things down and create friction. As a result, space for honest reflection, inquisition, and learning can be difficult to find and prevent new solutions from emerging. Standard practices, policies, and programs become deeply entrenched, even when they are problematic and suboptimal in achieving development outcomes.

This space is where dissent can play a powerful role by shaking things up in ways that transform systems and force parties to act outside of their comfort zones. Constructive dissent became a hallmark of mine starting in my days on Capitol Hill. By leveraging all the congressional tools at my disposal, such as legislation, reports, and hearings, I worked with others to challenge the status quo of US development policy in Afghanistan, Pakistan, Sri Lanka, and elsewhere.

This approach can result in a positive impact in the long run despite the short-term pains.

EMOTIONAL INTELLIGENCE

16. **Development diplomats require high levels of emotional intelligence.** There is something unique about the art of the development deal. Whether negotiating a way forward on Afghanistan's future or navigating Nepal's complex political party dynamics to advance economic growth, technical briefings, and expertise only took us so far. Making logical arguments based on evidence and rational thought worked well when putting together briefing papers at a desk, but the actual negotiations often played out differently than the official talking points anticipated.

Being able to successfully read the room, adapt policy responses in real-time, and think on one's feet are critical emotional intelligence skills for any development diplomat. Development diplomats should routinely practice and learn emotional intelligence skills such as active listening, building cultural awareness, and deepening knowledge of social justice movements. Connecting head and heart across cultures is critical in a global network.

17. **Development diplomats need to be flexible and agile.** Plan, plan, plan. That is what good bureaucrats do to execute policies and programs. Strong project management is the heart of any successful development initiative demanding adherence to deadlines, paper, procedures, and processes. While planning and preparation are critical skills for success, being flexible and agile proves to be as important for development diplomats.

Often during my overseas trips, our strategies did not go as planned. Our schedules changed last minute, security threats interrupted our priorities, and our partners offered conflicting ideas for how things should go. Negotiations with government counterparts did not always yield the intended outcome. Being overly rigid or under-appreciating the political fluidity of the moment led to frustrations on all sides. Development diplomats need to be strong project managers that can adapt to changing deadlines, political pressures, and external shocks to help keep things on track. Flexibility and agility are critical skills for development diplomacy.

18. **Development diplomats need to be emotionally prepared for working in unsafe environments.** The world is increasingly complex and interconnected with security, political, health, economic, and cybersecurity threats that transcend our borders. Sometimes this means navigating active war zones. Other times, it means living through the turmoil of post-conflict peace and reconstruction or security breaches, including cybersecurity threats. Training development diplomats on security protocols, personal safety, and other best practices is critical so they are better equipped to face potential dangers.

One of the hardest parts of my career involved navigating personal security threats in places like Sri Lanka, Afghanistan, and Pakistan. Despite the emotional turmoil, I physically survived these situations in part because I benefited from diplomatic security training. All development diplomats working in fragile environments should be physically trained and emotionally prepared for the heightened risks they face. They should never be afraid to ask for help.

DIVERSITY

19. Development diplomats must look like the people they represent and serve. Like many power centers globally, Washington and other western capitals are dominated by an expert culture run by connected networks. Breaking through these networks to identify and recruit new talent as expert witnesses, consultants, hires, and thought leaders requires a fundamental shift in ways of working at every level of power. Taking the time to identify and diversify points of view across socioeconomic, racial, gender, sexual, and geographic backgrounds can lead to new thinking and solutions, as I saw on Capitol Hill in diversifying the witness bench.

The next generation of development diplomats needs to reflect and represent the people they serve. Valuing diversity goes beyond racial, gender, and sexual orientation lenses to include varied geographic and local perspectives. Too often in development, power and resources are still captured by organizations and governments in rich countries who comfortably work within their white networks of power through consultants, contractors, thought leaders, and funders. In this colonial model of development, there is no equal partnership between those with power and the poor. There must be a shift of power to the poor and to women, especially from international and national networks to local networks at the grassroots levels where organizing, innovation, and resilience take place and are often led by women community leaders.[316] Diversifying the system remains deeply challenging and an uphill battle all development diplomats will need to take on.

---

316 Fatema Z. Sumar and Tara R. Gingerich, "The Future of Humanitarian Action is Local," *Stanford Social Innovation Review* 18, no. 2 (Spring 2020): 46.

20. **Development diplomats will have to rethink the role of travel to do their work.** Before COVID-19, frequent overseas travel for foreign policy and development work was common and part of the job. In my US government career from 2006 to 2018, I traveled three-quarters of a million miles to advance development diplomacy. The pace of travel and the accompanying lifestyle made it challenging to manage a healthy work-life balance and did not sufficiently consider the carbon footprint of our work.

As we create more green, sustainable, and healthy pathways in the post-COVID era, we will need to rethink the role of travel in advancing development diplomacy. While traveling will still be essential for building relationships, trust, and conducting oversight activities, we can aim to better leverage new technologies and virtual platforms to reduce the amount of physical travel needed. Getting this balance right will be our collective challenge and opportunity.

21. **Development diplomacy must create pathways for young parents, especially women, to survive and thrive.** Parents or caregivers managing international careers struggle with the responsibilities of caring for a family. Women must be actively supported to succeed as development diplomats. Workplace policies and cultural norms still have a long way to go to provide the needed flexibility and support, especially for new moms to succeed.

I faced numerous challenges in balancing a young family of three kids. I internalized many of the workplace obstacles, finding creative ways to breastfeed, juggling calendars to squeeze in pediatrician appointments, or staying up at odd hours to cook meals for the entire week in anticipation of being on the road. I did not challenge workplace norms in the early years of my career, but slowly over time, it came at a cost to my own emotional and physical health. These types of experiences are not sustainable nor empowering. Development diplomats need to actively change the culture of international careers to support working moms and caregivers, especially as we consider the pathways telework and more flexible working locations could open. Otherwise, we risk women not having a seat at the development diplomacy table, including in senior roles. We must start this journey of development diplomacy by focusing on the unique needs of women.

These twenty-one recommendations offer ways to invest in the next generation of development diplomats. Schools and training institutes can consider these insights alongside a suggested curriculum for development diplomats. Taken together, this formula outlines a new way of working together to fight poverty.

As Walter Gretzky, father of hockey's great Wayne Gretzky liked to say, "Go to where the puck is going, not where it has been."[317] Perhaps I was listening to Nageeb all along.

---

317 Christopher Berry, "The Meaning of Skate to Where the Puck Is Going, Not Where It Has Been," ChristopherBerry.ca, January 14, 2021.

DESIGNING A CURRICULUM FOR
DEVELOPMENT DIPLOMATS

Suggested Courses	Suggested Competencies
-Politics of Domestic & International Public Policy -Psychology and Negotiations for Policy Analysis -Econometrics and Statistics -Microeconomic and Macroeconomic Analysis -Political Economy Analysis of Development -National Security and Foreign Policy Fundamentals -Project Design and Impact Measurement -Congressional Oversight of Foreign Policy and Aid -US Executive Branch and Foreign Assistance -Role of Civil Society in Public Policy -Foreign Language -Gender, Inequality, and Inclusion	-Understanding of foreign policy, national security, international development, and foreign assistance -Ability to analyze economics of public policy including use of quantitative and qualitative analytical tools -Appreciation for social and emotional skills needed to navigate bureaucracies and organizational politics -Familiarity with complex government structures across executive and legislative branches -Experience in diplomatic negotiations and correspondence such as policy memos and cables -Knowledge of project management and budget analysis -Strong public speaking and presentation skills including use of new digital platforms -Fluency in at least one foreign language

SUMMARY OF 21 RECOMMENDATIONS FOR DEVELOPMENT DIPLOMATS

MONEY

1. Development diplomats must realize *how* money is spent is just as important as *how much* is spent.

2. Development diplomats should leverage a range of development financing options.

3. Development diplomats should plan for long-term, sustainable, and inclusive growth.

4. Development diplomats must invest resources seriously in women and girls.

BUREAUCRACY

5. Development diplomats should organize and think regionally, even on bilateral projects.

6. Development diplomats can work across bureaucratic silos to connect the dots on shared development priorities.

7. Development diplomats must rise above bureaucratic turf wars.

POLITICS

8. Development diplomats must navigate political waters for long-term buy-in on development priorities.

9. Development diplomats may need to create political momentum to advance development projects.

10. Development diplomats can help countries prioritize competing development demands.

11. Development diplomats must engage with those in power today and consider those who could be in power tomorrow.

12. Development diplomats may fail in one context but can apply the learnings elsewhere.

LANGUAGE

13. Development diplomats should learn the language of both foreign policy and international development.

14. Development diplomats must learn to speak the language of others.

15. Development diplomats can voice constructive dissent from time to time.

EMOTIONAL INTELLIGENCE

16. Development diplomats require high levels of emotional intelligence.

17. Development diplomats need to be flexible and agile.

18. Development diplomats need to be emotionally prepared for working in unsafe environments.

DIVERSITY

19. Development diplomats must look like the people they represent and serve.

20. Development diplomats will have to rethink the role of travel to do their work.

21. Development diplomacy must create pathways for young parents, especially women, to survive and thrive.

CONCLUSION

The silence threatened to take over the room and end the meeting on a strained note.

Why is it so quiet? As my mind wandered, my colleague gently nudged me, pointing out that the room was waiting for me to respond to Indian Prime Minister Manmohan Singh.

"Sorry sir...yes sir, sorry, my father grew up in Bombay on Mohammedali Road," I stammered and blushed, unprepared for this informal exchange with the Prime Minister at the tail end of his meeting with Senator Kerry in February 2010.[318]

In his crisp, pressed, white *salvar khameez*, black vest, and blue turban, Prime Minister Singh epitomized the grace and elegance of his distinguished office. I tried to focus on taking diligent notes but got star-struck instead. I could not process the fact of sitting here in the Prime Minister's New Delhi

---

318 "John Kerry in Delhi, Meets Manmohan Singh," *The New Indian Express*, updated May 16, 2012.

residence in Panchavati, sipping chai and eating biscuits as if I dined every day with the world's dignitaries.

I became so wrapped up in what my father in heaven must think of his eldest daughter, who is just one generation removed from India and his childhood poverty, being in the same room as India's leader, that I completely missed the Prime Minister's question regarding my origins.

In a gentle voice, Prime Minister Singh kindly responded, "He would be proud of you. Keep fighting to help others," using a similar phrase to my father's so many years ago on the New Jersey Turnpike. My life came full circle.

As a fourteen-year-old Girl Scout, I never could have imagined the richness of an international career and the impact I could have through the eyes of a diplomat, politician, policymaker, development official, and mother. I never expected one day I would become a development diplomat. Throughout this journey, I felt the urgency to be creative, see past the historic problems, and seize the moment to make change happen, whatever my level or rank. This book is my story, which no doubt has some unique elements, but overall, it is a journey about how we can do more together than we can apart while celebrating the differences between us. By purposely bridging the foreign policy and international development divide, development diplomacy can help us tackle poverty once and for all.

We have less than ten years to end the injustice of poverty to meet the 2030 Sustainable Development Goals. I emphasize the word "injustice" here because poverty is not inevitable but rather man-made in the laws we create, the companies we support, and the politicians we elect. Poverty is the result of inequality in how our societies are organized, with the few rich individuals getting richer while the masses of the poor get poorer. The good news is since we created poverty, we can *choose* to end it. If we are going to succeed by 2030, we need new ways to have a transformative impact at scale. Development diplomacy can be a powerful new tool in our arsenal.

Too many of us in foreign policy and international development careers work deep within our lanes, perfecting our expertise. We may be rewarded for defending our organization's turf at the expense of a broader shared mission, one bigger than individual objectives. The worlds between us can become vast and the chasm deep. There are legitimate fears that by working together, development will become politicized and taken over by politicians and policymakers who may instrumentalize development projects for their broader aims. The truth is, we live in political environments where political buy-in and support for fighting poverty are essential for structural changes to take root. We must understand both sides of this coin and be strategically smarter about how to pursue transformative, sustainable, and inclusive long-term development.

Working jointly becomes easier if we study together at the outset of our careers, starting in graduate schools and training programs. It becomes more second nature if we are not taught to think in silos but to work across the aisle. The answer is not to artificially separate the two fields. Instead, there must be greater understanding and appreciation for the unique roles each field can play and how together they can yield more sustainable and inclusive development outcomes that can withstand political headwinds.

As we train the next generation of development diplomats, we must be gender transformative in our approach, recognizing the critical role women play in this space. Likewise, the next generation needs to represent the true diversity of the people it serves, intentionally breaking through racial, social, economic, geographic, and other barriers to support greater inclusion and equity efforts.

Just as in World War II when President Roosevelt, Prime Minister Churchill, and world leaders planned for a post-war peace by creating new institutions and architecture, we must come together to rebuild a global future where no one faces the injustice of poverty. Our challenges today are as monumental as they were over seventy-five years ago. Our passion and commitment to meet them head-on remain strong. As my father said, we cannot rest until everyone has the same opportunities wherever they are in the world. Let us get to work together.

GRATITUDE

Writing my first book was like having a fourth child: a labor of love. Although I harbored fantasies of putting pen to paper for over a decade, it took three things to make it happen: the COVID-19 pandemic, the Creator Institute with my cohort of first-time authors, and the courage to stop talking and start typing.

COVID-19 turned all our lives upside down, including mine. I lost my paternal uncle, Zulfikar Gunja, to the politics of the pandemic and mourned the non-COVID deaths of my mother-in-law Anar Sumar and grandmother-in-law Nurkhanu Sumar. They were unable to see their beloved grandchildren and great-grandchildren, respectively, due to pandemic border closures.[319] Even through the heartbreak of losing loved ones and the stress of managing remote work and school, the pandemic gave me the gift of time slowed down, allowing me to be fully home. I used this time to reconnect with my children, heal from a career in overdrive,

---

319 Fatema Z. Sumar, "COVID-19 Killed My Uncle, His Name was Zulfikar," *Medium*, May 5, 2020.

and learn how to write a book thanks to the Creator Institute. I am indebted to all those who partnered with me to turn a dream into a reality.

While writing can be solitary and stressful, I felt supported every step of the way by a community of champions who loaned their eyes and ears to provide input on the manuscript. Special thanks to India Adams, Doug Frantz, David Wade, David McKean, Mara Bolis, Tariq Ahmad, Michelle Strucke, Andrew Imbrie, Steve Feldstein, Richard Kessler, Saroj Kumar Jha, Salman Zaheer, Sunil Khosla, Himesh Dhungel, Nilmini Rubin, Gregory Kausner, Nickie Monga, Dilafruz Khonikboyeva, and Nageeb Sumar.

My love to Kristina Wallender, Bridget Snell, Deepti Gupta-Patel, Hena Kazmi, Sujata Gadkar-Wilcox, and other friends for listening to me talk through my writing in excruciating detail for months on end. My appreciation to Eric Koester, Brian Bies, Cassandra Caswell-Stirling, Jessica Fleischman, Linda Berardelli, Cynthia Tucker, Amanda Brown, Gjorgji Pejkovski, Tea Jagodić, Nikola Tikoski, Vladimir Dudaš, and all the editors at New Degree Press who worked tirelessly with me every step of the way to cross the finish line. My gratitude to my cousin Mushtaq Gunja and my sister Arwa Gunja who stepped in at critical moments to help me on editing and marketing, respectively.

Many people across multiple US government agencies took the time to review the manuscript and provide clearance or feedback on behalf of the US government. I am grateful to Cameron Alford, Richard McCarthy, Morgan Williams, Jonathan Brooks, Caroline Nguyen, Tom Kelly, and colleagues at the US Millennium Challenge Corporation; Behar Godani and colleagues at the US State Department, including current or former US Ambassadors Anne Patterson, Susan M. Elliott, Alaina Teplitz, Randy Berry, Patricia A. Butenis, Atul Keshap, Robin Raphel, and Michael Klecheski; and former USAID Mission Directors William Frej and Beth Dunford.

Pursuing a career as a development diplomat happened by accident. Along the way, it took a village of champions who instilled in me the foundational skills I needed to succeed. To the late and great Michael Kenny and John Calimano, who taught me in high school how to write and speak, respectively, I soaked in every word you said. To my East Brunswick, New Jersey public school teachers, and Delaware Raritan Girl Scout leaders in particular, Alan Brodman and Sally Quaranta, respectively, thank you for being such great role models.

To Joyce Muchan, Mary Katzenstein, John Templeton, Ann Corwin, Christopher Kojm, Anne-Marie Slaughter, and my Cornell and Princeton families, I walked through doors you opened for me. To my Senate Foreign Relations Committee and Oxfam friends, I learned how to speak truth to power from each of you. To Doug Frantz, Nisha Biswal, Sonal Shah, Shelley Goode, Jonathan Nash, Michael Deich, and mentors through every phase of my career, I found my inner voice when you pushed me to lead. Finally, to John Kerry, I sat at the table because you pulled out a chair.

Embarking on a career of public service happened by choice. My family and Islamic faith instilled in me a deep ethos to take care of others. For this north star, I thank first and foremost my parents Zahir and Sakina Gunja, my in-laws Salim and Anar Sumar, my great-aunt and great-uncle Umme and Burhani Massey, my grandmother-in-law Nurkhanu Sumar, my siblings and siblings-in-law, and the Gunja, Khambaty, Sumar, and Hirji clans who poured the concrete of my life's foundation.

Most importantly, dreams do not come true without guardian angels. To my husband Nageeb Sumar and our three inspirational daughters Zahra, Safya, and Insiya, I get to fly because you part the clouds. Any successes I have had are due to your unconditional love and support. This book is because of you.

ABOUT THE AUTHOR

Globally, with nearly one out of every three people living in poverty, Fatema Z. Sumar believes we must tackle the root causes to create lasting solutions. She is a mission-oriented change leader and author, creating a more equal world by transforming global systems to reach vulnerable populations. She wrote this book to share stories from her own journey to inspire others to invest in development diplomacy.

Fatema has a distinguished career, leading efforts to advance inclusive and sustainable development in emerging markets and fragile countries. In 2021, President Biden appointed Fatema as the Vice President of Compact Operations at the U.S. Millennium Challenge Corporation, an independent U.S. government foreign aid agency that reduces poverty through economic growth.

She previously served as the Deputy Assistant Secretary for South and Central Asia at the U.S. Department of State, where she led U.S. efforts to expand regional economic and energy connectivity and as a Presidential Management Fellow (PMF). In Congress, Fatema worked for three US

Senators, including as a Senior Professional Staff Member on the U.S. Senate Foreign Relations Committee. She also worked in civil society at Oxfam America and the American Civil Liberties Union.

Fatema sits on Advisory Boards for Princeton, Cornell, and Indiana universities. Her work has been published in the *Stanford Social Innovation Review*, *The New Republic*, *The Hill*, and other outlets. She is a frequent guest speaker and has testified before the U.S. House of Representatives and U.S. Senate.

Fatema graduated with a Master of Public Affairs from Princeton University's School of Public and International Affairs, where she received the prestigious Stokes Award, and a Bachelor of Arts in Government from Cornell University. She studied abroad at the American University in Cairo.

Fatema and her husband live in Lexington, Massachusetts with their three inspirational daughters. When not at her computer or on her phone, you can find her exploring new places near and far, repurposing leftovers in the kitchen, or in a downward dog on her yoga mat.

APPENDIX

INTRODUCTION

Cochran, Eliza. "6 Facts About Women's Rights in Mongolia." *The Borgen Project* (blog). December 17, 2020. https://borgenproject.org/womens-rights-in-mongolia/.

Hiraga, Masakao, Ikuko Uochi, and Gabriela R.A Doyle. "Counting the Uncounted—How the Mongolian Nomadic Survey is Leaving No One Behind." *World Bank Blogs.* April 18, 2020. https://blogs.worldbank.org/opendata/counting-uncounted-how-mongolian-nomadic-survey-leaving-no-one-behind.

"MCC Mongolia Water Compacts Starts 5-Year Timeline with Entry into Force." US Millennium Challenge Corporation. Press release, April 5, 2021. https://www.mcc.gov/news-and-events/release/release-040521-mongolia-entry-into-force.

"MCC Regional Deputy Vice President Visits Mongolia, Meets with Senior Government Officials on MCC Compact Development Progress." US Millennium Challenge Corporation. Press release, December 6, 2017. https://www.mcc.gov/news-and-events/release/release-120617-sumar-mongolia-trip.

"Rural Women and the Millennium Development Goals." Inter-Agency Task Force on Rural Women. United Nations. 2012. Accessed May 10, 2021. https://www.unwomen.org/en/news/in-focus/commission-on-the-status-of-women-2012/facts-and-figures.

Sessions, Karen. "Congressional Notification Transmittal Sheet." US Millennium Challenge Corporation. June 11, 2018. https://assets.mcc.gov/content/uploads/cn-061118-mongolia-intent-to-sign.pdf.

Weatherford, Jack. *Genghis Khan and the Making of the Modern World*. New York: Crown Publishing Group, 2004.

"The World Bank in Mongolia Overview." The World Bank. Updated April 6, 2021. https://www.worldbank.org/en/country/mongolia/overview.

PART I

Morrison, Toni. "The Truest Eye." Interview by Pam Houston. *O, The Oprah Magazine*. November 2003. https://www.oprah.com/omagazine/toni-morrison-talks-love.

CHAPTER 1

"1: End Poverty in all its Forms Everywhere." The World Bank. Accessed June 5, 2021. https://datatopics.worldbank.org/sdgatlas/archive/2017/SDG-01-no-poverty.html.

"5 Shocking Facts about Extreme Global Inequality and How to Even It Up." Oxfam International. Accessed May 10, 2021. https://www.oxfam.org/en/5-shocking-facts-about-extreme-global-inequality-and-how-even-it.

"ADS Chapter 102 Agency Organization." US Agency for International Development. Revised June 27, 2017. https://www.usaid.gov/sites/default/files/documents/1868/102_0.pdf.

"Agencies: Overview." ForeignAssistance.gov. Updated January 22, 2021. https://www.foreignassistance.gov/agencies.

Azcona, Ginette. "From Insights to Action Gender Equality in the Wake of COVID-19." UN Women. 2020. https://www.unwomen.org/-/media/headquarters/attachments/sections/library/publications/2020/gender-equality-in-the-wake-of-covid-19-en.pdf?la=en&vs=5142.

Beaumont, Peter. "Decades of Progress on Extreme Poverty Now in Reverse Due to COVID." The Guardian. February 3, 2021. https://www.theguardian.com/global-development/2021/feb/03/decades-of-progress-on-extreme-poverty-now-in-reverse-due-to-covid.

Becker, Bastian. "Colonial Legacies in International Aid: Policy Priorities and Actor Constellations." In *From Colonialism to International Aid. Global Dynamics of Social Policy*, edited by Carina Schmitt, 161-185. Palgrave Macmillan, Cham, 2020. https://doi.org/10.1007/978-3-030-38200-1_7.

Chen, James. "Bretton Woods System and Agreement." Investopedia. Updated April 28, 2021. https://www.investopedia.com/terms/b/brettonwoodsagreement.asp.

"Climate Change and the Developing World: A Disproportionate Impact." US Global Leadership Coalition. March 2021. https://www.usglc.org/blog/climate-change-and-the-developing-world-a-disproportionate-impact/.

"Climate Change: Overview." The World Bank. Updated March 23, 2021. https://www.worldbank.org/en/topic/climatechange/overview.

General Assembly Resolution 70/1. *Transforming Our World: The 2030 Agenda for Sustainable Development*. A/RES/70/1. December 25, 2015. https://sdgs.un.org/2030agenda.

Ghizoni, Sandra Kollen. "Creation of the Bretton Woods System." Federal Reserve History. November 22, 2013. https://www.federalreservehistory.org/essays/bretton-woods-created.

"Goal 1: Eradicate Extreme Poverty & Hunger." United Nations.
Accessed June 5, 2021.
https://www.un.org/millenniumgoals/poverty.shtml.

"Half a Billion People Could Be Pushed into Poverty by
Coronavirus, Warns Oxfam." Oxfam International. Press
release, April 9, 2020.
https://www.oxfam.org/en/press-releases/half-billion-
people-could-be-pushed-poverty-coronavirus-warns-oxfam.

"The IMF and the World Bank." International Monetary Fund.
Accessed April 10, 2021.
https://www.imf.org/en/About/Factsheets/
Sheets/2016/07/27/15/31/IMF-World-Bank.

"India, China Played Central Role in Global Poverty Reduction:
United Nations." *Press Trust of India*. Updated July 7, 2015.
https://www.ndtv.com/india-news/india-china-played-
central-role-in-global-poverty-reduction-united-
nations-778980.

"Inequality and Poverty: The Hidden Costs of Tax Dodging."
Oxfam International. Accessed May 10, 2021.
https://www.oxfam.org/en/inequality-and-poverty-hidden-
costs-tax-dodging.

"Inequality Crisis Worsens as World Bank and IMF Persist with
Failed Policies." Bretton Woods Project. April 4, 2019.
https://www.brettonwoodsproject.org/2019/04/inequality-
crisis-worsens-as-bank-and-imf-persist-with-failed-policies/.

Ingram, George. "What Every American Should Know about US Foreign Aid." Brookings Institution. October 15, 2019. https://www.brookings.edu/opinions/what-every-american-should-know-about-u-s-foreign-aid/.

Kabeer, Naila. "Gender Equality, the MDGs and the SDGs: Achievements, Lessons and Concerns." *International Growth Centre* (blog). October 1, 2015. https://www.theigc.org/blog/gender-equality-the-mdgs-and-the-sdgs-achievements-lessons-and-concerns.

Knoy, Laura. "Transcript: 75 Years Ago: N.H.'s Bretton Woods Conference Reshaped World Economic Policy." *The Exchange*. New Hampshire Public Radio. July 8, 2019. https://www.nhpr.org/post/75-years-ago-nhs-bretton-woods-conference-reshaped-world-economic-policy#stream/0.

Lakner, Christoph, Nishant Yonzan, Daniel Gerszon Mahler, R. Andres Castaneda Aguilar, and Haoyu Wu. "Updated Estimates of the Impact of COVID-19 on Global Poverty: Looking Back at 2020 and the Outlook for 2021." *World Bank Blogs*. January 11, 2021. https://blogs.worldbank.org/opendata/updated-estimates-impact-covid-19-global-poverty-looking-back-2020-and-outlook-2021.

"Marshall Plan." HISTORY. Updated June 5, 2020. https://www.history.com/topics/world-war-ii/marshall-plan-1.

"Mega-rich Recoup COVID-losses in Record-Time Yet Billions Will Live in Poverty for at Least a Decade." Oxfam International. Press release, January 25, 2021. https://www.oxfam.org/en/press-releases/mega-rich-recoup-covid-losses-record-time-yet-billions-will-live-poverty-least.

"The Millennium Challenge Account." White House of President George W. Bush. Accessed April 20, 2021. https://georgewbush-whitehouse.archives.gov/infocus/developingnations/millennium.html.

"Millennium Development Goals Report 2015." United Nations. 2015. https://www.un.org/millenniumgoals/2015_MDG_Report/pdf/MDG%202015%20rev%20(July%201).pdf.

"Millennium Summit (6–8 September 2000)." United Nations. Accessed June 5, 2021. https://www.un.org/en/events/pastevents/millennium_summit.shtml.

"News on Millennium Development Goals." United Nations. Accessed June 5, 2021. https://www.un.org/millenniumgoals/.

"Office of the Administrator." US Agency for International Development. Updated January 20, 2017. https://www.usaid.gov/who-we-are/organization/leadership.

Patrick, Stewart M. "Remembering the Atlantic." *Council on Foreign Relations* (blog). August 16, 2011. https://www.cfr.org/blog/remembering-atlantic-charter.

"Poverty: Overview." The World Bank. Updated October 7, 2020.
https://www.worldbank.org/en/topic/poverty/overview.

Runde, Daniel F. "US Foreign Assistance in the Age of Strategic
Competition." Center for Strategic and International Studies.
May 14, 2020.
https://www.csis.org/analysis/us-foreign-assistance-age-
strategic-competition.

Seary, Emma. "50 Years of Broken Promises." Oxfam
International. October 2020.
https://oxfamilibrary.openrepository.com/bitstream/
handle/10546/621080/bn-50-years-broken-promises-aid-
231020-en.pdf.

Sharma, Ritu. "Foreign Aid 101 A Quick and Easy Guide to
Understanding US Foreign Aid, Fifth Edition." Oxfam
America. 2021.
https://webassets.oxfamamerica.org/media/documents/
ForeignAid_5thedition_FINAL.pdf.

"United Nations Conference on Environment and Development,
Rio de Janeiro, Brazil, 3–14 June 1992." United Nations.
Accessed June 5, 2021.
https://www.un.org/en/conferences/environment/rio1992.

"United Nations Secretary General's Road map for Financing
the 2030 Agenda for Sustainable Development 2019-2021."
United Nations. 2019.
https://www.un.org/sustainabledevelopment/sg-finance-
strategy.

"USAID History." US Agency for International Development. Updated May 7, 2019. https://www.usaid.gov/who-we-are/usaid-history#.

"US International Development Finance Corporation Begins Operations." US International Development Finance Corporation. January 2, 2020. https://www.dfc.gov/media/press-releases/us-international-development-finance-corporation-begins-operations.

World Investment Report 2014: Investing in the SDGs: An Action Plan. UN Conference on Trade and Development. United Nations. 2014. https://unctad.org/system/files/official-document/wir2014_en.pdf.

Worley, William. "Breaking: DFIF Merged with FCO." *Devex*. June 16, 2020. https://www.devex.com/news/breaking-dfid-merged-with-fco-97489.

Young-Powell, Abby. "What Happens When an Aid Department Is Folded?" *Devex*. December 18, 2019. https://www.devex.com/news/what-happens-when-an-aid-department-is-folded-96262.

CHAPTER 2

"Office of Foreign Assistance: About Us." US Department of State. Accessed February 9, 2021. https://www.state.gov/about-us-office-of-foreign-assistance/.

"Bureau of Economic and Business Affairs: Our Mission." US Department of State. Accessed July 28, 2021. https://www.state.gov/bureaus-offices/under-secretary-for-economic-growth-energy-and-the-environment/bureau-of-economic-and-business-affairs/.

"Bureau of International Organization Affairs: Our Mission." US Department of State. Accessed July 28, 2021. https://www.state.gov/bureaus-offices/under-secretary-for-political-affairs/bureau-of-international-organization-affairs/.

"Bureau of Population, Refugees, and Migration: Our Mission." US Department of State. Accessed July 28, 2021. https://www.state.gov/bureaus-offices/under-secretary-for-civilian-security-democracy-and-human-rights/bureau-of-population-refugees-and-migration/.

Casabona, Liza. "What is the Function of the 150 Account?" *The Borgen Project* (blog). April 17, 2015. https://borgenproject.org/what-is-the-function-150-account-how-international-aid-measures-up-in-the-federal-budget/.

"Diplomacy: The US Department of State at Work." US Department of State. Accessed February 9, 2021. https://careers.state.gov/learn/what-we-do/.

"Extended, Remodeled New State Building." US Department of State. Office of the Historian. Accessed June 5, 2021. https://history.state.gov/departmenthistory/buildings/section29.

"Feed the Future." Feed the Future. Accessed June 5, 2021.
https://www.feedthefuture.gov.

"National Security Council." The White House.
Accessed June 5, 2021.
https://www.whitehouse.gov/nsc/.

Nolan, Sarah Nitz. "The Congressional Committee Map:
Key Congressional Committees engaged in US Foreign
Assistance." InterAction. Accessed February 9, 2021.
https://www.interaction.org/aid-delivers/foreign-assistance-
overview/the-congressional-committee-map/.

"Office of Management and Budget." The White House. Accessed
June 5, 2021.
https://www.whitehouse.gov/omb/.

Policicchio, Mel. "Stokes Award Winners Look Ahead to
Washington." Princeton University School of Public and
International Affairs. July 7, 2016.
https://spia.princeton.edu/news/stokes-award-winners-look-
ahead-washington.

"Power Africa." US Agency for International Development.
Accessed June 5, 2021.
https://www.usaid.gov/powerafrica.

Salinger, Adva. "Q&A: What Exactly does the State
Department's 'F' Bureau do?" Devex. August 14, 2019.
https://www.devex.com/news/q-a-what-exactly-does-the-
state-department-s-f-bureau-do-95463.

"Translator-Interpreter Program." Cornell University Public
    Service Center. Accessed May 10, 2021.
    https://cornell.campusgroups.com/tip/home/.

"The United States President's Emergency Plan for AIDS Relief."
    US Department of State. Accessed June 5, 2021.
    https://www.state.gov/pepfar/.

Weed, Matthew C. and Serafino, Nina M. "US Diplomatic
    Missions: Background and Issues on Chief of Mission
    (COM) Authority." Congressional Research Service. March
    10, 2014.
    https://crsreports.congress.gov/product/pdf/R/R43422/3.

PART II
"John Kerry: 'How do you Ask a Man to Be the Last Man to
    Die for a Mistake?' Vietnam Veterans against the War
    Testimony—1971," Speakola. Accessed June 6, 2021.

CHAPTER 3
Biden Jr., Joseph R. "Remarks by President Biden on the Way
    Forward in Afghanistan." Treaty Room at The White House.
    Transcript. April 14, 2021.
    https://www.whitehouse.gov/briefing-room/speeches-
    remarks/2021/04/14/remarks-by-president-biden-on-the-
    way-forward-in-afghanistan/.

Bowman, Bertie. *Step by Step: A Memoir of Living the American
    Dream*. New York: One World, 2009.

Chapple, Amos. "Afghanistan Under the Taliban." *Radio Free Europe/Radio Liberty*. February 11, 2019. https://www.rferl.org/a/afghanistan-under-the-taliban-in-photos/29763626.html.

"Committee History and Rules." Committee on Foreign Relations. US Senate. Accessed March 16, 2021. https://www.foreign.senate.gov/about/history/.

Gettleman, Jeffrey and Schmitt, Eric. "US Kills Top Qaeda Militant in Southern Somalia." *The New York Times*. September 14, 2009. https://www.nytimes.com/2009/09/15/world/africa/15raid.html.

"Human Rights Abuses Exacerbating Poverty in Afghanistan, UN Report Finds." *UN News*. March 30, 2010. https://news.un.org/en/story/2010/03/334042-human-rights-abuses-exacerbating-poverty-afghanistan-un-report-finds.

"Interview: Vali Nasr." *PBS Frontline*. October 25, 2001. https://www.pbs.org/wgbh/pages/frontline/shows/saudi/interviews/nasr.html.

National Commission on Terrorist Attacks Upon the United States. *The 9/11 Commission Report: Final Report of the National Commission on Terrorist Attacks Upon the United States*, by Thomas H. Kean and Lee H. Hamilton. Y 3.2:T 27/2/FINAL, July 22, 2004. https://govinfo.library.unt.edu/911/report/911Report.pdf.

Kerry, John. "Transcript: Kerry Testifies Before Senate Panel, 1971." National Public Radio. Radio Broadcast. April 25, 2006. https://www.npr.org/templates/story/story. php?storyId=3875422.

Nagourney, Adam. "Obama Wins Election." *The New York Times*. November 4, 2008. https://www.nytimes.com/2008/11/05/us/ politics/05campaign.html.

Staats, Sarah Jane. "New House Foreign Affairs Committee Chairman Howard Berman Vows to Reassert Authorizers Role in Overhaul of US Foreign Assistance." Center for Global Development. March 12, 2008. https://www.cgdev.org/blog/new-house-foreign-affairs-committee-chairman-howard-berman-vows-reassert-authorizers-role.

"The Taliban and Afghan Women." Feminist Majority Foundation. Accessed May 15, 2021. https://feminist.org/our-work/afghan-women-and-girls/the-taliban-afghan-women/.

"Terrorist Groups: Afghan Taliban." Counter Terrorism Guide. Accessed May 15, 2021. https://www.dni.gov/nctc/groups/afghan_taliban.html.

US Congress. Senate. Committee on Foreign Relations. *Afghanistan's Impact on Pakistan.* 111th Congress, 1st session, October 1, 2009. S. Hrg. 111–295. https://www.foreign.senate.gov/imo/media/doc/100109_Transcript_Afghanistans%20Impact%20on%20Pakistan.pdf.

US Congress. Senate. Committee on Foreign Relations. *Countering the Threat of Failure in Afghanistan.* 111th Congress, 1st session, September 17, 2009. S. Hrg. 111–291. https://www.foreign.senate.gov/imo/media/doc/091709_Transcript_Countering%20the%20Threat%20of%20Failure%20in%20Afghanistan.pdf.

US Congress. Senate, Committee on Foreign Relations. *Exploring Three Strategies for Afghanistan.* 111th Congress, 1st session, September 16, 2009. S. Hrg. 111–321. https://www.foreign.senate.gov/imo/media/doc/091609_Transcript_Exploring%20Three%20Strategies%20for%20Afghanistan.pdf.

US Congress. Senate. Committee on Foreign Relations. *Perspectives on Reconciliation Options in Afghanistan.* 111th Congress, 2nd session, July 27, 2010. S. Hrg. 111–761. https://www.foreign.senate.gov/imo/media/doc/072710_Transcript_Perspectives%20on%20Reconciliation%20Options%20in%20Afghanistan.pdf.

"Working on Capitol Hill." Yale Law School Career Development Office. August 2013. https://www.law.berkeley.edu/files/careers/CDO_Working_On_Capitol_Hill_Public-3.pdf.

CHAPTER 4

Bent, Bill. "Life on a Secure Compound in a War Zone is Somewhat Surreal." American Foreign Service Association. September 14, 2014. https://afsa.org/serving-embassy-kabul.

Central Intelligence Agency. "Afghanistan." The World Factbook. Updated June 9, 2021. https://www.cia.gov/the-world-factbook/countries/afghanistan/.

Graham-Harrison, Emma. "Afghanistan's Garmsir is a Success for NATO—but its Future Remains Uncertain." The Guardian. December 12, 2012. https://www.theguardian.com/world/2012/dec/12/afghanistan-helmand-success-nato-uncertain.

Hill, John E. Through the Jade Gate to Rome: A Study of the Silk Routes during the Later Han Dynasty, 1st to 2nd Centuries CE. Charleston: BookSurge, 2009.

Kerry, John. "Chairman Kerry Delivers Speech on Afghanistan." Council on Foreign Relations' Washington, DC office. US Senate Committee on Foreign Relations. Transcript, October 26, 2009. https://www.foreign.senate.gov/press/go/chairman-kerry-delivers-speech-on-afghanistan.

Maizland, Lindsay and Laub, Zachary. "The Taliban in Afghanistan." Council on Foreign Relations. Updated March 15, 2021. https://www.cfr.org/backgrounder/taliban-afghanistan.

Nosworthy, Madeline O. "Jirga/Shura (Afghanistan)." Global Informality Project. School of Slavonic and East European Studies. Updated April 24, 2020. https://www.in-formality.com/wiki/index.php?title=Jirga_/_Shura_(Afghanistan).

Park, Catherine. "What to Know about the C130 Hercules Military Aircraft." 11 Alive. May 2, 2018. https://www.11alive.com/article/news/what-to-know-about-the-c130-hercules-military-aircraft/85-547997239.

Taylor, Alan. "Afghanistan in the 1950s and 60s." The Atlantic. July 2, 2013. https://www.theatlantic.com/photo/2013/07/afghanistan-in-the-1950s-and-60s/100544/.

US Congress. Senate. Committee on Foreign Relations. *Afghanistan's Narco War: Breaking the Link between Drug Traffickers and Insurgents.* 111th Congress, 1st session. August 10, 2009. Committee Print. https://fas.org/irp/congress/2009_rpt/afghan.pdf.

CHAPTER 5

Associated Press. "Afghan President's Political Rival Accepts Runoff." *WBUR.* October 21, 2009. https://www.wbur.org/news/2009/10/21/afghanistan-19.

Associated Press. "Karzai Endorses Afghan Runoff Election." *WBUR.* October 20, 2009. https://www.wbur.org/news/2009/10/20/afghanistan-18.

Associated Press. "Results in Afghan Election Fraud Probe
Expected." *WBUR*. October 17, 2009.
https://www.wbur.org/news/2009/10/17/bc-as-afghanistan-3.

Boone, Jon and Beaumont, Peter. "Afghanistan Poll Legitimacy
Fears as Taliban Violence Keeps Voters Away." *The
Guardian*. August 20, 2009.
https://www.theguardian.com/world/2009/aug/20/
afghanistan-elections-taliban-attack-voters.

Eikenberry, Karl. Interview by Renee Montagne. "Ambassador
Eikenberry to Leave Afghanistan." *Morning Edition*.
National Public Radio. Radio broadcast. July 8, 2011.
https://www.npr.org/2011/07/08/137696298/ambassador-
eikenberry-to-leave-afghanistan.

Kerry, John F. *Every Day is Extra*. New York: Simon & Schuster,
2018.

Kerry, John, and Lugar, Richard. "Senate Unanimously Passes
Kerry-Lugar Pakistan Aid Package." US Senate Committee
on Foreign Relations. Press release, September 24, 2009.
https://www.foreign.senate.gov/press/chair/release/senate-
unanimously-passes-kerry-lugar-pakistan-aid-package.

"Kerry Meets Gilani." *The Nation*. October 19, 2009.
https://nation.com.pk/19-Oct-2009/kerry-meets-gilani.

Kippen, Grant. "Afghanistan: Electoral Complaints Commission—Press Conference 12 May 2009." ReliefWeb. Transcript. May 12, 2009. https://reliefweb.int/report/afghanistan/afghanistan-electoral-complaints-commission-press-conference-12-may-2009.

"Obama Signs Kerry-Lugar Bill into Law." *Dawn.* October 16, 2009. https://www.dawn.com/news/913807/obama-signs-kerry-lugar-bill-into-law.

"Pakistani Public Opinion." Pew Research Center's Global Attitudes & Trends Project. August 13, 2009. https://www.pewresearch.org/global/2009/08/13/pakistani-public-opinion/.

PTI. "Security Situation in Afghan Linked with Stability in Pak." *The Economic Times.* Updated December 2, 2009. https://economictimes.indiatimes.com/news/politics-and-nation/security-situation-in-afghan-linked-with-stability-in-pak/articleshow/5293492.cms?from=mdr.

Siddique, Abubakar. "Karzai Campaign Declares Victory," *RadioFreeEurope/Radio Liberty.* Updated August 21, 2009. https://www.rferl.org/a/Mixed_Turnout_Violence_Seen_On_Afghan_Election_Day_As_Vote_Count_Begins/1804215.html.

Sieff, Kevin. "Mortenson Returns to Afghanistan, Trying to Move Past His 'Three Cups of Tea' Disgrace." *The Washington Post*. October 12, 2014. https://www.washingtonpost.com/world/asia_pacific/mortenson-returns-to-afghanistan-trying-to-move-past-his-three-cups-of-tea-disgrace/2014/10/12/9774ae90-402f-11e4-b03f-de718edeb92f_story.html.

Starr, Barbara, Elise Labott, Ivan Watson, Tricia Escobedo, and Samson Desta. "US 'Extremely Concerned' about Taliban Movements in Pakistan." *CNN*. April 24, 2009. https://www.cnn.com/2009/WORLD/asiapcf/04/24/pakistan.taliban.control.gilani/index.html.

Tavernise, Sabrina and Landler, Mark. "Allies Press Karzai to Accept Election Audit Results." *The New York Times*. October 17, 2009. https://www.nytimes.com/2009/10/18/world/asia/18afghan.html.

Tempest, Rone. "Afghan Rebel Gateway: Peshawar: Many Lured by Intrigue." *Los Angeles Times*. May 12, 1986. https://www.latimes.com/archives/la-xpm-1986-05-12-mn-3200-story.html.

Trevithick, Joseph. "The US State Department Has Its Own Sprawling Air Force, Here's What's in Its Inventory." *The Drive*. October 4, 2018. https://www.thedrive.com/the-war-zone/24017/the-u-s-state-department-has-its-own-sprawling-air-force-heres-whats-in-its-inventory.

US Congress. Senate. US Senate Foreign Relations Committee. "The US Senate Foreign Relations Committee Suite." Addendum to *The US Senate Foreign Relations Committee Suite* brochure. S. Pub. 115-9. Revised April 2018. https://www.senate.gov/art-artifacts/publications/pdf/room-foreign-relations.pdf.

Von Hippel, Karin and Shahid, Shiza. "The Politics of Aid: Controversy Surrounds the Pakistan Aid Bill." Center for Strategic & International Studies. October 19, 2009. https://www.csis.org/analysis/politics-aid-controversy-surrounds-pakistan-aid-bill.

CHAPTER 6

Burke, Jason. "Former Sri Lankan Army Chief Convicted for War Crimes Claim." *The Guardian*. November 18, 2011. https://www.theguardian.com/world/2011/nov/18/former-sri-lankan-army-chief-jailed.

Dibbert, Taylor. "Sri Lanka's NGO Clampdown." *Foreign Policy*. July 25, 2014. https://foreignpolicy.com/2014/07/25/sri-lankas-ngo-clampdown/.

Nasaw, Daniel. "Sri Lanka Blasts US Report on Human Rights Abuses." *The Guardian*. October 22, 2009. https://www.theguardian.com/world/2009/oct/22/sri-lanka-state-department-report.

Polgreen, Lydia. "US Report on Sri Lanka Urges New Approach." *The New York Times*. December 6, 2009.

"Sri Lanka Ignores Calls by Aid Groups for Better Access to War
Refugees." *The New York Times.* May 22, 2009.
https://www.nytimes.com/2009/05/23/world/asia/23lanka.
html.

US Congress. Senate. Committee on Foreign Relations. *Sri
Lanka: Recharting US Strategy After the War.* 111th Congress,
1st session, December 7, 2009. Committee Print 111-36.
https://www.govinfo.gov/content/pkg/CPRT-111SPRT53866/
pdf/CPRT-111SPRT53866.pdf.

CHAPTER 7

AlMukhtar, Sarah and Rod Nordland. "What Did the US Get for
$2 Trillion in Afghanistan?" *The New York Times.* December
9, 2019.
https://www.nytimes.com/interactive/2019/12/09/world/
middleeast/afghanistan-war-cost.html.

Baker, Peter, Helene Cooper, and Mark Mazzetti. "Bin Laden is
Dead, Obama Says." *The New York Times.* May 1, 2011.
https://www.nytimes.com/2011/05/02/world/asia/osama-bin-
laden-is-killed.html?searchResultPosition=22.

Bureau of Political-Military Affairs. "US Government
Counterinsurgency Guide." United States Government
Interagency Counterinsurgency Initiative. US Department of
State. January 2009.
https://2009-2017.state.gov/documents/organization/119629.pdf.

"The Cost of Inaction Afghanistan Humanitarian Crisis." UN Office for the Coordination of Humanitarian Affairs. Updated on reliefweb.int on May 25, 2021. https://reliefweb.int/sites/reliefweb.int/files/resources/afg-cost-of-inaction-20210523.pdf.

DeYoung, Karen. "Afghan Nation-Building Programs Not Sustainable, Report Says." *The Washington Post.* June 7, 2011. https://www.washingtonpost.com/national/national-security/afghan-nation-building-programs-not-sustainable-report-says/2011/06/07/AG5cPSLH_story.html?tid=a_inl_manual.

Dilanian, Ken. "US Risks Wasting Billions More in Afghanistan Aid, Report Says." *Los Angeles Times.* June 17, 2011. https://www.latimes.com/archives/la-xpm-2011-jun-17-la-fg-afghan-aid-test3-story.html.

"Douglas Frantz—Participant." The Aspen Institute. Accessed June 6, 2021. https://csreports.aspeninstitute.org/Roundtable-on-Artificial-Intelligence/2017/participants/details/488/Douglas-Frantz.

George, Susannah. "Civilian Casualties in Afghanistan Hit Record Highs as U.S. Forces Withdraw, U.N. Mission Reports." *The Washington Post.* July 26, 2021. https://www.washingtonpost.com/world/2021/07/26/afghan-civilian-casualties/.

Kerry, John. "Chairman Kerry Opening Statement at Nomination Hearing for Ambassador to Afghanistan." US Senate Committee on Foreign Relations. Press release, June 8, 2011. https://www.foreign.senate.gov/press/chair/release/chairman-kerry-opening-statement-at-nomination-hearing-for-ambassador-to-afghanistan.

Koop, Avery. "Mapped: The 25 Poorest Countries in the World." Insider. April 22, 2021. https://markets.businessinsider.com/news/stocks/mapped-the-25-poorest-countries-in-the-world-1030335981.

Pforzheimer, Annie. "Protecting Wider US Interests after a Troop Withdrawal." Center for Strategic and International Studies. May 26, 2021. https://www.csis.org/analysis/protecting-wider-us-interests-after-troop-withdrawal.

Rosenberg, Eli. "Key Moments in the Downfall of Anthony Weiner." *The New York Times.* October 28, 2016. https://www.nytimes.com/2016/10/29/nyregion/key-moments-in-the-downfall-of-anthony-weiner.html?searchResultPosition=4.

Sahibzada, Habiburahman, Sayed Murtaza Muzaffari, Tobias Haque, and Muhammad Waheed. "Afghanistan Development Update: Setting Course to Recovery." The World Bank, April 2021. https://thedocs.worldbank.org/en/doc/e406b6f24c2b7fdeb93b56c3116ed8f1-0310012021/original/Afghanistan-Development-Update-FINAL.pdf.

Slaughter, Anne-Marie. "To Make Big Change, Start Small: Have the Conversation with Your Boss." LinkedIn. October 3, 2015. https://www.linkedin.com/pulse/make-big-change-start-small-have-conversation-your-boss-slaughter/.

Slaughter, Anne-Marie. "Why Women Still Can't Have It All." *The Atlantic*. July/August 2012. https://www.theatlantic.com/magazine/archive/2012/07/why-women-still-cant-have-it-all/309020/.

Thier, Alex. "Sustainable Assistance for Afghanistan." *Impact Blog, US Agency for International Development*. August 1, 2011. https://blog.usaid.gov/2011/08/sustainable-assistance-for-afghanistan/.

US Congress. Senate. Committee on Foreign Relations. *Afghanistan: Right Sizing the Development Footprint*. 112th Congress, 1st session, September 8, 2011. S. Hrg. 112-201. https://www.foreign.senate.gov/imo/media/doc/090811_Transcript_Afghanistan.pdf.

US Congress. Senate. Committee on Foreign Relations. *Evaluating Goals and Progress in Afghanistan and Pakistan*. 112th Congress, 1st session, June 23, 2011. S. Hrg. 112-103. https://www.foreign.senate.gov/imo/media/doc/062311_Transcript_Evaluating%20Goals%20and%20Progress%20in%20Afghanistan%20and%20Pakistan.pdf.

US Congress. Senate. Committee on Foreign Relations.
Evaluating US Foreign Assistance to Afghanistan. 112th
Congress, 1st session, June 8, 2011. Committee Print 112-21.
https://www.foreign.senate.gov/imo/media/doc/SPRT%20
112-21.pdf.

PART III

His Highness the Aga Khan. "Address to Both Houses of the
Parliament of Canada in the House of Commons Chamber."
February 27, 2014. Special Joint Session of Canadian
Parliament, Ottawa, Canada. Speech transcript.
https://www.akdn.org/speech/его-высочество-ага-хан/
address-both-houses-parliament-canada-house-commons-
chamber.

CHAPTER 8

Batsaikhan, Uuriintuya and Marek Dabrowski. "Central Asia
Twenty-five Years after the Breakup of the USSR." *Russian
Journal of Economic* 3, no. 3 (2017).
https://www.sciencedirect.com/science/article/pii/
S2405473917300429.

"CASA-1000 Central Asia South Asia Electricity Transmission
and Trade Project Regional Environmental Assessment."
Central Asia South Asia Electricity Transmission and Trade
Project. February 2014.
http://www.casa-1000.org/Docs/0104/CASA-1000%20
REA%20Main%20February-14%20Final.pdf.

"Day 18: Afghanistan-Uzbekistan Friendship Bridge."
Intentionally International (blog). June 11, 2018. Accessed
February 18, 2021.
https://intentionallyinternational.com/2018/06/11/day-18-
afghanistan-uzbekistan-friendship-bridge/.

Editors of Encyclopaedia Britannica. "Soviet invasion of
Afghanistan." *Encyclopedia Britannica.* May 11, 2020.
https://www.britannica.com/event/Soviet-invasion-of-
Afghanistan.

"GNI per Capita, Atlas Method (Current US$)." The World Bank.
Accessed February 18, 2021.
https://data.worldbank.org/indicator/NY.GNP.PCAP.CD.

Menendez, Robert. "Chairman Menendez Meets with President
Karzai to Discuss Afghanistan's Future." US Senate Foreign
Relations Committee. Press release, February 20, 2013.
https://www.foreign.senate.gov/press/chair/release/
chairman-menendez-meets-with-president-karzai-to-
discuss-afghanistans-future.

Menendez, Robert. "Chairman Menendez Meets with Pakistani
President Zardari on Counter-Terrorism and Bilateral
Cooperation." US Senate Foreign Relations Committee.
Press release, February 22, 2013.
https://www.foreign.senate.gov/press/chair/release/
chairman-menendez-meets-with-pakistani-president-
zardari-on-counter-terrorism-and-bilateral-cooperation.

Nichol, Jim. "Central Asia: Regional Developments and
Implications for US Interests." Congressional Research
Service. March 21, 2014.
https://fas.org/sgp/crs/row/RL33458.pdf.

Ruttig, Thomas. "Crossing the Bridge: The 25th Anniversary of
the Soviet Withdrawal from Afghanistan." Afghan Analysts
Network. February 15, 2014.
https://www.afghanistan-analysts.org/en/reports/context-
culture/crossing-the-bridge-the-25th-anniversary-of-the-
soviet-withdrawal-from-afghanistan/.

"Secretariat for CASA-1000 Power Transmission Project Fact
Sheet." US Agency of Development. Updated September 14,
2020.
https://www.usaid.gov/sites/default/files/
documents/2020_09_14_CASA_Secretariat_Fact_Sheet_
ENG.pdf.

Siddiqui, Sabena. "CASA Project and Energy Dynamics across
Central, South Asia." *Al Arabiya*. Updated May 20, 2020.
https://english.alarabiya.net/views/news/middle-
east/2018/11/08/Can-CASA-project-shift-energy-dynamics-
across-Central-South-Asia-.

US Congress. Senate. Committee on Foreign Relations. *Central
Asia and the Transition in Afghanistan*. 112th Congress, 1st
session, December 19, 2011. Committee Print.
https://www.foreign.senate.gov/imo/media/doc/71639.pdf.

US Department of State. "US Announces $15 Million in Funding for CASA-1000 Electricity Project." US Department of State Archived Content 2009 to 2017. Media Note. December 11, 2013.
https://2009-2017.state.gov/r/pa/prs/ps/2013/218629.htm.

"US Support for the New Silk Road." US Department of State Archived Content 2009 to 2017. Accessed May 15, 2021.
https://2009-2017.state.gov/p/sca/ci/af/newsilkroad/index.htm.

"The World Bank in the United States: Overview." The World Bank. Updated December 1, 2020.
https://www.worldbank.org/en/country/unitedstates/overview.

The World Bank. "Poverty Continues to Decline, but Pace of Poverty Reduction is Slowing in Central Asia." Press release 2020/ECA/17, October 17, 2019.
https://www.worldbank.org/en/news/press-release/2019/10/17/poverty-continues-to-decline-but-pace-of-poverty-reduction-is-slowing-in-central-asia.

CHAPTER 9

"CASA-1000: Pakistan, Afghanistan Agree Electricity Transit Fee," *The Express Tribune*, October 11, 2014.
https://tribune.com.pk/story/774116/casa-1000-pakistan-afghanistan-agree-electricity-transit-fee.

"Kabul Hosts International Nowruz Festival." *ToloNews.*
Updated March 28, 2014.
https://tolonews.com/afghanistan/kabul-hosts-
international-nowruz-festival.

Leiby, Richard. "Who is Robin Raphel, the State Department
Veteran Caught Up in Pakistan Intrigue? *The Washington
Post.* December 16, 2014.
https://www.washingtonpost.com/lifestyle/style/
who-is-robin-raphel-the-state-department-veteran-
caught-up-in-pakistan-intrigue/2014/12/16/cfa4179e-8240-
11e4-8882-03cf08410beb_story.html.

Michel, Casey. "What Happens to Uzbek Opposition to CASA-
1000 if Karimov is Dead?" *The Diplomat,* September 2, 2016.
https://thediplomat.com/2016/09/what-happens-to-uzbek-
opposition-to-casa-1000-if-karimov-is-dead/.

"Power Interconnection Project to Strengthen Power Trade
Between Afghanistan, Turkmenistan, Pakistan." *Asian
Development Bank.* February 28, 2018.
https://www.adb.org/news/power-interconnection-
project-strengthen-power-trade-between-afghanistan-
turkmenistan-pakistan.

"Prime Minister, Muhammad Nawaz Sharif Arrived in
Dushanbe, Tajikistan for Two Day Official Visit." Office of
the Prime Minister. Islamic Republic of Pakistan. June 17,
2014.
https://pmo.gov.pk/news_details.php?news_id=216.

Sumar, Fatema Z. "A Transformation: Afghanistan Beyond 2014." US Department of State Archived Content 2009 to 2017. April 30, 2014. https://2009-2017.state.gov/p/sca/rls/rmks/2014/225439.htm.

"Uzbekistan Supports CASA-1000 Project—Kamilov." *The Tashkent Times*. November 29, 2018. https://tashkenttimes.uz/world/3235-uzbekistan-supports-casa-1000-project-kamilov.

"World Bank Group Invests in Energy Trade between Central Asia and South Asia." The World Bank. March 27, 2014. https://www.worldbank.org/en/news/press-release/2014/03/27/world-bank-group-invests-energy-trade-central-south-asia.

CHAPTER 10

"Afghanistan vs. Nepal: Economic Indicators Comparison." Georank. Accessed May 25, 2021. https://georank.org/economy/afghanistan/nepal.

Blon, Anil. "Dwarika's Hotel Kathmandu." Hotels in Nepal, Responsible Nepal Tours. May 14, 2020. https://responsiblenepaltours.wordpress.com/2020/05/14/dwarikas-hotel-kathmandu/.

Brown, Nick M. "Millennium Challenge Corporation: Overview and Issues." Congressional Research Service. Updated October 3, 2019. https://fas.org/sgp/crs/row/RL32427.pdf.

Buckley, Michael. *Meltdown in Tibet: China's Reckless Destruction of Ecosystems from the Highlands of Tibet to the Deltas of Asia.* New York: St. Martin's Press, 2014.

"Nepal Adopts Secular Constitution Amid Violent Protests." International Justice Resource Center. September 30, 2015. https://ijrcenter.org/2015/09/30/nepal-adopts-secular-constitution-amid-violence-and-deadly-protests/.

"Power Politics Delays MCC in Nepal." *Nepali Times.* May 8, 2021. https://www.nepalitimes.com/here-now/power-politics-delays-mcc-in-nepal/.

"Readout of MCC CEO's Trip to Nepal." US Millennium Challenge Corporation. February 20, 2015. https://www.mcc.gov/news-and-events/release/release-022014-readout-of-mcc.

Rose, Sarah and Franck Wiebe. "An Overview of the Millennium Challenge Corporation." Center for Global Development. January 27, 2015. https://www.cgdev.org/publication/ft/overview-millennium-challenge-corporation.

Saldinger, Adva. "MCC Signs $500M Compact with Nepal to Improve Power, Roads." *Devex.* September 15, 2017. https://www.devex.com/news/mcc-signs-500m-compact-with-nepal-to-improve-power-roads-91031.

Shrestha, Prithvi Man. "Nepal, US Expected to Sign Pact
Within a Year." *The Kathmandu Post*. February 13, 2015.
https://kathmandupost.com/money/2015/02/13/nepal-us-
expected-to-sign-pact-within-a-year.

Sumar, Fatema Z. "Helping Nepal Develop New Sources of
Energy." *US State Department DipNote* (blog). March 27,
2015.
http://2007-2017-blogs.state.gov/stories/2015/03/27/helping-
nepal-develop-new-sources-energy.html.

Sumar, Fatema Z. "Opinion: MCC Has Engaged in a $500
Million Compact with Nepal. Here's Why." *Devex*. February
15, 2018.
https://www.devex.com/news/opinion-mcc-has-engaged-in-
a-500-million-compact-with-nepal-here-s-why-92119.

US Embassy Kathmandu. "Millennium Challenge Corporation
Discusses Next Steps with Government of Nepal." US
Embassy in Nepal. Press release, October 7, 2016.
https://np.usembassy.gov/millennium-challenge-
corporation-discusses-next-steps-government-nepal/.

"US and Nepal Sign $500 Million Compact." US Millennium
Challenge Corporation. Press release, September 14, 2017.
https://www.mcc.gov/news-and-events/release/release-
091417-nepal-signing-event.

Vaughn, Bruce. "Nepal: Political Developments and US
Relations." Congressional Research Service. Updated
December 4, 2015.
https://crsreports.congress.gov/product/pdf/R/R44303.

CHAPTER 11

Associated Press. "AP Explains: The Latest in Sri Lanka's Political Crisis." *The Astorian*. Updated November 12, 2018. https://www.dailyastorian.com/news/world/ap-explains-how-sri-lanka-plunged-into-political-crisis/article_16dc3cof-06e6-54f4-95ea-88d53bd16doc.html.

Barry, Ellen and Dharisha Bastians. "Sri Lankan President Concedes Defeat After Startling Upset." *The New York Times*. January 8, 2015. https://www.nytimes.com/2015/01/09/world/asia/sri-lanka-election-president-mahinda-rajapaksa.html.

Bruce-Lockhart, Anna. "5 Things to Know About Sri Lanka's Economy." World Economic Forum. August 17, 2015. https://www.weforum.org/agenda/2015/08/5-things-to-know-about-sri-lankas-economy/.

Hewage, Kithmina. "Year in Review: Sri Lanka's Road to Recovery in 2019." Stimson Center South Asian Voices. January 3, 2020. https://southasianvoices.org/year-in-review-2019-sri-lankas-road-to-recovery/.

Hussein, Asiff. "The Jewels of Sarandib—Sri Lanka as Seen through Arabian Eyes." *Roar Media*. November 13, 2017. https://roar.media/english/life/history/the-jewels-of-sarandib-sri-lanka-as-seen-through-arabian-eyes.

Igoe, Michael. "In Sri Lanka, with 'Great Power Competition' Comes Great Headaches for MCC." *Devex*. August 5, 2020. https://www.devex.com/news/in-sri-lanka-with-great-power-competition-comes-great-headaches-for-mcc-97844.

"Millennium Challenge Corporation Approves $480 Million Grant to Sri Lanka to Expand Economic Opportunities and Reduce Poverty." *Colombo Page*. April 26, 2019. http://www.colombopage.com/archive_19A/Apr26_1556286277CH.php.

"Policy & History." US Embassy in Sri Lanka. Accessed June 5, 2021. https://lk.usembassy.gov/our-relationship/policy-history/.

Rich, Ben R. *Clarence Leonard (Kelly) Johnson 1910–1990: A Biographical Memoir.* Washington: National Academies Press, 1995.

"Selection Process." US Millennium Challenge Corporation. Accessed March 19, 2021. https://www.mcc.gov/who-we-select/selection-process.

"Sri Lanka Attacks: What We Know about the Easter Bombings." *BBC News*. April 28, 2019. https://www.bbc.com/news/world-asia-48010697.

Sumar, Fatema Z. "Congress Should Decrease Politicization at the Millennium Challenge Corporation." *The Hill*. September 8, 2018. https://thehill.com/opinion/white-house/405671-congress-should-decrease-politicization-at-the-millennium-challenge.

US Embassy Colombo. "Statement on Decision of Millennium Challenge Corporation Board." US Embassy in Sri Lanka. December 17, 2020. https://lk.usembassy.gov/statement-on-decision-of-millennium-challenge-corporation-board/.

US Millennium Challenge Corporation. "Millennium Challenge Corporation Board of Directors Selects Burkina Faso, Sri Lanka, Tunisia for New Compacts." Press release, December 14, 2016. https://www.mcc.gov/news-and-events/release/release-121416-board-meeting-dec-2016.

"US Millennium Challenge Corporation Partners with Sri Lanka to Promote Economic Opportunity." *The Daily FT.* January 31, 2017. https://www.ft.lk/article/594961/US-Millennium-Challenge-Corporation-partneres-with-Sri-Lanka-to-promote-economic-opportunity#sthash.3gCIMqiR.gbpl.

Williamson, John ed. "What is Political Economy?" In *The Political Economy of Policy Reform.* 3–19. Washington: Peterson Institute for International Economics, 1994. http://assets.press.princeton.edu/chapters/s6819.pdf.

CHAPTER 12

Azcona, Ginette, Antra Bhatt, Jessamyn Encarnacion, Juncal Plazaola-Castaño, Papa Seck, Silke Staab, and Laura Turquet. "From Insights to Action: Gender Equality in the Wake of COVID-19." UN Women. 2020. https://www.unwomen.org/-/media/headquarters/

attachments/sections/library/publications/2020/gender-equality-in-the-wake-of-covid-19-en.pdf?la=en&vs=5142.

"Closed Compact Report: Jordan Compact." US Millennium Challenge Corporation. September 2018. https://www.mcc.gov/resources/doc/closed-compact-report-jordan.

"COVID-19 and Its Economic Toll on Women: The Story Behind the Numbers." UN Women. September 16, 2020. https://www.unwomen.org/en/news/stories/2020/9/feature-covid-19-economic-impacts-on-women.

"Empowering Women & Girls." Clinton Global Initiative. Accessed June 5, 2021. https://www.un.org/en/ecosoc/phlntrpy/notes/clinton.pdf.

"Facts and Figures: Economic Empowerment." UN Women. Updated July 2018. https://www.unwomen.org/en/what-we-do/economic-empowerment/facts-and-figures.

"Fakhoury Urges MCC to Continue Support for Jordan after 'Successful' Projects." *The Jordan Times*. February 23, 2017. http://www.jordantimes.com/news/local/fakhoury-urges-mcc-continue-support-jordan-after-successful'-projects.

"More than a Pipe Dream." Oxfam. December 11, 2019. https://www.oxfamamerica.org/explore/stories/more-pipe-dream/.

Namrouqa, Hana. "Jordan World's Second Water-Poorest Country." *The Jordan Times.* October 22, 2104. http://www.jordantimes.com/news/local/jordan-world's-second-water-poorest-country#:~:text=AMMAN%20—%20Jordan%20now%20ranks%20as,government%20officials%20said%20on%20Wednesday.

"Nearly Energy Self-Sufficient Treatment and Recycling of Wastewater in the Region of Amman, Jordan." Suez Group. Accessed June 6, 2021. https://www.suez.com/en/our-offering/success-stories/our-references/as-samra-wastewater-and-biosolids-treatment-and-reuse.

Pirela, Claudia. "Women Plumbers Aid Jordan's Water Conservation Effort." US Millennium Challenge Corporation. February 22, 2017. https://www.mcc.gov/blog/entry/blog-022217-jordan-women-plumbers.

Sánchez-Páramo, Carolina, and Ana Maria Munoz-Boudet. "No, 70% of the World's Poor aren't Women, but That Doesn't Mean Poverty Isn't Sexist." *Let's Talk Development, World Bank Blogs.* March 8, 2018. https://blogs.worldbank.org/developmenttalk/no-70-world-s-poor-aren-t-women-doesn-t-mean-poverty-isn-t-sexist.

Sumar, Fatema Z. "Testimony for House Foreign Affairs Committee Hearing 'Jordan: A Key US Partner.'" US Millennium Challenge Corporation. 2016. https://docs.house.gov/meetings/FA/FA13/20160211/104369/HHRG-114-FA13-Wstate-SumarF-20160211.pdf.

"Water Sector in Jordan: More Women Being Trained as Skilled Workers." GIZ. Accessed June 5, 2021. https://www.giz.de/en/worldwide/64272.html.

"Why the Majority of the World's Poor Are Women." Oxfam International. Accessed March 8, 2021. https://www.oxfam.org/en/why-majority-worlds-poor-are-women.

"Women's Workplace Equality Index." Council on Foreign Relations. Accessed June 5, 2021. https://www.cfr.org/legal-barriers/.

World Bank Group. *Country Partnership Framework for Hashemite Kingdom of Jordan for the Period FY17-FY22*. World Bank Group. Report No. 102746-JO. June 15, 2016.

PART IV

Harris, Kamala. *The Truths We Hold*. New York: Penguin Publishing Group, 2019.

CHAPTER 13

"The Accra Agenda for Action." Organization for Economic Cooperation and Development. Accessed June 5, 2021. https://www.oecd.org/dac/effectiveness/45827311.pdf.

Criado Perez, Carolina. *Invisible Women: Data Bias in a World Designed for Men.* New York: Abrams Books, 2019.

"Financing for Development in the Era of COVID-19 and Beyond: Menu of Options for the Consideration of Heads of State and Government Part II." United Nations. September 2020. https://www.un.org/sites/un2.un.org/files/financing_for_development_COVID-19_part_ii_hosg.pdf.

Gollob, Sam and Michael E. O'Hanlon. "Afghanistan Index: Tracking Variables of Reconstruction and Security in Post-9/11 Afghanistan." Brookings Institution. August 2020. https://www.brookings.edu/wp-content/uploads/2020/08/FP_20200825_afganistan_index.pdf.

Grenier, Gilles and Weiguo Zhang. "The Value of Language Skills." IZA World of Labor. March 2021. https://wol.iza.org/articles/economic-value-of-language-skills/long.

Kharas, Homi and Dooley, Meagan. "Long-run Impacts of COVID-19 on Extreme Poverty." Brookings Institution. June 2, 2021. https://www.brookings.edu/blog/future-development/2021/06/02/long-run-impacts-of-covid-19-on-extreme-poverty/.

"Millennium Challenge Corporation, India Ministry of External Affairs Announce Cooperation to Promote Economic Growth." US Millennium Challenge Corporation. Press release, January 13, 2017. https://www.mcc.gov/news-and-events/release/pressstmt-011317-mcc-mea-joint-statement.

Munoz Boudet, Ana Maria, Paola Buitrago, *Bénédicte Leroy de la Brière, David Newhouse, Eliana Rubiano Matulevich, Kinnon Scott, and Pablo Suarez-Becerra.* "Gender Differences in Poverty and Household Composition through the Life-cycle: A Global Perspective." World Bank Group, Poverty and Equity Global Practice and Gender Global Theme. Policy Research Working Paper 8360, March 2018. https://documents1.worldbank.org/curated/en/135731520343670750/pdf/WPS8360.pdf.

Organization for Economic Cooperation and Development. *Global Outlook on Financing for Sustainable Development 2021* (report). Paris: OECD Publishing, November 9, 2020. https://www.oecd.org/dac/global-outlook-on-financing-for-sustainable-development-2021-e3c30a9a-en.htm.

Rossabi, Morris. "All the Khan's Horses." *Natural History.* October 1994.

Sampler, Larry and Jonathan Stivers. "Building the Bridges of the New Silk Road." *US Agency for International Development Impact Blog.* February 13, 2015.

https://blog.usaid.gov/2015/02/building-the-bridges-of-the-new-silk-road/.

US Congress. Senate. Committee on Foreign Relations. *Evaluating US Foreign Assistance to Afghanistan.* 112th Congress, 1st session, June 8, 2011. Committee Print 112-21. https://www.foreign.senate.gov/imo/media/doc/SPRT%20 112-21.pdf.

Williams, Paige. "The Remarkable Comeback of Przewalski's Horse." *Smithsonian Magazine.* December 2016. https://www.smithsonianmag.com/science-nature/ remarkable-comeback-przewalski-horse-180961142/.

CHAPTER 14

Berry, Christopher. "The Meaning of Skate to Where the Puck Is Going, Not Where It Has Been." ChristopherBerry.ca. January 14, 2021. https://christopherberry.ca/the-meaning-of-skate-to-where-the-puck-is-going-not-where-it-as-been/.

Sumar, Fatema Z. and Tara R. Gingerich. "The Future of Humanitarian Action is Local," *Stanford Social Innovation Review* 18, no. 2 (Spring 2020): 40-47. https://ssir.org/articles/entry/the_future_of_humanitarian_ action_is_local.

CONCLUSION

"John Kerry in Delhi, Meets Manmohan Singh." *The New Indian Express*. Updated May 16, 2012. https://www.newindianexpress.com/nation/2010/feb/15/john-kerry-in-delhi-meets-manmohan-singh-131793.html.

GRATITUDE

Sumar, Fatema Z. "COVID-19 Killed My Uncle, His Name was Zulfikar." *Medium*. May 5, 2020. https://medium.com/@FatemaDC/COVID-19-killed-my-uncle-his-name-was-zulfikar-afc8997b4b07.